Simply the Best
BABY NAME BOOK

Simply the Best
BABY NAME BOOK

The most complete guide
to traditional and new names

Stuart Wilson

PAN BOOKS

First published 2001 by Pan Books

This edition published 2013 by Pan Books
an imprint of Pan Macmillan, a division of Macmillan Publishers Limited
Pan Macmillan, 20 New Wharf Road, London N1 9RR
Basingstoke and Oxford
Associated companies throughout the world
www.panmacmillan.com

ISBN 978-1-4472-6597-9

A CIP catalogue record for this book is available
from the British Library.

Typeset by SX Composing DTP, Rayleigh, Essex

Visit **www.panmacmillan.com** to read more about all our books and to buy
them. You will also find features, author interviews and news of any author
events, and you can sign up for e-newsletters so that you're always first to hear
about our new releases.

*This book is dedicated to my mother, Bea,
whose lifelong interest in names inspired my
first researches in this area.*

Contents

Introduction

The last few decades have seen big changes in the amount of information available on the performance of first names. Major breakthroughs include the Registrar General's statistics for England and Wales, published as 'First name profiles' in *The Guinness Book of Names* by Leslie Dunkling, and the HMSO publication *First Names* by Emma Merry, which is based upon the National Health Service Central Register. The 'First name profiles' show the rise and fall of all names in popular use since 1900, latterly at five-year intervals. The book by Emma Merry shows the performance of the top hundred names for girls and boys from 1944 onwards, and also lists the top fifty for Greater London, Wales and the eight standard regions of England, giving a unique insight into the regional variations of names.

Between them, Leslie Dunkling and Emma Merry have revolutionized our understanding of how names are used, and I for one am happy to acknowledge my considerable debt to them. Other researchers on name use have also been at work: a good deal of statistical information is emerging in the United States with separate figures for Hispanic and African-American groups (as reported by Bruce Lansky, Leslie Dunkling and others), and the top fifty names are available for Australia.

Fascinating though all these statistics may be, they were bound to remain inaccessible to the average parent until some way could be found of translating the figures into a description of how each name performed. This proved a difficult task; but now a system has been developed to achieve this, and the results are contained in this book. For the first time in any name book every popular name is given a concise word picture describing its performance since 1900, thus enabling parents to follow the recent pattern of usage of that name.

So, in this book, the usage of popular names is seen as moving in a progression from 'occasional' through 'light' and 'heavy' usage to the ultimate stage of 'very heavy' use. This is based on the Registrar General's statistics as presented in 'First name profiles' relating to 10,000 same-sex births. Taking male names for example, '1' would mean one boy out of every 10,000 born that year received that name. Each of the terms from 'occasional' to 'very heavy' indicates a band of usage within this system:

Occasional use 1–49 out of every 10,000 births that year

Light use 50–149 out of every 10,000 births that year

Heavy use 150–299 out of every 10,000 births that year

Very heavy use 300+ out of every 10,000 births that year

As here I add dates to the levels of usage you can see at a glance whether the name is still popular. If a name shows a definite peak in performance, the year for this is stated, and if it fell out of general use the date for this is also given. If two dates are given, for example 'Occasional use from 1960 to 1985', this means that the name fell out of use after 1985. These comments provide a clear picture of the rise and fall of every name in popular use, giving parents insight into whether the name is maintaining its place, falling out of fashion or starting to revive again. However, parents should bear in mind that information on name performance is available only for those names that have been in general use long enough to show up on the statistics.

After the publication of my book *The Pan Guide to Babies' Names* (the first name book to be indexed by concept and source) I set up a name consultancy to advise parents on the choice of names. What emerged from this consultancy was the realization that modern parents are only interested in the recent performance of names. There is simply no evidence that parents have any interest in the history of a name beyond 1900, and a name's popularity in 1600 or 1700 is just not relevant to the process of choosing a name for a baby born today. For that reason no reference is made in this book to name performance before 1900.

Other surprises emerged during the consultancy process. For example, when I first began researching name use, I assumed that the average parent would be interested in famous bearers of a name. However, I discovered that most parents are sensible about this: they realize that a famous namesake will seem charismatic only for a limited time and may have fallen into obscurity (or even disgrace) by the time any baby named today reaches maturity. Since information on famous namesakes thus plays little or no part in the selection process, it is not included in this book.

Other more subtle aspects of name use clarified for me over this period. I began to see that fashions in name popularity reflect current trends in society. Hence the revival of interest in Celtic culture has focused attention on Celtic names; the ecology movement has made Native American names fashionable; and Japan's rise as an industrial power has highlighted Japanese names. The impact of Eastern religion and philosophy has helped popularize Sanskrit names, the rise of Islam has spread Arabic names and the increasing interest in native peoples has brought Polynesian names to the fore. Celtic names in particular have shown a substantial increase in popularity over the last two decades. This book includes a wide range of Celtic names: not only Welsh, Irish Gaelic and Scottish Gaelic, but also many names from Cornish and Breton sources.

It also became clear that too little allowance had previously been made in books of this kind for the increasing pace of modern life. Today's English-speaking parent is a busy person with no time to waste; that is why foreign language variants are listed here alphabetically by source, enabling readers to access swiftly and easily names from any favourite language tradition. I have given full coverage to the Celtic languages, distinguishing between a Scottish form like Hamish and the Scottish Gaelic original, in this case Seumas. The result of this approach is the most thorough and balanced listing of foreign language variants in any name book. I have also included a section 'Languages of the world'; if you come across any unfamiliar language in the text, this is the place to look. I have given the number of languages within each continent or area; and the total of 342 languages is more than double the number cited in any other name book. And there is one other thing to add about languages: as this book is designed for an English-speaking audience I have followed progressive American practice and omitted accents.

With the busy parent in mind, there is also no point listing all the possible alternative spellings of a name. I could have greatly increased the size of this book had I gone down that road but there is no evidence that the modern parent wants this approach. Parents are perfectly capable of creating their own version of a name by swapping *c* for *k*, *s* for *z*, *ie* for *y* and so on. Hence I give the main forms of each name only, leaving the reader free to develop their own spelling alternatives. Add to this the exciting new developments in blend names (combining the elements of two or more existing names) and the field is wide open for parents to create whatever name they wish.

This is a precious freedom that is highly developed in the English-speaking world, a product of our history and our willingness to experiment. It is seen at work in the tradition among Southern families in the United States of giving children stylish and unusual names, and through the creation of new names by black American families by using prefixes like *La-*, *Sha-* and *De-*. This development is interesting because the meaning of many of these names is secondary to their sound, their style, their resonance. Such a confident exercise in parent power is unfortunately by no means universal. In several European countries names have been chosen for centuries from approved lists of saints, apostles and 'persons known from ancient history'; no other names being permitted. In France, for instance, it was only as recently as January 1993 that all restrictions on names were finally lifted. In comparison to this, the English-speaking parent has enjoyed a remarkable degree of freedom in naming their child – a freedom which should be appreciated and cherished.

During the preparation of this book I devoted much effort to researching the best new names available. It is the attractiveness and vitality of new names which inspired me to write a name book in the first place and which sustained me during the years of research and writing. These names have quite a different appeal from that of traditional names, as a glance at the section 'Rising stars among the new names' will quickly demonstrate. Quite early in my research I became aware that alternative education in general and the Steiner/Waldorf system in particular is uniquely rich in new names. The Steiner/Waldorf system is a holistic form of education which aims to cover every level of development: physical, emotional, mental and spiritual. I wrote to all the Steiner/Waldorf schools in the English-speaking world, a total of 139 schools; many sent me extensive name lists and these yielded a remarkable number of new names.

I have also researched dictionaries, novels, television, films and all the other major name books to bring you the best new names. The result is a host of names from many countries – the most comprehensive listing of new names to appear in any name book. This rich harvest of new names gives you a bigger pool of attractive names to choose from – more names, more variety and more choice – all part of the modern trend towards empowering parents to choose exactly the right name for each child. After all, each baby is a unique human being, holding all the potential of a new life and a new world.

Even in the case of established names new uses can arise, and this can transform a name's popularity. A good example of this is the growing trend towards using male names for girls. These are often called gender-neutral or unisex names. This is an aspect of name usage that is complex and changing rapidly so I have devoted a whole section to it, with cross-references in the text wherever appropriate. This approach provides the most comprehensive information on gender-neutral names hitherto published.

Primarily, this book aims to address the needs of the English-speaking parent, which may be quite different from the needs of parents in other cultures. A name may be attractive because of its foreign and exotic sound, but push that foreignness too far and the English-speaking parent will reject it. Thus the Italian Anna may be preferred to the traditional English Ann, but many names – quite acceptable in their home culture – will seem too exotic for the average English-speaking parent. It has been my aim to heed this aspect of name choice but to include the maximum number of names that the English-speaking parent will find acceptable and attractive.

However you choose a name, do bear in mind that the

best name for your baby will be one you really resonate with, and feel your child will be happy with too. Your child's name is a gift that he or she will probably carry through a whole lifetime, so it is worthwhile spending some time choosing a good name. You now have the whole world of names in your hands, and I hope that somewhere here you will find the perfect name for your baby.

Choosing a name

1 If you feel drawn to several first names, try them out with the surname to see if they flow and sound right, especially when spoken aloud.

2 It often sounds better if the first name and the surname contain a different number of syllables. And a plain surname can be given a lift by a stylish first name. Thus two short names together – Jane Smith – may sound curt or insignificant, whereas Kayla Smith or Zaranda Smith suggest livelier personalities with more energy and style. Bear in mind that a longer surname can often sound better with a short first name, for example John Camberley.

3 Check for any meanings that may lurk in the combination of first name and surname. Ann and Eileen are both fine names but one would obviously want to avoid Ann Teak or Eileen Dover.

4 Avoid names that run together when you speak them, like Beryl Lane. Such names may be confusing to anyone encountering them for the first time.

5 If you choose a third (middle) name, make sure it sounds right with the other two names.

6 Remember that nicknames and shortened forms will be used whether you or the child like them or not. William Gill may sound fine but Bill Gill less so. Avoid all names that rhyme, like Mavis Davis, as they can easily verge upon the comic.

7 Check the initials of the full name. If you have a
surname beginning with *M* and call your daughter
Delia Isobel or Dalya Irissa her initials will be D.I.M. –
a fact that her peer group at school will probably not
allow her to forget.

8 Be cautious about naming a child after some
charismatic figure of the day. Names of this sort date
easily, and fall out of fashion with the decline of
interest in the hero or heroine concerned.

9 If you like a name but want to give it a new twist,
maybe a different spelling or a variant from another
language is the answer. If the name has been widely
used for any length of time you should find other
forms and variants in this book. They will be listed
under the most popular form of the name.

10 Be wary of names that are either too modern in a
weird and wacky way, or too obviously archaic. Try to
give your child an attractive name that will be within
his or her comfort zone. If you go to extremes in any
direction the child may have to put up with a good
deal of teasing.

11 Check the chosen name against the list given in the
'Gender-neutral names' on pages 10–32, just to make
sure there are no surprises in that area. As you will
see from that section, usage can vary from country to
country, and in an increasingly mobile age no one can
be sure which country or even which continent their
child may one day be living and working in.

Gender-neutral names

In recent years there has been a great increase in the use of neutral or unisex names that are not gender-specific. This whole area of naming can be confusing because usage varies between countries. Girls seem much less concerned about bearing a male name than boys do about bearing a female name, and parents in general seem to have taken this on board in choosing names for their children. That is why the movement is all in one direction – male names being taken over for use by girls.

Alongside the transferring of male names into wider use, there is the development of new forms specifically for girls. The original spelling of a name usually continues as the male form, while the new and imaginative spelling alternatives very often become accepted as names for girls, although this does not apply in every case. Even the general rule that end-spellings divide into *-i*, *-ie* and *-ey* for girls, and *-y* for boys is not entirely consistent. There is no rule that provides a universal guide in all cases, so it really is necessary to check out each chosen gender-neutral name to see where usage stands at present. Gender-neutral names are often in flux, so look out for changes as they occur. Above all, with gender-neutral names there is one guiding principle: if you're in doubt, play safe and don't choose it!

The following represents the most comprehensive listing of gender-neutral names currently available. The term 'English-speaking countries' is used here in a specific way: it means countries where the dominant and original language is English. Countries with original non-English languages such as Wales, Scotland and Ireland do not fall within this category for the purposes of this list.

The names in this section have been listed in groups for ease of comparison, and this overrides the normal alphabetical order. The groups begin with the most popular form of the name.

Name   Commentary

Aaron Boys and (very rarely) girls.

Adina Girls and (very rarely) boys.

Adrian, Adrien Boys and (very rarely) girls.

Adrienne Girls only.

Aeron Boys only in English-speaking countries.
  Girls and boys in Wales.

Aerona Girls only.

Ainslie, Ainsley Boys and (rarely) girls.

Ainslea, Ainslee Girls only.

Albany Girls only in English-speaking countries.
  Girls and boys in Ireland.

Alby Girls (Ailbhe) in English-speaking countries.
  Girls and boys (Ailbhe, Albert) in Ireland.

Ali Girls (Alison, Alice) and boys (Ali, Alastair, Alasdair, Alexander).

Alix Girls only (Alexandra).

Alex Boys (Alexander) and (rarely) girls (Alexandra).

Alexis Girls and (very rarely) boys.

Alpha Girls and (rarely) boys.

Alva Girls and (very rarely) boys.

Alvie Girls (Alvina) and boys (Alvin).

Amasa Girls and (very rarely) boys.

Anand Boys only.

Ananda Girls only in English-speaking countries. Girls and (rarely) boys in India.

Andrea Girls only in English-speaking countries. Boys only in Italy (Andrew).

Aindrea, Andra, Anndra Girls only (Andrea) in English-speaking countries. Boys only in Scotland (Andrew).

Angel Girls and (very rarely) boys.

Angie Girls (Angela) in English-speaking countries. Boys in Scotland (Angus).

Andy Boys only (Andrew).

Andie, Andee Girls only (Andrea).

Ara Girls and boys.

Ariel Girls and boys.

Arielle Girls only.

Asa Girls and boys.

Asher Boys and (very rarely) girls.

Ashley Girls and (rarely) boys in USA. Boys only in UK. No longer used (for boys) in Australia.

Ashleigh, Ashlie, Ashlea, Ashlee Girls only.

Ash Girls and boys.

Ashton Boys and (very rarely) girls.

Aspen Girls and boys.

Aubrey Boys only in UK. Girls and boys in USA.

Avery Girls and boys.

Bailey Boys and (very rarely) girls.

Barrie Boys and (rarely) girls.

Barri Girls only.

Bell Girls (Belle) and (very rarely) boys (Bell).

Bernie Boys (Bernard) and (rarely) girls (Bernice, Bernadette).

Beverley Girls and (very rarely) boys.

Billy, Bill Boys only (William).

Billie Girls (Wilhelmina) and (rarely) boys (William).

Blair Boys and (very rarely) girls.

Blake Boys and (rarely) girls.

Bo Girls and boys.

Bob Boys only (Robert).

Bobbi, Bobbie Girls only (Roberta, Robyn).

Bobby Boys (Robert) and (very rarely) girls (Roberta).

Brandon Boys and (very rarely) girls.

Brett Girls and boys.

Britt Girls and (rarely) boys.

Brook Girls and boys.

Brooke Girls only.

Brooks Boys only.

Calum Boys and (very rarely) girls.

Cameron Boys and (rarely) girls in USA. Boys only in UK and Australia.

Camron Boys only.

Canice Girls only in English-speaking countries. Boys and (rarely) girls in Ireland.

Carey Girls and boys.

Carie, Cari Girls only.

Cary Boys and (rarely) girls.

Carol Girls and (very rarely) boys.

Carole Girls only.

Carroll Boys only.

Caryl Girls and (very rarely) boys.

Karol Girls and (rarely) boys in English-speaking countries. Boys only in Poland.

Karel Girls and (rarely) boys in English-speaking countries. Boys only in Czechoslovakia.

Carson Girls and boys.

Carter Boys and (rarely) girls.

Casey Girls and boys.

Casie, Caci, Kacee, Kaci, Kacie Girls only.

Kacy Boys and (rarely) girls.

Kasey, Kacey Girls and (rarely) boys.

Cass Girls (Cassandra) and boys (Cassidy).

Cassady Girls only.

Cassidy Boys and (very rarely) girls.

Cedar Girls and boys.

Celeste Girls only in English-speaking countries. Boys in France (Celestin).

Ceri Girls only in English-speaking countries. Girls and boys in Wales.

Chandra Girls only in English-speaking countries. Girls and boys in India.

Charlie Boys (Charles) and (rarely) girls (Charlotte).

Charlee, Charlea, Charleigh, Charli Girls only (Charlotte).

Charley, Charly Boys (Charles) and (rarely) girls (Charlotte).

Chris Girls (Christine) and boys (Christopher).

Kris Girls (Kristine) and boys (Kristian).

Chrissie, Chrissy Girls only (Christine).

Christian, Kristian Boys and (rarely) girls.

Kristiane Girls only.

Christie Girls (Christine) and boys (Christopher).

Christy Boys (Christopher) and (very rarely) girls (Christine).

Christee Girls only.

Clarrie Girls (Clara) and (rarely) boys (Clarence).

Claude Boys only in English-speaking countries. Girls and boys in France.

Clem Girls (Clementine) and boys (Clement).

Clemmie Girls only (Clementine).

Cody Boys and (rarely) girls.

Codey Girls and boys.

Codi, Codie, Codee Girls only.

Kody Boys and (rarely) girls.

Kodey Girls and boys.

Kodi, Kodie, Kodee Girls only.

Colby Boys and (rarely) girls.

Colbi, Colbee Girls only.

Cory, Corry, Korey, Kory, Korry Boys only.

Corey, Corrie, Korrie Boys and (rarely) girls.

Cori, Corie, Corree, Corrye, Kori, Korie, Korri Girls only.

Coty Girls and (very rarely) boys.

Courtney Girls and (rarely) boys in USA. Girls and boys in UK and Australia.

Courtni, Courtnie, Courtnay, Courtny, Courtnee, Cortney, Kortney, Kortny, Kortni, Kourtney, Kourtni Girls only.

Crystal Girls and (very rarely) boys.

Krystal, Krystel, Krystle, Kristal, Kristel, Kristle Girls only.

Cymry Girls and boys.

Cymri, Cymrie, Kymry, Kymri Girls only.

Cyrille Girls only in English-speaking countries. Boys only in France (Cyril).

Dacey Girls and boys.

Dacee, Daci, Daycey, Dayci Girls only.

Dakota Girls and (rarely) boys.

Dale Boys and (rarely) girls.

Dayle Girls only.

Dallas Girls and boys.

Dana Girls and (rarely) boys.

Danny, Dan Boys only (Daniel).

Danni, Dannii, Dannie, Danney, Dannee Girls only (Danielle).

Daniele Girls only (Danielle) in English-speaking countries. Boys only in Italy (Daniel).

Dara Girls and (very rarely) boys in English-speaking countries. Boys and (rarely) girls in Ireland.

Darby Girls and boys.

Darcy Girls and boys.

Darci, Darcie, Darcee, Darcey Girls only.

Darryl Boys and (very rarely) girls.

Daryl Girls (Darlene) and boys.

Dee Girls and boys.

Del Girls and (very rarely) boys.

Derry, Derrie Girls and (rarely) boys.

Deri Girls only.

Darrie Boys only.

Devan, Devin Boys and (very rarely) girls.

Devon Boys and (very rarely) girls.

Devona, Devonna Girls only.

Dodi Boys only (Daud).

Dodie Girls only (Dorothy).

Dolly Girls only (Dolores) in English-speaking countries. Girls and boys in Scotland (a Highland form of Donald).

Dominique Girls and boys (Dominic) in France. In USA the name is widely used for girls, but usage for boys occurs only within the black community.

Dominic Boys only.

Don Boys only (Donald) in English-speaking countries. Girls and boys in Wales, where it is the name of a Celtic goddess.

Donny Boys only (Donald).

Donnie, Donni, Donnee, Donney Girls only (Donna).

Drew Boys (Andrew) and (rarely) girls.

Dusty Boys only (Dustin) in USA. Girls only in UK.

Dusti, Dustey, Dustee Girls only.

Eddie Boys (Edward) and (rarely) girls (Edwina).

Eden Girls and boys.

Elan Girls and boys.

Elice, Ellice Girls (Alice) and boys (Ellis).

Elisha Boys only in UK. Girls and boys in USA.

Emlyn Boys and (very rarely) girls (Emily).

Emmanuel Boys only. In Jewish communities the form Immanuel is preferred.

Emmanuelle Girls only.

Emer Girls and boys.

Erin Girls and (rarely) boys.

Eryl Girls and boys.

Esme Girls and (very rarely) boys.

Esmee Girls only.

Evan Boys and (very rarely) girls.

Evelyn Girls only.

Evelyne Girls only.

Ezra Boys and (very rarely) girls.

Fallon Girls and boys.

Faron Girls and (rarely) boys.

Fern Girls and (rarely) boys.

Fernley Girls and boys.

Flann Boys and (rarely) girls.

Flavia Girls only.

Flavien, Flavienne Girls only.

Flavian Boys only.

Florian Boys and (very rarely) girls.

Floriane, Florianne, Floriana Girls only.

Flynn Boys and (rarely) girls.

Fran Girls (Frances) and (rarely) boys (Francis).

Frances Girls only.

Francis Boys and (very rarely) girls.

Frank Boys only (Francis).

Frankie Girls (Frances) and boys (Francis).

Frankee, Franki, Frankey, Franky Girls only (Frances).

Freddie Boys and (rarely) girls (Freda).

Fynn Boys and (rarely) girls.

Gabriel Boys only in English-speaking countries. Girls and (rarely) boys in Germany and Austria.

Gabriell, Gabrielle Girls only.

Gabriele Girls only in English-speaking countries and in Germany. Boys only in Italy (Gabriel).

Gabby Girls and boys.

Gabi, Gabbi, Gabee Girls only.

Ganesh, Ganesha Boys and (very rarely) girls.

Garnet Girls and (rarely) boys.

Garnett Boys only.

Garnetta, Garnette Girls only.

George Boys and (very rarely) girls (Georgina, Georgia).

Georgie Boys (George) and (very rarely) girls (Georgina, Georgia).

Georgi, Georgy, Georgey Girls only (Georgina, Georgia).

Gervaise, Gervais, Gervase, Garvais Boys and (very rarely) girls.

Jervaise, Jervayse, Jervaese Girls only.

Gill Girls (Gillian) and (rarely) boys (Gilbert) in English-speaking countries. Boys only in Germany (Giles).

Jill Girls only.

Ginette Girls and (very rarely) boys (Eugene).

Ginger Girls and (rarely) boys.

Greer Girls and (very rarely) boys.

Gwyn Boys and (rarely) girls (Gwyneth).

Hansi Boys (Hans) and (rarely) girls (Johanna).

Happy Girls and boys.

Harper Girls and boys.

Henry Boys only.

Henri Girls (Henrietta) in English-speaking countries. Boys only in France (Henry).

Henrie, Henree, Henrey Girls only (Henrietta).

Heulyn Girls only in English-speaking countries. Girls and boys in Wales.

Hilary, Hillary Girls and (rarely) boys.

Hunter Boys and (rarely) girls.

Hyacinth Girls and (very rarely) boys.

Inge Girls (Ingeborg) and boys (Ingemar).

Innes Girls (Ines) and boys (Angus).

Ira Boys and (very rarely) girls.

Isla Girls only.

Islay Boys only (rare male form of Isla).

Jack Boys only (John).

Jackie, Jacky Girls (Jacqueline) and (rarely) boys (John).

Jacki, Jacqui, Jaquie Girls only (Jacqueline).

Jade Girls and (very rarely) boys.

Jaden Boys and (rarely) girls.

Jaeden, Jadean, Jayden, Jadee, Jaydee Girls only.

Jael Girls and (very rarely) boys.

Jaime, Jamie, Jayme Girls (Jamesina) and boys (James).

Jaymee, Jaymie, Jaymey Girls only (Jamesina).

Jaomi Girls and boys.

Jan Girls and boys.

Janne Girls (a Danish form of Johanna) and boys (a Swedish form of Jan).

Janis Girls only in English-speaking countries. Boys only in Latvia (John).

Jarrah Girls and (very rarely) boys.

Jasper Boys and (very rarely) girls.

Jay Boys and (rarely) girls.

Jaye Girls only.

Jayce, Jaycey Boys only.

Jaycee, Jayci, Jaci Girls only.

Jean Girls only in English-speaking countries. Boys only in France (John).

Jeanne, Jeannie, Jeanie Girls only (Jean).

Gene Boys and (very rarely) girls.

Jerry Boys (Jerald) and (rarely) girls (Jeraldine).

Jerri, Jeri Girls only (Jeraldine).

Gerry Boys (Gerald) and (rarely) girls (Geraldine).

Geri Girls only (Geraldine).

Jervaise, Jervayse, Jervaese: see **Gervaise**.

Jessie, Jessey Girls (Jessica) and (rarely) boys (Jesse).

Jess Boys only (Jesse).

Jesse Boys and (very rarely) girls (Jessica).

Jessy, Jessi, Jessa Girls only (Jessica).

Jewel Girls and (very rarely) boys.

Joan Girls only in English-speaking countries. Boys in Spain (a Catalan form of John).

Jocelyn, Jocelin Girls and (rarely) boys.

Joss Boys only (a form of Jocelin or Jocelyn).

Joe Boys only (Joseph).

Jo Girls (Joanna, Josephine) and boys (Joseph).

Jodi, Jodie Girls only (Judith).

Jody Girls (Judith) and (rarely) boys (Joseph).

Joel Boys and (rarely) girls.

Joelle Girls only.

Johan Girls (Johanna) and boys (John).

Johnny Boys only in most English-speaking countries. Boys and (rarely) girls in USA.

Jordan Girls and boys in UK and USA. Boys only in Australia.

Jorden, Jordin, Jordyn, Jordene Girls only.

Jordon Boys only.

Jude Boys and (rarely) girls (Judith).

Julie Girls and (very rarely) boys (Julian, Jules).

Juniper Girls and boys.

Justine Girls and (very rarely) boys.

Kacy, Kacey, Kasey: see **Casey**.

Kai Girls and boys.

Kay Girls and (very rarely) boys.

Kanoa Girls and boys.

Karol, Karel: see **Carol**.

Kayle Boys and (rarely) girls.

Kayleigh, Keeley Girls only.

Kelly Girls and boys.

Kellie, Kelli, Kelley, Kellee Girls only.

Kelsey Boys only.

Kelcie, Kelcey Girls only.

Keola Girls and (rarely) boys.

Kendall Girls and boys.

Kendelle, Kendyll, Kyndall Girls only.

Kenya Girls only in English-speaking countries. Boys only in Russia, where it is a form of Innokenti meaning innocent.

Kerry Girls and boys.

Kerri, Kerrie, Kerree, Kerrey Girls only.

Kim Girls (Kimberley) and (rarely) boys (Kimball).

Kym Girls only.

Kimberley, Kimberly Girls and (rarely) boys.

Kimberleigh, Kimberlea, Kimberlee, Kimberlie Girls only.

Kingsley Boys and (rarely) girls.

Kirby Girls and boys.

Kirbi, Kirbey, Kirbee Girls only.

Kody, Kodey, Kodi, Kodie, Kodee: see **Cody**.

Kohana Girls and (rarely) boys.

Kori, Korie, Korri, Kory, Korey, Korry: see **Corey**.

Kourtney, Kourtni, Kortney, Kortni, Kortny: see **Courtney**.

Kris: see **Chris**.

Kristian, Kristiane: see **Christian**.

Kristal, Kristel, Kristle, Krystal, Krystel, Krystle: see **Crystal**.

Kyle Boys and (rarely) girls.

Kyla Girls only.

Lakotah Girls and (very rarely) boys.

Lamar Girls and boys.

Lani Girls and (very rarely) boys.

Laurence Boys and (very rarely) girls.

Laurie Girls (Laura) and boys (Laurence).

Lawrie Boys only (Lawrence).

Lauren Girls and (rarely) boys (Laurence).

Loren Girls (Lauren) and boys (Laurence).

Lavon Girls (Lavonne) and (very rarely) boys (Lavon – invented name used mainly by Mormon families).

Leaf Girls and boys.

Lee Girls and boys in USA. Boys only in UK.

Leigh Girls only.

Leighton Boys and (rarely) girls.

Lennox Boys and (rarely) girls.

Leslie Girls and boys.

Lesley, Lesli, Leslee Girls only.

Linden Boys and (very rarely) girls.

Lindsay, Linsey, Linsay Girls and (rarely) boys.

Lindsey, Lyndsay, Lynsey, Lyndsey, Lynzee, Linzi Girls only.

Logan Boys and (very rarely) girls.

Loren Girls and (rarely) boys (Laurence).

Lorne Girls and (very rarely) boys.

Lou Girls (Louise) and boys (Louis).

Louie Boys only (Louis).

Lucian Boys only.

Lucien Boys and (very rarely) girls.

Lucienne Girls only in English-speaking countries. Boys only in France (Lucian).

Luke Boys only in English-speaking countries. Boys and girls in Hawaii (Lucy).

Lyn Girls only in English-speaking countries. Girls and boys (Llywelyn) in Wales.

Lynn Girls and (very rarely) boys.

Mackenzie Girls and (rarely) boys in England and USA. Boys only in Scotland. Boys and (rarely) girls in Canada, Australia and New Zealand.

Macy Boys and (rarely) girls.

Madison Girls and (rarely) boys.

Maddison Boys and (very rarely) girls.

Mallory Girls and (very rarely) boys.

Mandy Girls (Amanda) and (rarely) boys (Mandel).

Marion Girls and (very rarely) boys.

Marian Girls only in English-speaking countries. Boys only in Poland (Marius).

Marlin Girls (Marlene) and boys (Merlin).

Marty Girls (Martha) and boys (Martin).

Maxi, Maxie Girls (Maxine) and boys (Maximillian).

Mel Girls (Melanie) and boys (Melvin).

Meredith Girls and boys.

Meredyth, Meredithe Girls only.

Merle Girls only in UK and Australia. Boys and (rarely) girls in USA.

Merlin Boys only.

Merlyn, Merlane Girls only.

Micah Boys and (very rarely) girls.

Micha Girls only.

Michal Boys (Michael) in France and Poland. Girls in English-speaking countries.

Michael Boys and (very rarely) girls.

Mo Girls (Maureen) and (rarely) boys (Maurice).

Morgan Girls and boys in English-speaking countries. Boys only in Wales.

Morgen Girls and boys.

Morgane, Morgyn, Morgann Girls only.

Morgun, Morrgan Boys only.

Morven Boys and (very rarely) girls.

Motya Girls (Matrona) in English-speaking countries.

Boys only in Russia (Matthew).

Murphy Girls and boys.

Murry Boys and (very rarely) girls.

Nakotah Girls and (rarely) boys.

Nanda Girls only in USA. Boys only in India.

Nicky Girls (Nicola) and boys (Nicholas).

Nicki, Nickie, Nikki Girls only (Nicola).

Nicola Girls only in English-speaking countries.
  Boys only in Italy (Nicholas).

Nicole Girls only in English-speaking countries.
  Girls and (rarely) boys in France (Nicholas).

Nicol Girls (Nicole) and boys (Nicholas).

Nico Girls (Nicola) in English-speaking countries. Boys
  and (rarely) girls in Italy (Nicolo).

Noel Boys and (rarely) girls.

Noelle Girls only.

Ocean Girls and boys.

Ollie Girls (Olivia, Olga) and boys (Oliver).

Olly Boys only (Oliver).

Ophrah Girls and (rarely) boys.

Owny Boys and (rarely) girls.

Paige Girls only in UK. Girls and (rarely) boys in USA.

Page Boys only.

Payge Girls only.

Paris Boys and (rarely) girls in USA. Boys only in
  Europe, in France a form of Patrice (Patrick).

Pat Girls (Patricia) and boys (Patrick).

Patsy Girls (Patricia) and (very rarely) boys (Patrick).*

---

* Patsy is used in USA as a slang term for a dupe or victim.

Phil Girls (Philippa) and boys (Philip).

Phyl, Phyll Girls only (Phyllis).

Phoenix Girls and (rarely) boys.

Precious Girls and boys.

Quinn Boys and (rarely) girls.

Quin, Quinna, Quinne Girls only.

Quint Boys only.

Randall Girls and boys.

Randel, Randelle Girls only.

Randy Boys only (Randolph) in USA and Canada.

Randi, Randie, Randee, Randii Girls only (Miranda or Randall) in USA.*

Raven Girls and boys.

Regan Girls and boys.

Reganne, Regane Girls only.

Reine Girls in English-speaking countries. Boys in Sweden (Reinhold).

Rene Girls (Irene) and (rarely) boys (Reginald).

Rick, Ricky, Rickie, Rickey Boys only (Richard).

Ricki, Rikki, Rikky Girls only (Erica).

Riley Girls and boys.

Rylee, Rylie, Ryley, Rylea, Ryleigh Girls only.

Rio Girls and boys.

Ripley Girls and boys.

* Randi, Randie and Randy are not used at all in UK due to the different perception of randy as a word. This stems from its two separate origins: 1. (Scottish) loud-spoken, vigorous, boisterous; 2. (English) lustful, lecherous. *Webster's Dictionary* emphasizes the Scottish origin of randy whereas the *Concise Oxford Dictionary* stresses its English source. It seems reasonable to suppose that usage of the name Randy began in USA and Canada among families of Scottish descent.

River Girls and boys.

Rob, Robb Boys only (Robert).

Robbie, Robby Boys (Robert) and (rarely) girls (Roberta).

Robbi Girls only (Roberta).

Robin Girls and (very rarely) boys.

Robyn Girls only.

Rohan Girls and boys.

Rohana, Rohane Girls only.

Ronnie Girls (Veronica) and boys (Ronald).

Rory Boys and (very rarely) girls.

Rowan Girls and boys.

Rowane, Rowayne, Rowaine, Rowann, Rowanne, Ro Girls only.

Rube, Ruby Girls (Ruby) and boys (Reuben).

Rusty Girls and boys.

Ryan Boys and (very rarely) girls.

Ryana, Riane, Ryenne Girls only.

Sage Girls and boys.

Sal Girls (Sally) in English-speaking countries. Boys in Italy (Salvatore) and Spain (Salvador).

Sam Girls (Samantha) and boys (Samuel).

Sammy, Sammie Boys only (Samuel).

Sandie Girls (Alexandra) and (rarely) boys (Alexander).

Sandy Boys (Alexander) and (rarely) girls (Alexandra).

Sandi, Sandee Girls only.

Sasha Girls and (rarely) boys in English-speaking countries. Boys only in Russia (Alexander).

Sacha Girls and (rarely) boys in English-speaking

countries. Boys only in France (Alexander).

Sascha Girls and (rarely) boys in English-speaking countries. Boys only in Germany and Austria (Alexander).

Sashia, Saschae, Sashah Girls only.

Schuyler Boys and (very rarely) girls.

Selwyn Boys and (very rarely) girls.

Seraiah Girls and boys.

Seren Girls only in English-speaking countries. Girls and (rarely) boys in Wales.

Shane Boys and (very rarely) girls.

Shannon Girls and (rarely) boys.

Shannan, Shanna, Shanene, Shanine, Shanneen Girls only.

Shannen, Shanon Boys and (rarely) girls.

Shanti Girls and (very rarely) boys.

Shantih, Shantie Girls only.

Sharman Boys (Sherman) and (rarely) girls (Charmian).

Shaun Boys and (rarely) girls.

Shauna, Shaunna, Shaune, Shaunee, Shaunie, Shauney Girls only.

Shawn Boys and (rarely) girls.

Sean Boys and (very rarely) girls.

Shawna, Shawnna, Shawne Girls only.

Shea Girls and (very rarely) boys.

Shelby Girls and (rarely) boys.

Shelley Girls and (very rarely) boys.

Shiloh, Shilo Girls and boys.

Shiloe Girls only.

Shirley Girls and (very rarely) boys.

Shura Girls in English-speaking countries. Boys in Russia (Sasha).

Sidney Boys only.

Sydney Boys and (rarely) girls.

Sydnie, Sydnee Girls only.

Simcha Boys and (rarely) girls.

Simone Girls only in English-speaking countries. Girls (rarely) and boys in Italy (Simon).

Sky Girls and boys.

Skyler Boys only.

Skylar Girls only.

Sloan Boys only.

Sloane Girls only.

Sly Boys (Silvester) and (very rarely) girls.

Sol Girls and boys (Solomon).

Spencer Boys and (rarely) girls.

Stacy, Stacey Girls (Anastasia) and (rarely) boys (Eustace).

Staci, Stacee, Staicie, Staicy, Staycee, Stayci Girls only.

Steve Boys only (Stephen).

Stevie Girls (Stephanie) and boys (Stephen).

Steffi Girls only (Stephanie).

Storm Girls and (rarely) boys.

Sunny Girls only.

Sonny Boys only.

Syra Girls and (very rarely) boys.

Tally Girls and (rarely) boys.

Tam Girls only (Tasmin) in English-speaking countries.

Boys only in Scotland (Thomas).

Tangye Girls and boys.

Taylor Girls and (rarely) boys.

Terah Girls and (very rarely) boys.

Terry Boys and (rarely) girls.

Terri, Terrie, Terrey Girls only (Teresa).

Tierney Boys and (rarely) girls.

Tony Boys only (Antony).

Toni Girls only (Antonia).

Topaz Girls and boys.

Topaza, Topaze, Topayze Girls only.

Torrance Girls only.

Torrence Boys only.

Tory, Tori Girls (Victoria) and boys (Torrence).

Torie, Torey, Torya, Torye Girls only (Victoria).

Torrey, Torri, Torrie, Torry Boys only (Torrence).

Tracey, Traci Girls only.

Tracy Girls and (very rarely) boys.

Tristan Boys and (rarely) girls.

Troy Boys and (rarely) girls.

Troi, Troia, Troya, Troyla Girls only.

Tyler Boys and (rarely) girls.

Val Girls (Valerie) and boys (Valentine).

Valentine Boys and (very rarely) girls.

Vanya Girls only (Vanessa or Vania) in English-speaking countries. Boys only in Russia (John).

Vania Girls only.

Vivian Girls only in USA. Boys and (rarely) girls in other English-speaking countries.

Vivienne Girls only.

Vivien Girls only in English-speaking countries. Boys only in France (Vyvyan).

Vyvyan Boys only.

Viv Girls (Vivienne) and (very rarely) boys (Vyvyan).

Wallis Boys (Wallace) and (very rarely) girls.

Westin Boys and (rarely) girls.

Whitley Girls and (very rarely) boys.

Whitney Girls and (very rarely) boys.

Whitnee, Whitnie, Whitny, Whytne Girls only.

Willow Girls and (very rarely) boys.

Wyllow, Wylow, Willoe, Wyloe Girls only.

Winnie Girls (Winifred) and (rarely) boys (Winston).

Wyn, Wynne Girls and (rarely) boys.

Yancy Boys only.

Yancey, Yancie Girls only.

Zenda Girls and boys (Eugene).

Zephyr Girls and (rarely) boys.

Zefira, Zefyr Girls only.

Zhenya Girls in English-speaking countries (Yevgenia). Boys in Russia (Yevgeni). Both names are forms of Eugene.

Languages of the world

The names in this book are drawn from a total of 342 languages; these are listed below under the appropriate continent or area. If you come across a name entry citing an unfamiliar language, simply refer to this section to find out which area the name comes from. If you wish to find out more about the geographical origins of these languages I suggest you consult the table of the world's languages which forms Appendix 3 in *The Cambridge Encyclopedia of Language* by David Crystal. This lists nearly a thousand living languages in alphabetical order, and gives information on language families and where each language is spoken. Another useful resource is *The Melting Pot Book of Baby Names* by Connie Lockhart Ellefson, which enables you to research names country by country.

The total of 342 languages given here may seem large (more than double the number cited in any other name book) yet this is only a small proportion of all living languages which are estimated to number between five and six thousand.

Europe

Armenian, Azerbaijani, Basque, Breton (Brezhoneg), Bulgarian, Catalan, Cornish, Corsican, Czech, Danish, Dutch, Esperanto, Estonian, Etruscan, Finnish, Flemish, French, Frisian, Galician, Gaulish, Georgian, German, Gheg, Greek, Hungarian (Magyar), Icelandic, Irish Gaelic,

Italian, Latin, Latvian, Lithuanian, Macedonian, Maltese, Manx Gaelic, Middle English, Norman French, Norwegian, Old English, Old French, Old German, Old Norse, Polish, Portuguese, Romanian (Rumanian), Romany, Russian, Sardinian, Scottish Gaelic, Serbo-Croatian (Serbian, Croatian), Sicilian, Slovenian (Slovene), Spanish, Tosk, Ukrainian, Welsh, Yiddish.

(56 languages)

The more general terms Celtic, Scandinavian and Slavonic are used when it is uncertain which language is the source of the name.

Middle East

Akkadian, Arabic, Aramaic, Assyrian, Avestan, Babylonian, Chaldean, Egyptian, Hebrew, Hittite, Pashto, Persian (Farsi), Phoenician, Phrygian, Syriac, Turkish.

(16 languages)

The terms Iranian and Semitic are used when it is uncertain which language is the source of the name.

Africa

Abaluhya, Afrikaans, Akan, Amharic, Ashanti, Ateso, Babudja, Baduma, Bambara, Bantu, Bari, Bemba, Benin, Chichewa, Comorian, Dagomba, Dinka, Diola, Dogon, Dutoro, Efik, Ewe, Fante, Fultani, Ga, Gurma, Hausa, Haya, Ibibio, Ibo (Igbo), Idoma, Kakwa, Kamba, Kikuyu, Kirundi, Kiswahili, Lingala, Loma, Luganda (Ganda), Lumasada, Lunyole, Luo, Mahona, Malagasy, Masai, Mashona, Meru, Muarusha, Muganda, Musamia, Musoga, Mwera, Ndali, Ngoni, Nsenga, Nyakyusa,

Nyanja (Chewa), Nyika, Ochi, Oromo, Ovimbundu, Rukiga, Rukonjo, Runyankore, Runyoro, Rutooro, Rwanda, Shona, Somali, Sotho, Sudanese, Sukuma, Swahili, Swazi (Swati, Siswati), Tarok, Tiv, Tonga, Tswana, Twi, Umbundu (Umbundi), Urhobo, Usenga, Uset, Wahungwe, Watamare, Xhosa, Yao, Yoruba, Zande (Azande), Zaramo, Zezuru, Zulu.

(92 languages)

The terms African and Nigerian are used when it is uncertain which language is the source of the name.

Asia
(including Malaysia and Indonesia)

Andamanese, Assamese, Balinese, Bengali, Bisayan, Burmese, Cambodian (Khmer), Chinese, Dari, Dravidian, Dzongkha, Formosan, Gujarati, Hindi, Ilocano, Indonesian, Japanese, Javanese, Kashmiri, Kazakh, Kirghiz, Korean, Koya, Laotian (Lao), Malay, Maldivian (Divehi), Mandar, Mongolian (Khalkha), Nepalese (Nepali), Nicobarese, Pali, Punjabi (Panjabi), Rajasthani, Sadani, Sanskrit, Santali, Sikkimese, Sinhala (Singhalese), Sumatran, Sunda, Tagalog (Philipino), Tajiki (Tadzhik), Tamil, Thai, Tibetan, Timori, Todas (Toda), Turkmen, Urdu, Uzbek, Vietnamese.

(51 languages)

Oceania
(including Australia and Papua New Guinea)

Aborigine, Bislama (Vanuatuan), Carolinian, Chamoro, Fijian, Futuna, Gilbertese, Hawaiian, Hiri Motu, Maori, Marquesan, Marshallese, Nauruan, Palauan, Papuan,

Rapanui, Samoan, Solomonese, Tahitian, Tasmanian, Tongan, Tuvaluan.

(22 languages)

The term Polynesian is used when it is uncertain which language is the source of the name.

The Americas

Abnaki, Aleutian, Algonquian, Apache, Arapaho, Araucanian, Arawakan, Arikaran, Athapascan, Aymara, Aztec, Blackfoot, Caddoan, Carib, Carrier, Cherokee, Cheyenne, Chickasaw, Chinook, Chippewa, Choctaw, Chumash, Clallam, Coahuila, Comanche, Coos, Costanoan, Creek, Crow, Dakota, Delaware, Dene, Diegueno, Eskimo, Fox, Gosiute, Hichiti, Hokan, Hopi, Illinois, Iroquoian (Iroquois), Kansa, Karok, Keresan, Kickapoo, Kiowa, Klamath, Kootenai, Laguna, Lenape, Luiseno, Maidu, Mandan, Mayan, Menominee, Miwok, Mohave, Mono, Moquelumnan, Muskogean (Muskogee), Nahuatl (Nahua), Navajo, Nayas, Nez Perce, Ojibwa, Omaha, Osage, Otoe, Paiute, Papago, Patwin, Pawnee, Pennicook, Pima, Pomo, Ponca, Potawatomi, Quapaw, Quechua, Salinian, Salish, Sarcee, Sauk, Seminole, Seneca, Shasta, Shoshone (Shoshoni), Sioux (Lakotah), Siwash, Spokane, Sranan, Taos, Tewa, Tlingit, Tsimshian, Tupi-Guarani, Twana, Ute, Washo, Winnebago, Wintun (Wintu), Wyandot, Yurok, Zapotec, Zuni.

(105 languages).

The term Native American is used when it is uncertain which language is the source of the name.

Rising stars among the new names

When writing this book I was amazed at the sheer quantity of attractive new names now emerging, names that have a style and vitality quite different from the appeal of traditional names. Some new names have great potential, and I have selected a few to represent the many rising stars of the future:

Girls

Aroha, Bianca, Carys, Dara, Elenya, Fontayne, Geneth, Halena, Ilora, Jeony, Kayla, Loretha, Melina, Neola, Ohana, Paz, Questa, Roshana, Seren, Takara, Uhura, Vanora, Willow, Xena, Yola, Zaranda.

Boys

Alvar, Brymer, Clyde, Dillon, Egan, Farrel, Galen, Harley, Ieuan, Jeston, Kyle, Lorin, Micah, Niran, Orlan, Payton, Quinn, Ryan, Sandor, Torin, Uffa, Vance, Westley, Xavier, Yanto, Zade.

The best of the new names sound beautiful to the ear of an English-speaker and have a positive meaning. My own favourites include (for girls): Keela (Irish Gaelic – so beautiful that only poets can describe her); Topanga (Indonesian – support, hence caring, supportive) and Wauna

(Miwok – snow geese calling as they fly overhead). And (for boys): Musoke (Rukonjo – born while a rainbow was in the sky) and Takoda (Sioux – friend to all).

The Angel of the Name

In traditional cultures, the process of naming a child was given much thought and was often framed within some kind of ceremony. Carter Revard writes of a complex rite practised by the Native American Osage tribe in which a person representing 'Sky Nation' sat in the north of the ceremonial circle and one representing the Earth sat in the south. Through this ceremony the child was able to 'enter the circle of being'.

A similar degree of attention to the naming of a child may be found in many other traditional cultures. The ancient Jewish esoteric brotherhood of the Essenes, for example, had a tradition which they called the Angel of the Name. They believed that before a child is born, the incoming soul chooses a name which reflects its essential quality and aspirations for its new life on earth. This name is entrusted to an angel whose task it is to communicate intuitively to the parents the name which the soul has chosen. Usually the angel seeks to contact the mother of the child as being the more sensitive and intuitive parent, but in the case of a very down-to-earth mother and a sensitive father, the angel contacts the father.

Many people believe that names hold our very essence. So if as a parent you suddenly have a strong feeling that the name just *has* to be —, this may be the name which the angel has been trying to communicate. If both parents are unable to agree upon the proffered name, perhaps it could be considered as a second or middle name. Then later on the child can choose for himself or herself, and can adopt the second name as their name if they truly resonate with it.

A–Z names for girls

A

Aba Fante; born on Thursday.

Abbie A form of Abigail. Occasional use 1975–85.

Abigail Hebrew; father's joy. Occasional use from 1900, peaking in light use in 1990. *Other forms*: Abagail, Abbie, Abby, Gail, Gale, Gayle. *Variants*: Abaigeal (Irish Gaelic); Gala (Norwegian).

Abiona Yoruba; born during a journey.

Abra Hebrew; earth mother. *Other form*: Abrial. *Variants*: Abarrance (Basque); Abrielle (French); Abriana (Italian).

Acacia Greek; from the name of the tree meaning innocent.

Acantha Greek; from the name of the tree meaning thorny.

Acima Hebrew; the Lord will judge. *Other forms*: Acyma, Akima.

Ada Old English; happy. Heavy use at its peak in 1900, but then went into a sharp decline and fell out of use by 1950. A small revival in 1965 was not sustained. *Other forms*: Addie, Aeda, Etta. *Variants*: Aida (French, Italian); Adah (Hebrew).

Adabelle A blend of Ada and Belle (Isabel).

Adalee A blend of Ada and Lee.

Adalina A blend of Ada and Lina.

Adamina Hebrew; red earth. A feminine form of Adam.

Adamma Ibo; child of beauty.

Adantha A blend of Ada and Samantha.

Adara, Adra Greek; beauty. Or Sanskrit; consideration.

Adeana Hebrew; desire, aspiration.

Adela A form of Adele. Occasional use in 1935, and 1965–70.

Adelaide Old German; nobility. Occasional use from 1900, but fell out of use by 1950. A revival in 1985 was not sustained. *Other forms*: Adalaida, Adeline. *Variants*: Adelka (Czech); Elke (Dutch); Adalheid, Heidi (German); Akela (Hawaiian); Ailis (Irish Gaelic); Adelaida (Italian, Spanish); Ela (Polish); Adaliya (Russian).

Adele Old German; noble. Occasional use from 1935, with a small but steady increase since 1975. *Other forms*: Adela, Adelle, Adalia, Adelia, Athala, Della, Delle. *Variants*: Adelka, Dela (Czech); Adele Adelina, Adette (French); Akela (Hawaiian); Adel (Hungarian); Ailis (Irish Gaelic); Adelina (Italian); Ela (Polish); Adeliya (Russian); Adelita, Lela (Spanish).

Adeliza A blend of Adele and Liza (Elizabeth).

Adelle A form of Adele. Occasional use from 1980 to 1985.

Adena Hebrew; noble.

Adeola Yoruba; honour confers a crown.

Aderyn Welsh; bird, hence a free spirit.

Adesina Nigerian; she has unlocked the path. A name often given to a first-born daughter.

Adiel, Adielle Hebrew; ornament of God.

Adina Hebrew; slender.

Adiva Hebrew; pleasant, gentle.

Adoncia Latin; sweet.

Adonia Greek; beautiful.

Adria From Hadria in northern Italy. A feminine form of Adrian.

Adrienne Greek; dark, mysterious. A name linked to the Adriatic Sea, probably named for its dark water. Occasional use 1935–65, reviving in 1985. *Other forms*: Adrah, Adrea, Adrina. *Variants*: Adri (Dutch); Adriane (German); Adriana (Italian).

Adwen Welsh; white, blessed.

Aelita Welsh; berry.

Aeres Welsh; heiress.

Aerin Welsh; heiress. A feminine form of Aerion.

Aerlyn A blend of Aeres and Lynda.

Aerona Welsh; battle.

Aethnen Welsh; aspen.

Afina Romanian; blueberry.

Agatha Greek; good, kind. *Other forms*: Agace, Aggie. *Variants*: Agathe (French, German); Agathi (Greek); Agotha (Hungarian); Agata (Irish Gaelic); Agnesina (Italian); Atka (Polish); Agafia, Ganya (Russian); Agueda (Spanish); Agda (Swedish).

Agnes Greek; pure. Light use at its peak in 1900, but declined rapidly and fell out of use by 1970. *Other forms*: Agneta, Agnola, Anese, Annais, Annice, Annis, Ina, Nancy, Nesta, Neysa. *Variants*: Anezka (Czech); Agnies (French); Agni (Greek); Aigneis (Irish Gaelic); Agnella, Agneta (Italian); Jaga (Polish); Agnessa, Nessa, Nyusha (Russian); Aneska, Aneya, Neza (Slavonic);

Ines, Inez, Ynez (Spanish); Agneta (Swedish); Nessie, Nesta (Welsh).

Ahulani Hawaiian; heavenly shrine.

Ahura Avestan; Lord. Ahura-Mazda was the supreme beneficent deity in Zoroastrian mythology.

Ahuva Hebrew; love, beloved.

Aia Hebrew; wife.

Aideen Scottish Gaelic; fire. A feminine form of Aidan.

Aiko Japanese; beloved.

Ailani Hawaiian; ruler, leader.

Ailbhe Possibly Irish Gaelic; white.

Aileen An Irish form of Helen. Occasional use from 1900. Other form: Ailene. *Variants*: Aili (Finnish); Ailinn (Portuguese).

Ailsa From the Scottish island name Ailsa Craig, which is derived from Old Norse; Island of Alfsigr, a name meaning elf victory.

Aimee A French form of Amy. Occasional use from 1925, peaking in 1990. *Other forms*: Aimi, Aimie, Aimy, Aymy.

Aina Scandinavian; always, hence constancy and loyalty.

Aine Irish Gaelic; brightness, splendour, delight.

Aingeal Irish Gaelic; angel.

Aisha Arabic; woman. *Other forms*: Aesha, Asha, Ayesha, Aysha, Aytza, Yiesha. *Variants*: Iesha, Ishana, Ishanda (Persian).

Aislin, Aisling, Aishling Irish Gaelic; dream, vision.

Aithne Irish Gaelic; little fire.

Aiyana Native American; forever flowering.

Ajanta Sanskrit; realm of the mountain goat.

Akasha Sanskrit; space.

Akela Polynesian; noblewoman.

Akima, Aki, Japanese; born in autumn.

Akina Japanese; bright flower.

Akira Japanese; intelligence. *Other form*: Akura.

Akiva Hebrew; to protect.

Akora Kora with the *A-* prefix.

Alamea Hawaiian; ripe, precious.

Alameda Native American; cottonwood grove.

Alana Possibly Scottish Gaelic; bright, handsome. A feminine form of Alan. Occasional use from 1955 peaking in 1990. *Other forms*: Alaina, Alaine, Alanis, Alayne, Lanna. *Variant*: Aleni (Greek).

Alani Hawaiian; orange.

Alanza Spanish; noble and eager.

Alaqua Seminole; sweet-gum tree.

Alatna Athapascan; river.

Alaula Hawaiian; dawn.

Albany Irish Gaelic; Scotland. *Other forms*: Albanie, Albanye. (See Gender-neutral names.)

Alcina Greek; sea maiden. *Other forms*: Alcine, Alcyne.

Aldara Greek; winged gift.

Aldora Old English; noble gift.

Aledwen Probably Welsh; to pour forth. A feminine form of Aled.

Aleshanee Coos; she plays all the time.

Alethea Greek; truth. *Other forms*: Alethia, Alithea. *Variant*: Aletea (Italian).

Alexandra Greek; protector. Occasional use from 1925 peaking in light use in 1990. *Other forms*: Alexa, Alexandrina, Alexia, Alexis, Alix, Lexi, Lexine. *Variants*:

Leska, Lexa, Shuka (Czech); Alexandrie, Alexandrine, Sandrine (French); Alexis (German); Aleka, Ritsa (Greek); Alexa, Elka, Lekszi (Hungarian); Alastriona (Irish Gaelic); Alessandra (Italian); Aleska, Ola (Polish); Aleksandra, Alya, Alesha, Lelya, Lesya, Olesya, Sanya, Shura (Russian); Alexina (Scottish); Cesya, Seska, Zandora (Slavonic); Alandra, Alejandra, Jandina, Dina, Xandra (Spanish).

Alexia A form of Alexandra. Occasional use from 1965.

Alexis A form of Alexandra. Popularized by the television series *Dynasty*. Occasional use 1950–85. *Other forms*: Alexi, Alexia, Alexsis, Alexxis, Alexys, Lexis. *Variants*: Alexia (German); Alessia (Italian).

Algoma Native American; valley of flowers.

Ali A form of Alice or Alison. (See Gender-neutral names.)

Alianne A blend of Alice and Anne.

Alibeth A blend of Alice and Elizabeth.

Alice Old German; nobility. Very heavy use at its peak in 1900, but declined rapidly into occasional use. Recovered in 1955, and climbed back to light use by 1990. *Other forms*: Adelicia, Alecia, Aleka, Alicia, Alise, Alisha, Alissa, Allison, Alys, Alyssa, Elissa, Ilyssa, Licia. *Variants*: Alisha (Czech); Alix (French); Alexie, Alise, Elise, Ilse (German); Alecea, Alizka (Greek); Alika (Hawaiian); Ilisha (Hebrew); Aliz, Lici (Hungarian); Ailis, Ailish, Eilis (Irish Gaelic); Alicia (Italian); Alissa (Polish); Elica (Romanian); Alisa, Alya (Russian); Ailidh, Ailis (Scottish Gaelic); Alyosha, Elza, Lyssa (Slavonic); Alicia, Licha (Spanish); Elsa, Elsena (Swedish); Alys (Welsh).

Alicia An Italian form of Alice. Occasional use from 1900, peaking in 1990.

Alida, Elida Spanish; noble. *Variants*: Alette (French); Aleda, Alyda (German); Aleta (Greek); Aletta (Italian); Alita (Spanish).

Alienor Greek; light. *Other form*: Aliea.

Alika Nigerian; outstanding beauty.

Alima Arabic; musical.

Alina Celtic; fair. *Variants*: Alene (Dutch); Alya (Russian).

Alisandra A blend of Alice and Sandra.

Alisha A Czech form of Alice. Occasional use from 1975 peaking in 1990.

Alison A form of Alice. Light use from 1935 rising to a peak of heavy use in 1965. *Other forms*: Allison, Allyson, Alyson. *Variant*: Allsun (Irish Gaelic).

Alissa A form of Alice. Occasional use from 1980. *Other forms*: Alisha, Alyssa.

Aliza A blend of Alix (Alexandra) and Elizabeth.

Allison A form of Alison. Occasional use from 1950, peaking in 1965.

Allyson A form of Alison. Occasional use from 1955.

Alma Hebrew; maiden. Occasional use from 1900, peaking in 1925 and falling out of use in 1965. *Other forms*: Aluma, Elma.

Almedha Breton; kind. *Other form*: Almita.

Almira Arabic; princess.

Alodie Old English; rich.

Aloha Hawaiian; greetings, love.

Alohi Polynesian; bright, shining.

Aloma From the name of the plant.

Alonza Old German; eager for battle.

Alora A blend of Alice and Lora (Laura).

Aloysia Old German; glorious battle. *Other form*: Aloisa.

Alpha Greek; the first. (See Gender-neutral names.)

Alpowa Nez Perce; a spring.

Alta Latin; highest, best, supreme. *Other forms*: Altaya, Altura.

Althea Greek; wholesome. Occasional use from 1965. *Other forms*: Altheda, Altheya.

Aluinn Scottish Gaelic; beautiful.

Alula Latin; winged one.

Alva Possibly Irish Gaelic; healing, strength. Almha was the name of an Irish goddess of legendary strength. *Other form*: Alvada.

Alvina Old German; friend to all. *Other forms*: Alvena, Alvyna, Elvina. *Variants*: Alva (Dutch); Alwina (German); Alba (Spanish).

Alvira Old German; elf arrow.

Alvita Latin; vivacious.

Alya Arabic; sublime. *Other form*: Alyosha.

Alyena A character in the novel *Tribesmen of Gor* by John Norman.

Alyra, Alura Old English; wise counsellor.

Alyson A form of Alison. Occasional use from 1950 peaking in 1965.

Alyssa Greek; wise. *Other form*: Alyssum.

Alzena Arabic; woman.

Ama Ewe; born on Saturday. Or Esperanto; loving.

Amabel Latin; lovable.

Amabeth A blend of Amanda and Elizabeth.

Amadelle A blend of Amanda and Delia.

Amaka Zulu; fragrance.

Amalandra A blend of Amalia and Sandra.

Amalia Arabic; hopeful. Or Old German; industrious. *Other forms*: Amala, Amalya. *Variant*: Amalie (German).

Amalina A blend of Amanda and Carolina (Caroline).

Amalinda A blend of Amanda and Linda.

Amalissa A blend of Amanda and Alice.

Amanda Latin; lovable. Light use from 1950 peaking in heavy use in 1965. *Other forms*: Manda, Mandy. *Variants*: Amandine (French); Amata (Spanish).

Amara Greek; eternally beautiful. Or Sanskrit; immortal.

Amaranda, Ameranda Blends of Amanda or Miranda.

Amaranta From *Amarant*, a book of botanical fantasy by Una Woodruff, which describes the mythical island of Amarantos.

Amarantha Greek; unfading. *Other forms*: Amarante, Amaranthe.

Amarel, Amarella Blends of Amara and Ella.

Amarena, Amarina, Amaryna Blends of Amara and Rena.

Amarinda Greek; long-lived.

Amarintha A blend of Amara and Cynthia.

Amaris Hebrew; whom God has promised.

Amaryllis Greek; fresh stream.

Amasa Hebrew; bearer of burdens. (See Gender-neutral names.)

Amathea, Amathia, Amathette Blends of Amanda and Anthea.

Amaya Japanese; night rain.

Amba Sanskrit; universal mother.

Amber Arabic; the name of the resinous jewel.

Occasional use from 1970, peaking in 1990. *Other forms*:
Amberly, Ambra, Ambur.

Ambika Sanskrit; benevolent mother.

Ambrosine Greek; immortal. A feminine form of
Ambrose. Occasional use 1925–35. *Other form*:
Ambrosyne.

Ameerah, Amera Arabic; princess.

Amelia Old German; industrious. Popularized by the
novel *Amelia* by Henry Fielding. Occasional use from
1900 rising into light use in 1990. *Other forms*: Amalia,
Ameline, Amelita, Amielia, Emelina, Emily, Millie,
Milly. *Variants*: Amalia (Czech); Amelie, Emalie
(French); Amalie, Amelie (German); Aimilios (Greek);
Emilia, Ilma, Mali, Malika (Hungarian); Aimiliona
(Irish Gaelic); Amalia (Italian); Amalija (Latvian); Ama,
Melcia (Polish); Amalija (Russian); Amilia (Scottish);
Amelita, Nuela (Spanish); Amalia (Swedish).

Amelinda Latin; beloved and pretty.

Amera A blend of Amy and Vera. *Other forms*: Ameral,
Amyra.

Amethyst Greek; from the name of the gem meaning not
drunken. (The stone was supposed to prevent
intoxication.) *Other forms*: Amathyst, Ametha.

Amhara Amharic; from the name of the Amhara people
of Ethiopia.

Amica Latin; friend.

Amina Arabic; faithful. *Other form*: Ameena.

Aminda A blend of Amina and Linda.

Aminta, Amintha, Aminda Latin; loving.

Amira Hebrew; speech.

Amma Old Norse; grandmother.

Amoretta Latin; little loved one. *Other form*: Amorah.

Amrita Sanskrit; immortal, giving immortality. The name of a goddess in the Hindu Vedas.

Amy Latin; love. Light use in 1900, but declined and fell out of use by 1965. Revived in 1970, and rose into heavy use by 1990. *Other forms*: Ami, Amia, Amie, Amii, Amye, Esme, Isme. *Variants*: Aimee, Amelie, Esme (French); Amalia, Amadea (Italian); Ema (Romanian); Amaliya (Russian); Amada, Amata (Spanish); Amata (Swedish); Anwyl (Welsh).

Anaba Navajo; she returns from war.

Anabeth, Annabeth Blends of Ann and Elizabeth.

Anaelle Hebrew; pure fire (or light) of heaven. The Essenes called Anael the Angel of Air, and linked this angel to Friday.

Anahera Maori; angel.

Anahita Persian; spotless. The Persian goddess of the waters.

Anais French/Greek; fruitful.

Anala Hindi; fine.

Ananda Sanskrit; happiness, bliss. *Other forms*: Anandi, Anandini. (See Gender-neutral names.)

Anastasia Greek; resurrection. Popular for babies born at Easter. Occasional use from 1980. *Other forms*: Anastasie, Anstice, Asia, Nastassia, Nestia, Stacey, Stacy, Stasya, Tansy, Tasya. *Variants*: Anastazie, Staska (Czech); Anastasie (French, German); Annstas (Irish Gaelic); Nastasia (Italian); Asya (Latvian); Nastusya (Lithuanian); Anastazja (Polish); Anya, Asya, Nastasya, Nastusha, Stasya, Tasenka, Tasya (Russian); Tasia (Spanish).

Andeana Spanish; walker.

Andora A blend of Ann and Dora.

Andra, Andriana Old Norse; breath.

Andrea Greek; brave. Light use from 1935, peaking in 1965 and now in a steady decline. *Other forms:* Andee, Andie, Andra, Adreana, Andriana. *Variants*: Andere (Basque); Ondrea (Czech); Andree (French); Aindrea (Irish Gaelic); Andreana (Italian).

Andris Welsh; very fair.

Anela Hawaiian; angel.

Anella, Annella Blends of Ann and Ella.

Angel Greek; being of light, angel. *Variants*: Andel (Czech); Ange (French); Anjel (Hungarian); Aniol, Anjali (Polish).

Angela Greek; angel. Light use from 1925, peaking in heavy use in 1965, and now in decline. *Other forms*: Angeleta, Angelica, Angelina, Angelita, Angi, Angie, Angy. *Variants*: Andela, Andelka (Czech); Angele, Angelique (French); Anjela, Angelika (German); Angelica, Angeliki (Greek); Anakela (Hawaiian); Angyalka (Hungarian); Aingeal (Irish Gaelic); Aniela (Italian); Aniela, Anjana, Anjani (Polish); Anhelina, Gelya, Lina (Russian); Anja, Anjali, Anjelica (Slavonic); Angelita (Spanish); Angyles (Welsh).

Angelika A German form of Angela. *Other form*: Angelica. *Variants*: Angelique (French); Angelike (German).

Angelina A diminutive of Angela. Occasional use from 1900 to 1980. *Other forms*: Angeleen, Angelena, Angelene, Angeline, Angelyn, Anjelina. *Variant*: Angeline (French).

Angeline A form of Angelina. Occasional use 1950–65. Fell out of use in 1970, but showed a small revival in 1990.

Angeni Native American; spirit.

Angharad Welsh; much loved. Occasional use from 1985. *Other forms*: Anchoret, Ancreta, Angahard, Ankerita, Ingaret.

Angwen Welsh; beautiful.

Ani Hawaiian; beautiful.

Anika Hausa; sweetness of face. Occasional use from 1980. *Other forms*: Aneka, Anica, Anicka, Annika, Annyka.

Anila Sanskrit; wind. Anil is the wind god in Hindu mythology.

Anira A blend of Ann and Vera.

Anisa A blend of Ann and Lisa.

Anisha Possibly Sanskrit; without a master.

Anita A diminutive of Ann. Occasional use from 1900, peaking in 1965 and falling out of use in 1990. *Other form*: Anyta.

Ann, Anne Hebrew; graceful. Ann was traditionally the most popular spelling of this name, although it was overtaken briefly by Anne in 1965. Both forms peaked in light usage in the 1950s, and the decline has since been a steady one, especially for Anne which fell out of use in 1990. *Other forms*: Ana, Anica, Anina, Anita, Anitra, Anna, Annaleen, Annalette, Annette, Annice, Annora, Nana, Nancy, Nanette, Nanine, Nita. *Variants*: Anna (Armenian); Ane (Basque); Annick (Breton); Anna (Bulgarian); Anca, Aninka, Anuska, Andula (Czech); Hanne (Danish); Anke, Anneke (Dutch); Anniki (Finnish); Annette, Nanette, Ninon (French); Annchen, Anneliese, Hanna, Hanne, Nettchen (German); Nana, Noula (Greek); Ana, Ane (Hawaiian); Anais, Chana, Enye, Hana, Hannah (Hebrew); Anci, Anika, Annuska, Anyu, Nina (Hungarian); Aine (Irish

Gaelic); Anna, Annetta, Annina (Italian); Ance, Aneta, Ansenka, Anyuta, Asya (Latvian); Annike, Annze, Ona, Onele (Lithuanian); Ania, Aniela, Anka, Hania, Hanka (Polish); Anicuta (Portuguese); Ana (Romanian); Anechka, Anja, Annina, Anninka, Anoushka, Annuska, Annya, Anya, Asya, Naina, Nina, Ninka (Russian); Annag (Scottish Gaelic); Anara, Annika (Slavonic); Ana, Anica, Anita, Nanor, Nita (Spanish); Annika (Swedish); Aneta, Nyura (Ukrainian).

Anna An Italian form of Ann. Never as popular as Ann or Anne until it began to overtake them in the late 1970s. Peaking in light use in 1980, it has maintained its position, and is now more widely used than either of the two alternative spellings.

Annabel Latin; lovable. Occasional use from 1965. *Other forms*: Anabel, Anabella, Annabelle, Annabla. *Variants*: Anabela (Hawaiian); Annabla (Irish Gaelic); Annabella (Italian); Anabla (Scottish Gaelic).

Annabelle A form of Annabel. Occasional use from 1965 to 1985.

Annabeth A blend of Ann and Elizabeth.

Annada A blend of Ann and Ada.

Annalee, Annalia Blends of Ann and Lee.

Annalyn A blend of Anna and Lyn. *Other form*: Annalynde.

Annamarie A blend of Anne and Marie. Occasional use from 1970.

Annathea A blend of Anna and Anthea.

Anneka A Dutch diminutive of Ann.

Annelisa A blend of Anne and Lisa. *Other forms*: Analisa, Analise, Annalise. *Variants*: Annelise (Danish); Annaliese (German).

Annemarie A blend of Anne and Marie. Occasional use 1965–80.

Anne-Marie A blend of Anne and Marie. Occasional use from 1965. *Other forms*: Annamarie, Annemarie, Annmarie, Ann-Marie.

Annette A diminutive of Anne. Light use from 1935. *Other forms*: Anetra, Anette, Annetta.

Annie A form of Ann. Very heavy use in 1900, but declined sharply and fell out of use in 1960. There was a small revival in 1990.

Annis A form of Agnes. Occasional use 1925–80. *Other forms*: Annice, Annys.

Annjanette A blend of Ann and Janette. *Other form*: Anjani.

Annmarie A blend of Ann and Marie. Occasional use 1960–85.

Ann-Marie A blend of Ann and Marie. Occasional use from 1965.

Annwyl Welsh; dear.

Anoka Sioux; on both sides.

Anona Latin; ninth born. *Other form*: Annona.

Anora Hebrew; grace.

Anouhea Hawaiian; soft fragrance.

Anouska A Russian form of Ann. Occasional use from 1980. *Other form*: Anoushka.

Ansara Arabic; helper.

Anthea Greek; flowery. Occasional use from 1935 but fell out of use by 1980. *Other forms*: Anthia, Anthella.

Anthelia A blend of Anthea and Delia.

Antoinette From the Roman family name Antonius. A French feminine form of Anthony. Occasional use from

1960. *Other forms*: Antonette, Antonietta, Netta, Onita.

Antonia From the Roman family name Antonius. A feminine form of Anthony. Occasional use from 1950. *Other forms*: Toni, Tonia, Tonya. *Variants*: Andonine (Basque); Anthoine, Antoinette, Toinette (French); Antonie (German); Antonella, Antonietta (Italian); Antonina, Nina, Tola (Polish); Antonette, Tonya (Russian); Antonieta, Antonina, Tona (Spanish); Antonetta (Swedish).

Anusha Sanskrit; a star name in Hindu astrology.

Anwen Welsh; very fair.

Anya A Russian form of Ann. Occasional use from 1975.

Anzu Japanese; apricot.

Ao Maori; planet earth.

Aolani Hawaiian; heavenly cloud.

Aostra Greek/Egyptian; sunrise, dawn.

Apaksi Seminole; tomorrow.

Aphra Hebrew; young deer.

April Latin; to open (hence springtime). Occasional use from 1950 peaking in 1975. *Other forms*: Averyl, Avril. *Variants*: Ebrel (Cornish); Avril, Avrille (French); Aibrean (Irish Gaelic); Abril (Spanish); Aprili (Swahili); Ebrilla (Welsh).

Aquarelle French; watercolour.

Ara Old German; eagle. Or Maori; path, awake. *Variant*: Aram (Armenian). (See Gender-neutral names.)

Arabah Hebrew; desert.

Arabella Old German/Latin; beautiful eagle. *Other forms*: Arabel, Arabelle. *Variants*: Arabelle, Belle (French); Orabella (Italian); Arabela (Spanish).

Araminta Latin; loving.

Arani Maori; orange.

Arantha A blend of Ara and Samantha.

Aranya Sanskrit; of the forest.

Ardana Sanskrit; restless

Ardath Hebrew; flowering field.

Ardelia, Ardelle, Ardis Latin; enthusiastic.

Arden Old English; valley of the eagle. *Other form*: Ardenne.

Arella Hebrew; angel.

Arene Basque; holy one.

Aretha Greek; virtue. *Other forms*: Areta, Arista, Aritha, Arytha. *Variant*: Arette (French).

Ariadne Greek; holy one. *Variants*: Ariane (French); Ariana (Italian).

Arial Welsh; vigour.

Arian Welsh; silver.

Ariane Greek; holy one. *Other forms*: Ariana, Arianna. *Variants*: Arianne (French); Arianna (Italian).

Arianwen Welsh; silver white.

Ariel Hebrew; lioness of God. *Variant*: Ariele (Italian). (See Gender-neutral names.)

Ariella Hebrew; lioness of God. *Variant*: Arielle (French).

Arinda A blend of Ara and Linda.

Arinna Hittite; goddess of the sun.

Arista Greek; the best.

Arita Maori; eager. *Other form*: Areeta.

Aritha A Greek wood nymph. *Other form*: Arytha.

Arlene Celtic; promise. Occasional use from 1935. *Other forms*: Arlana, Arleen, Arlena, Arlette, Arleyne, Arlina, Arlyn, Harlene.

Arletta Old German; girl. *Other form*: Arlette.

Arlynn A blend of Arlene and Lynn.

Armelle French/Celtic; princess.

Armida Latin; little warrior.

Armina Old German; warrior.

Arna Hebrew; cedar tree. *Other forms*: Arnelle, Arnette.

Aroha Maori; love.

Aruna Sanskrit; dawn.

Arvada Danish; eagle.

Arwen Welsh; fair, fine. *Other forms*: Arwenna, Arwyn, Arwynne.

Asa Japanese; morning. (See Gender-neutral names.)

Asenka Russian; graceful.

Asgell Welsh; chaffinch.

Asha Sanskrit; wish, desire, aspiration.

Ashira Hebrew; wealthy.

Ashleigh Old English; ash wood. Occasional use from 1975, rising sharply in 1990. *Other forms*: Ashlea, Ashlee, Ashlie.

Ashley Old English; ash wood. *Other form*: Ash. (See Gender-neutral names.)

Ashlyn, Ashlynn, Ashlin, Ashlynne Old English; ash tree pool.

Ashura Swahili; born during the Islamic holy month of Ashur.

Asima Arabic; protector.

Asmita Sanskrit; self-respect.

Aspen Old German; from the name of the tree in the poplar family. (See Gender-neutral names.)

Asta Greek; star.

Astara Azerbaijani; a place-name in Azerbaijan.

Astra Latin; star. *Variants*: Asta (Danish); Astrea (Hungarian).

Astraea Greek; star-maiden. In Greek mythology Astraea was the daughter of Zeus and Themis.

Astrid Old Norse; divine beauty. *Variants*: Asta, Sassa (Swedish).

Asvina Hindi; born during Libra.

Atalie Scandinavian; pure. *Other forms*: Atalia, Talia, Talie.

Atalya Spanish; guardian.

Atanua Marquesan; dawn. The name of the daughter of the Marquesan god Atea.

Atara Hebrew; crown. *Other forms*: Atandra, Atarah.

Athalia Hebrew; God is exalted.

Athene Greek; wisdom. Athena was the Greek goddess of wisdom.

Atifa Arabic; affection, sympathy.

Atiya Arabic; gift.

Aubrey Old German; elf ruler. *Other forms*: Aubray, Aubree, Aubri. *Variant*: Aubrie (French). (See Gender-neutral names.)

Audrey Old English; noble strength. Peaked in heavy use in 1935, but then declined and fell out of use by 1985. *Other forms*: Audra, Audrene, Audrie, Audry, Awdrey. *Variant*: Audra (French).

Aulani Hawaiian; royal messenger.

Aura Greek; breath, a subtle energy field around the body.

Aurelia Latin; golden. *Variants*: Aurelne (Basque); Aurele, Aurelie (French); Aurel (German); Aureliana (Italian); Aurelio (Spanish).

Auriol, Auriole Latin; golden.

Aurora Latin; dawn. *Variant*: Aurore (French).

Auroraleah A blend of Aurora and Leah.

Autumn From the name of the season.

Ava Latin; bird, hence a free spirit. *Other form*: Avia.

Avalon Latin; island. An island paradise in Celtic mythology.

Avasa Hindi; independent.

Avatara Sanskrit; saviour, divine teacher.

Avelene Old French; hazel tree. *Other forms*: Avelina, Aveline. *Variant*: Aibhlinn (Irish Gaelic).

Avellane, Avellaine From the French name for a heraldic cross.

Avena Old English; oatfield.

Averil A form of Avril. Occasional use 1925–50.

Avery Old English; elf (hence wise) counsel. A form of Alfreda, a feminine version of Alfred. (See Gender-neutral names.)

Avesta Persian; knowledge, wisdom.

Avielle Hebrew; God is my father.

Avis Latin; bird, hence a free spirit. Occasional use from 1925. *Other form*: Avicia. *Variants*: Havoise (French); Aveza (German).

Avisha Hebrew; gift of God.

Aviva, Aviyah Hebrew; springtime. *Other forms*: Avika, Avri.

Avril Old English; boar battle. Occasional use from 1925, peaking in 1950 and now in decline. *Other forms*: Averil, Everelle.

Awanata Miwok; turtle.

Awapa Paiute; at cedar spring.

Awena Welsh; muse.

Awenita Native American; a fawn.

Aya Hebrew; fly swiftly.

Ayala, Ayla Hebrew; deer. *Other form*: Aaliyah.

Ayame Japanese; the iris flower.

Ayana Amharic; beautiful flower.

Ayanna Hindi; innocent.

Ayita Cherokee; first in the dance.

Ayla A character in the novel *Clan of the Cave Bear* by Jean M. Auel.

Aymara Aymara; the name of a tribe in Bolivia and Peru.

Ayne A form of the Scottish dialect word aine, meaning own, hence my own child

Ayomi Yoruba; my gift, my joy.

Ayumi Japanese; progress.

Aza Arabic; comfort.

Azaela Greek; from the name of the flowering plant Azalia.

Azami Japanese; thistle flower.

Azara From the plant name.

Azea The name of a civilization in the novel *In Conquest Born* by C.S. Friedman.

Azena Zena with the *A-* prefix.

Azina Zina with the *A-* prefix.

Azizah Arabic; cherished, precious. *Variant*: Aziza (Swahili).

Azmera Amharic; harvest.

Azura Persian; sky blue. *Variant*: Azzura (German).

B

Badra, Badria Dari; moonlike.

Bahira Arabic; dazzling, brilliant.

Bakula Hindi; flower.

Bali Sanskrit; strength. Bali is the name of a monkey king in Hindu mythology. Also linked to the name of the Pacific island.

Baraka Hebrew; blessing.

Barantha A blend of Barbara and Samantha.

Barbara Greek; stranger. Peaked in heavy use in 1950 but now in rapid decline. *Other forms*: Babette, Bara, Barbarella, Barbarette, Barbi, Barby, Barica. *Variants*: Bara, Baruska (Czech); Barbra (Danish); Barbe (French); Babette (German); Voska (Greek); Babara (Hawaiian); Bairbre (Irish Gaelic); Babetta, Barbarina, Barina (Italian); Varvara, Vara, Varya (Russian); Bebe (Spanish); Barbe, Barby, Varina, Varinka, Varuna, Varvara (Slavonic), Barbro (Swedish).

Barielle Probably Hebrew; excellence of the Lord.

Barika Swahili; successful.

Barri A form of Berenice. *Other form*: Barrie. (See Gender-neutral names.)

Barrie-Anne A blend of Barrie and Anne.

Barrie-Jane A blend of Barrie and Jane.

Beatrice Latin; bringer of happiness. Peaked in light use in 1900, but then declined rapidly and fell out of use by 1960. There was a small revival in 1980. *Other forms*: Bea, Beatie, Beatrix, Beatty, Bebe, Bettrys, Trixie, Trixy. *Variants*: Blazena (Czech); Beatrix (French, German, Dutch); Beatrisa, Bice (Italian); Beatrise (Latvian); Beatriz (Portuguese), Beatrisa (Russian); Beitris

(Scottish Gaelic); Beatriz, Ticha, Trisa (Spanish); Bettrys (Welsh).

Beatrix A form of Beatrice. Occasional use 1925–55. It fell out of use but revived again in 1990.

Becca Irish Gaelic; small, neat.

Becky A form of Rebecca. Occasional use from 1980.

Bela Hungarian; bright.

Belantha A blend of Bella (Isabel) and Samantha.

Belicia Spanish; dedicated to God.

Belinda Latin; wise beauty. Occasional use from 1955, peaking in 1965. *Other forms*: Bell, Belle, Bella, Blenda, Linda, Lynda, Velinda. *Variants*: Belle (French); Belita, Bella (Spanish).

Bemba Bemba; the name of a tribe in Zimbabwe.

Bena Hebrew; wise. *Other form*: Benna.

Benita A Spanish form of Benedicta. Latin; to bless. *Variants*: Benoite (French); Benedikta (German); Benedetta (Italian); Benita (Spanish).

Berenice A form of Bernice. Occasional use 1935–75.

Berinthia Probably invented by Vanbrugh for his play *The Relapse*. *Other forms*: Berantha, Berynthia.

Berlynn A blend of Bertha and Lynn.

Bernadette Old German; bold as a bear. A feminine form of Bernard. Occasional use from 1950 peaking in 1960. *Other forms*: Berna, Bernadine, Bernadotte, Bernarda, Bernela, Bernetta, Bernine, Bernita. *Variants*: Bernadetta (Italian); Bernarda, Dina (Polish); Bernadina (Spanish).

Bernice Greek; bringer of victory. Occasional use from 1900 but fell out of use in 1975. *Other forms*: Berenice, Bernelle, Bernine, Bernita, Bunny, Neigy, Nicia, Nixie,

Pherenice, Vernice. *Variants*: Berenice (French); Berenike (German); Bearnas (Scottish Gaelic); Bernita (Spanish).

Bernie A form of Bernice or Bernadette. (See Gender-neutral names.)

Bertha Old German; bright. Occasional use from its peak in 1900 to 1960. *Variants*: Berthe, Bertille (French); Bertel (German); Berta (Italian, Spanish); Berit (Swedish).

Beryl Greek; precious stone. The Spanish gold topaz. Light use from 1900 peaking in 1935. Fell out of use in 1985. *Other forms*: Berrura, Beryle.

Beth A form of Elizabeth. Occasional use from 1975.

Bethan A blend of Beth and Ann. Occasional use from 1995.

Beth-Anna A blend of Beth and Anna.

Bethany Hebrew; house of figs. Occasional use from 1980 rising sharply to light use in 1990. *Other forms*: Bethane, Bethania, Bethena, Bethia, Bethira, Bethita.

Bethia Hebrew; daughter of God.

Betora A blend of Betty and Lora (Laura).

Betsy A form of Elizabeth. Occasional use from 1925 to 1970.

Betty A form of Elizabeth. Heavy use at its peak in 1925 but then declined and fell out of use in 1970. *Other forms*: Bette, Betti, Betsy, Betzy, Biddy, Boski. *Variants*: Bette (French); Bette, Betti (German); Betta, Bettina (Italian); Beithidh (Scottish Gaelic); Belita (Spanish).

Betty-Jean A blend of Betty and Jean.

Betty-Jo A blend of Betty and Joanna.

Betty-Lou A blend of Betty and Louise.

Beulah Hebrew; married woman. Occasional use from 1925 falling out of use in 1970. *Other forms*: Beula, Beullah.

Beverley Old English; beaver stream. Light use from 1935, peaking in 1960, and has declined steadily since then. *Other forms*: Bev, Beverlee, Beverly, Buffy.

Beverly A form of Beverley. Occasional use 1950–70.

Beverlyann A blend of Beverly and Ann.

Bianca Italian; white. Occasional use from 1975. *Other forms*: Biancha, Biancia. *Variants*: Blanche (French); Blanka (German); Bluinse (Irish Gaelic); Blanca (Italian); Vianca (Spanish).

Bijou French; small and elegant, like a jewel.

Billie A form of Wilhelmina. (See Gender-neutral names.)

Billie-Jean A blend of Billie and Jean.

Billie-Jo A blend of Billie and Joanna.

Blaise, Blaze Old English; fiery torch. *Variant*: Blas (Spanish).

Blake Old English; pale, shining. (See Gender-neutral names.)

Blanche French; white. Occasional use from 1900, falling out of use in 1965. *Other forms*: Bellanca, Blancha, Blinny, Branca. *Variants*: Bela (Czech); Blanchette (French); Blanka (German); Bluinse (Irish Gaelic); Bianca (Italian); Branca (Portuguese); Blanca (Spanish); Blenda (Swedish).

Blodwen Welsh; white flower. Occasional use from 1925, falling out of use in 1950. *Other form*: Blodwyn. *Variants*: Blejwyn (Cornish); Blathnaid (Irish Gaelic).

Blossom Old English; to open into flower. Occasional use in the 1960s, but then fell out of use. *Variant*: Bluma (German).

Bluette From the plant name. *Other forms*: Blu, Blue.

Blysse Old English; perfect joy. *Other forms*: Blisse, Blyss.

Blythe Old Norse; joyful, blithe.

Bo Chinese; precious. (See Gender-neutral names.)

Bobbie A form of Roberta. Occasional use in 1955 and 1990.

Bobbie-Ann A blend of Bobbie and Ann.

Bobbie-Jo A blend of Bobbie and Joanna.

Bobbie-Lee A blend of Bobbie and Lee.

Bodhi Sanskrit; enlightenment, bliss.

Bonita Spanish; pretty. Occasional use from 1950. *Other form*: Nita. *Variant*: Bona (Italian).

Bonnie Scottish; beautiful. Occasional use from 1980. *Other forms*: Bonnee, Bonnetta.

Botan Japanese; peony. In Japan this is a name that would traditionally be given to a child born in June.

Brandi, Brandie, Brandy Dutch; burnt wine.

Brandy-Lynn A blend of Brandy and Lynda.

Brangane Welsh; white raven.

Branwen Welsh; beautiful raven.

Breana, Breanne Celtic; dark-haired beauty. *Other forms*: Breanna, Brenna.

Bree, Breena Irish Gaelic; fairy palace.

Breelyn A blend of Bree and Lynda.

Brenda Irish Gaelic; little raven. Heavy use peaking in 1935 and then declining till it fell out of use in 1980. *Other forms*: Brenna, Brendelle, Brendette.

Brendella A blend of Brenda and Ella.

Brendina A blend of Brenda and Dinah. *Other forms*: Brendene, Brendine.

Brendora A blend of Brenda and Dora.

Brenna Irish Gaelic; raven-haired.

Brett A form of Brittany. Occasional use from 1950. *Other forms*: Bret, Bretta, Brette. (See Gender-neutral names.)

Briallen Welsh; primrose.

Briana, Brianne Possibly Irish Gaelic; strong. Feminine forms of Brian. *Other forms*: Briahna, Brianne. *Variant*: Brienne (French).

Briantha A blend of Briana and Samantha.

Bridget Irish Gaelic; the high one. Occasional use from 1900. *Other forms*: Bedelia, Berget, Biddy, Breda, Breege, Bridgette, Bridie, Brietta, Brigid, Brita, Britte, Bryde. *Variants*: Pirkko (Finnish); Brigitte (French); Birgit, Brigitta (German); Berek (Greek); Breege, Brid, Brighid, Brigid (Irish Gaelic); Bree, Brigida (Italian); Birget (Norwegian); Bryga, Brygida (Polish); Brigida, Gidita (Spanish); Birgitte, Brigitta, Britt, Britta (Swedish); Bryde, Ffaod (Welsh).

Brie From the name of the cheese-making region in France.

Brieanne A blend of Brie and Anne. *Other form*: Brieann.

Brijette A blend of Bridget and Jette.

Brina Slavonic; protector.

Brisa Spanish; beloved.

Britt A form of Bridget. *Other forms*: Brita, Britta. (See Gender-neutral names.)

Brittany Latin; from Britain. Occasional use from 1990 in UK, although used widely in USA. *Other forms*: Britney, Brittaney, Brittanie, Brittney, Brittny.

Bronanda A blend of Bronwen and Wanda.

Bronessa Welsh; white.

Bronnen Cornish; waterside plant, rush.

Bronwen Welsh; white breast. *Other forms*: Bronia, Bronwyn.

Bronya Russian; armour.

Brook, Brooke Old English; dweller by the stream. (See Gender-neutral names.)

Brooklyn A blend of Brook and Lyn.

Brucena French; woods. A feminine form of Bruce.

Bruna Italian; brown-haired. A feminine form of Bruno. *Other forms*: Brunella, Brunetta.

Bryna Irish Gaelic; strength with virtue. *Other form*: Brynnah.

Bryola A blend of Bryna and Lola.

Bryony Greek; from the plant name. Occasional use from 1965. *Other forms*: Brioni, Brionie, Briony.

Buena Spanish; good.

C

Cachelle, Cachel French; hidden, hence hidden talents or wisdom.

Cachet French; prestige, authenticity.

Cadence Latin; movement of sound. *Variant*: Cadenza (Italian).

Cady Middle English; gentle.

Cahua Creek; place where cane grows.

Caietta Latin; to rejoice. A feminine form of Cai.

Cailin Scottish Gaelic; girl.

Caitanya A blend of Caitlin and Tanya.

Caitlin An Irish form of Catherine. Occasional use from 1985. *Other forms*: Cailey, Caitleen, Caitlene, Caitlon, Caitlyn, Caitria, Catlin, Cayley.

Caja Cornish; daisy.

Cala Arabic; castle.

Calabara Russian; grey squirrel.

Calabria Gaulish; white.

Calandra Greek; skylark. *Variants*: Calandre (French); Calandria (Spanish).

Calantha Greek; beautiful blossom. *Variant*: Calanthe (French).

Calara A blend of Calantha and Lara.

Caldora Greek; beautiful gift.

Caledonne, Caledonia Scottish Gaelic; Scotland.

Calella Celtic; handmaid.

Calendula Latin; marigold.

Calida Spanish; ardently loving.

Calinda A traditional Spanish dance.

Calista Greek; most lovely. *Other forms*: Calise, Calysta.

Calla, Callan, Cally, Callie Greek; beautiful.

Callena Old German; talkative.

Calliope Greek; beautiful voice. *Variant*: Kalliope (Greek).

Callula Latin; little beauty.

Caltha Latin; marigold.

Calypso Greek; concealer. A sea nymph in Greek mythology.

Camara A blend of Camilla and Mary.

Cambria Latin; from Wales.

Camelia From the flowering plant Camellia, named after the botanist George Joseph Kamel.

Cameo Italian; a carving (the term for a sculptured jewel).

Camilla Latin; attendant, messenger. Occasional use from 1955. *Other forms*: Camala, Camie, Camila, Cammilyn, Cammylle, Chamelle, Kamille, Millie, Milly. *Variants*: Kamila (Czech); Cami, Camille (French); Kamilla (German, Polish); Kamila (Hungarian); Komilla (Russian); Camila (Spanish).

Caminda A blend of Camilla and Linda.

Camira A blend of Camilla and Mira (Myra).

Canace Greek; daughter of the wind.

Candia Greek; woman from Candia (now called Heraklion) in Crete.

Candice Greek; fire white. Occasional use from 1975. *Other forms*: Canace, Canda, Candace, Candelle, Candi, Candis, Candise, Candy, Candyce, Kandace, Kandy, Kandyce.

Candida Latin; white. *Other form*: Candyda. *Variants*: Candi, Candide (French); Kandida (German).

Candora A blend of Candice and Dora.

Candra Sanskrit; moon.

Canice Irish Gaelic; pleasant person. (See Gender-neutral names.)

Canli A blend of zodiac signs Cancer and Libra.

Cantara Arabic; small bridge.

Cantrelle French; song.

Caomh Scottish Gaelic; loving.

Capay Wintun; stream.

Caprice Latin; head with bristling hair. *Other forms*: Capri, Caprise, Capryce, Kaprice, Kapryce.

Cara Irish Gaelic; friend. Or Italian; dear one. Occasional use from 1975. *Other forms*: Caralie, Carina, Carine, Kara, Karina. *Variants*: Carina (Italian); Carita (Spanish).

Carana A blend of Cara and Nana.

Caranda A blend of Cara and Amanda.

Carantha A blend of Cara and Samantha.

Caraway Greek; from the plant name.

Cardeil Scottish Gaelic; friendly.

Careen The name of one of Scarlett O'Hara's sisters in *Gone With The Wind* by Margaret Mitchell.

Carelle, Carella Old English; care, hence carer, caregiver.

Carema A blend of Cara and Emma.

Carey Old English; pleasant stream. Occasional use from 1965. *Other forms*: Cari, Carie, Karey. (See Gender-neutral names.)

Cariad Welsh; sweetheart.

Carilla Old German; farmer.

Carina Latin; a keel. Occasional use from 1955. *Other forms*: Carene, Carine, Caryn, Karina. *Variants*: Karina (German); Karna (Swedish).

Caris Greek; favour, grace. *Other forms*: Carissa, Carisse, Karissa.

Carissa Greek; beloved. *Variants*: Caressa, Karessa (French).

Carita Latin; compassion, charity.

Carla Old English; womanly. A feminine form of Charles. Occasional use from 1950 peaking in 1980. *Other forms*: Arla, Carene, Carila, Carletha, Carlia, Carlonda, Carlysle. *Variant*: Carlita (Spanish).

Carley A form of Carly. Occasional use 1975–85.

Carlie A form of Carly. Occasional use from 1960 peaking in 1980.

Carline Latin; from the plant name, meaning thistle.

Carlissa A blend of Cara and Lissa (Larissa).

Carly A form of Caroline. Light use from 1975 peaking in 1980. *Other forms*: Carlee, Carli, Carlie, Carley, Carlye, Karli, Karly.

Carmel Hebrew; vineyard. Occasional use from 1950. *Other forms*: Carmelia, Carmelitha, Carmelina, Carmelita, Carmesa, Carmila, Leeta. *Variants*: Carmela, Carmelina, Carmilla (Italian); Carmo (Portuguese); Carmelita, Melita (Spanish).

Carmen Latin; song. Occasional use from 1950. *Other forms*: Carmia, Carmaine, Carmene, Carmina, Carmita, Carmyn. *Variants*: Charmaine (French); Karmen (Hebrew); Carmine (Italian); Carmelita (Spanish).

Carol Old English; womanly. A feminine form of Charles. Heavy use 1950–60, but then declined steadily, and fell out of use in 1990. *Other forms*: Carel, Carilis, Carola, Carole, Carrol. *Variants*: Karel, Karole (Finnish); Carole (French); Karoll (Slavonic); Carlita, Carola (Spanish).

Carole A French form of Carol. Occasional use from 1935, peaking in light use in 1960 and falling out of use in 1990.

Carolinda A blend of Carol and Linda.

Caroline An Italian feminine form of Charles. Light use from 1900, peaking in 1960 and then slowly declining. *Other forms*: Arla, Carla, Carlene, Carley, Carline, Carly, Carlynne, Caro, Carol, Caroleen, Carolene, Carolina, Carolyn, Carolyne, Caron, Carrie, Cassie, Charla, Charlayne, Charleen, Charlene, Cherlene, Karla, Karlene, Karoline, Karolyn, Lina, Sharleen. *Variants*: Karolina, Karola (Czech); Lina (Finnish); Charlotte (French); Karoline, Lottchen (German); Carla, Carolina (Italian); Karlene (Latvian); Karolinka, Ina (Polish); Karolina (Scandinavian); Carolan (Slavonic); Carlota (Spanish); Lotta (Swedish).

Carolyn A blend of Carol and Lyn. Occasional use from 1950 peaking in light use in 1960. *Other forms*: Carolynne.

Caromel Latin; dear honey.

Caromy Celtic; friend. *Other forms*: Caromie, Karomy.

Caron Welsh; loving, kind. Occasional use 1955–70. *Other forms*: Carren, Carron.

Caronwen Welsh; fair love.

Carrie A form of Caroline. Occasional use from 1900. *Other forms*: Carri, Kari, Karri. *Variant*: Kari (Danish).

Carson Old English; son of the marsh dweller. (See Gender-neutral names.)

Caryl Welsh; loving, kind.

Carys Welsh; loved one.

Casey Irish Gaelic; watchful. *Other forms*: Kacey, Kasey. (See Gender-neutral names.)

Cassady Celtic; ingenious. A feminine form of Cassidy. (See Gender-neutral names.)

Cassandra Greek; entangler of men. Occasional use from 1900. *Other forms*: Casandra, Cass, Cassander, Cassey, Cassie, Caz, Sandie, Sandra, Sandy. *Variants*: Casandre, Kassandre (French); Casandra, Casita (Spanish).

Cassantha A blend of Cassandra and Samantha.

Cassara A blend of Cassandra and Sara.

Cassey A form of Cassandra. Occasional use from 1985. *Other form*: Cassie.

Cassia From the name of a plant which was made into a perfume. *Other forms*: Cassena, Cassya, Kassya.

Catherine Greek; pure. Light but steady use from 1900. *Other forms*: Caitlin, Caren, Caryn, Casey, Catarina,

Catharine, Cathleen, Cathryn, Cathy, Catrina, Catriona. *Variants*: Caitlin, Caitria, Cathleen, Caitriona, Catrin, Caitlin (Irish Gaelic); Catarina, Caterina (Italian); Catarina, Catia (Portuguese); Catriona, Catryna (Scottish Gaelic); Catrina (Slavonic); Catalina (Spanish); Cadi, Catrin (Welsh).

Cathleen An Irish form of Catherine. Occasional use from 1950 to 1970.

Cathryn A form of Catherine. Occasional use from 1960.

Cathy A form of Catherine. Occasional use 1960–75.

Catrina A Slavonic form of Catherine. Occasional use from 1955 to 1980.

Catriona A Scottish Gaelic form of Catherine. Occasional use from 1950. *Other forms*: Caitriona, Katriona, Triona. *Variant*: Caitriona (Irish Gaelic).

Cavatina Italian; little aria, usually melodic and graceful.

Cazantha A blend of Caz (Cassandra) and Samantha.

Ceanne A blend of Celia and Anne.

Cecilia Latin; dim-sighted. Occasional use from 1900, peaking in 1925, but fell out of use by 1950, probably because of the negative meaning of the name. A small revival in 1975 was not sustained. *Other forms*: Cacilie, Cecelia, Cecely, Cecille, Cecily, Celia, Cicely, Sisile. *Variants*: Cecilie, Cilka (Czech); Silja (Finnish); Cecile, Celie (French); Cacilie (German); Kiki, Kikilia (Hawaiian); Sile, Sisile (Irish Gaelic); Cesia (Polish); Sile, Sileas (Scottish Gaelic); Cecilla, Chila (Spanish); Cesya (Swedish).

Cedar Greek; from the name of the coniferous tree with fragrant wood, once considered a sign of wealth in those who possessed things made from it. (See Gender-neutral names.)

Ceilidh, Caylee Scottish Gaelic; gathering, celebration.

Celandine A flower name. Greek; the swallow.

Celantha A blend of Celia and Samantha.

Celara A blend of Celia and Lara.

Celeste Latin; heavenly. *Other forms*: Celestine, Celestina, Celestyna. *Variants*: Celestyna, Tyna (Czech); Celestine, Celie (French); Celestina (Italian, Spanish); Celina, Celinka, Celka (Polish); Cela, Celestyn, Celinka, Selinka (Russian).

Celia A form of Cecilia. Occasional use from 1900, peaking in 1950. *Other forms*: Ceilia, Ceileigh, Ceyla, Ceylin. *Variants*: Celie, Celine (French).

Celosia Greek; a flame.

Cemoche Hichiti; big sand.

Cerella, Cerelle Latin; springtime.

Ceri Welsh; loving, kind. Occasional use from 1960. *Other forms*: Ceria, Cerian, Cerri, Cerys.

Ceridwen Welsh; fair poetry. The name of the Welsh goddess of poetry. Occasional use from 1900.

Cerise French; cherry.

Cerka Serbo-Croatian; daughter.

Cerys Welsh; loving, kind.

Chai Hebrew; life.

Chaika Russian; seagull.

Chakra Sanskrit; wheel or circular vortex of energy.

Chalconel A modern invention meaning chalice of the elves.

Challah Hebrew; bread.

Challis, Challys Phonetic forms of chalice.

Chalona Lona with the *Cha-* prefix.

Chamara Mara with the *Cha-* prefix.

Chambray French; from the name of the lightweight fabric.

Chamella Mella (Melah) with the *Cha-* prefix.

Chana Cambodian; fragrant tree. *Other forms*: Chan, Chanae.

Chanda Sanskrit; great goddess. A name given in Hindu mythology to the goddess Devi.

Chandelle French; candle.

Chandra Sanskrit; moon. (See Gender-neutral names.)

Chanel From the name of the French perfume. Occasional use from 1980. *Other forms*: Chaneel, Chanell, Chanelle, Channelle, Shanel.

Chanelle A form of Chanel. Occasional use in 1980.

Chantal French; song. Occasional use from 1970. *Other forms*: Chantale, Chantalle, Chantay, Chantaye, Chantel, Chantelle, Chantille.

Chantel A form of Chantal. Occasional use from 1965, peaking in 1990.

Chantelle A form of Chantal. Occasional use from 1970, running parallel with Chantal until 1990, when it suddenly became seven times as popular. *Other forms*: Chantel, Chantela, Chantele, Chantella, Chantiel, Chantrel, Chantress, Chauntel, Chawntel, Chontel, Shantel, Shantelle.

Chantrea Cambodian; moon.

Chardae, Chardey, Charde Forms of Chardonnay, from the name of the wine-making grape variety originating in France, now grown all over the world. *Other forms*: Chardonay, Shardonay.

Charel, Charelle Blends of Charlotte and Ella.

Charis Greek; grace, beauty. *Other form*: Charisse.

Charity Latin; affection. Occasional use from 1900, falling out of use in 1980. *Other forms*: Carisa, Carissa, Charis, Charissa, Charrie, Chattie, Cherry, Sharity. *Variants*: Karita (Finnish); Carita (Italian); Caridad (Spanish).

Charla, Sharla Old English; womanly. Feminine forms of Charles.

Charleen A diminutive of Charlotte. Occasional use from 1980 to 1985. *Other forms*: Charlayne, Charlene.

Charlene A diminutive of Charlotte. Popularized by the television series *Neighbours*. Occasional use from 1980, although now declining. *Other forms*: Charla, Charlaine, Charlanna, Charlayne, Charleen, Charleesa, Charlena, Charlesina, Charline, Charlyn, Charlzina. *Variant*: Sharlene (French).

Charlie A form of Charlotte. *Other forms*: Charle, Charlea, Charlee, Charleigh, Charley, Charli, Charly, Charyl, Sharley, Sharli, Sharlie. (See Gender-neutral names.)

Charlinda, Sharlynda Blends of Charlotte and Linda.

Charlotte A French feminine form of Charles. Light use from 1900, although it almost disappeared in 1955. Since then, however, it has steadily increased and was in very heavy use by 1990. *Other forms*: Carla, Carlota, Carlotta, Charil, Charla, Charlayne, Charlene, Charline, Charlotta, Charyl, Cheryl, Karlene, Karlotta, Lola, Lotta, Lottie, Lotty, Sharlene, Sharline, Sharyl, Sherry, Sheryl, Totti. *Variants*: Karla (Czech); Lotje (Dutch); Lolotte (French); Karla, Karlotte, Lotte (German); Karlotta (Greek); Sarolta (Hungarian); Searlait (Irish Gaelic); Carlotta (Italian); Carlota (Spanish); Charlotta (Swedish).

Charlyanne A blend of Charly (Charlie) and Anne.

Charmaine A French form of Carmen. Occasional use from 1950. *Other forms*: Charma, Charmain, Charmalique, Charmane, Charmara, Charmayne, Charmene, Charmese, Charmine, Charmita, Charmyn.

Charmian Greek; drop of joy. Occasional use from 1955. *Other forms*: Charmiane, Charmyan.

Chava Hebrew; life.

Chavonne A phonetic form of Siobhan. *Other forms*: Chavanne, Chavon, Chavonna.

Chaya Hebrew; life.

Chaylee, Chayle Blends of Chaya and Lee. *Other form*: Chylan.

Chelsea Old English; landing place for chalk. Light use from 1985, showing a sharp increase in 1990. *Other forms*: Chelcie, Chelcy, Chelese, Chelsa, Chelsay, Chelsey, Chelsie, Chellise, Cheslee, Cheslie, Chessie, Kelsi, Shelsea. *Variant*: Kelsi (Scottish).

Chena Athapascan; river.

Chenetta French; oak tree. *Other forms*: Chenca, Chenette.

Chenille French; hairy caterpillar (hence the thick pile fabric).

Chenoa Sioux; white dove.

Chere French; dear one. *Other form*: Cher.

Cheredith, Cheredyth Blends of Chere and Edith.

Chereen, Cherene, Cheryna Blends of Chere and Doreen.

Cherella, Cherelle Blends of Chere and Ella.

Cherie French; dear one. Occasional use from 1950. *Other form*: Cheri.

Cherilyn, Cherilene Blends of Cheryl and Lyn.

Cherisa, Cherissa Blends of Cheryl and Lisa.

Cherita A blend of Cheryl and Rita.

Cherith, Cheryth Latin; love, cherish. *Variant*: Cherise (French).

Cherokee Cherokee; our people. From the name of the Native American nation.

Cherry A form of Cherie. Occasional use from 1955.

Cheryl A blend of Cherry and Beryl. Light use from 1950, peaking in 1965. *Other forms*: Charel, Cherelle, Cheryle, Cheryll, Cheryn.

Cheryl-Anne, Cherylann Blends of Cheryl and Anne.

Cheryl-Lee A blend of Cheryl and Lee.

Chesca A blend of Chere and Jessica. *Other form*: Cheska.

Chesna Slavonic; peaceful.

Chewelah Probably Spokane; snake, hence wisdom.

Cheyenne Cheyenne; from the name of the Native American nation.

Chi Chinese; life-force, breath. The fundamental energy of the universe in Taoist philosophy.

Chiara Italian; clear.

Chika Japanese; near and dear.

Chimena Greek; hospitable.

Chimwa Nyanja; stone, foundation.

China Persian; porcelain, china.

Chiquita Spanish; little one.

Chiriga Wahungwe; girl of poor parents.

Chirita From the name of the flowering plant.

Chloe Greek; young green shoot, hence blooming. Light use from 1970 with a marked increase in 1990. *Other forms*: Clea, Clo, Cloe, Cloey, Klea, Kloe, Klowie. *Variant*: Cloe (Italian).

Chlorella, Chlorel Blends of Chloris and Ella.

Chloris Greek; blooming.

Cho Korean; beautiful. *Other form*: Chonda.

Cholena Delaware; bird, hence a free spirit.

Choya Japanese; butterfly.

Chris A form of Christine. (See Gender-neutral names.)

Chrisanda A blend of Christine and Amanda.

Chrisantha A blend of Christine and Samantha.

Chrisselle A blend of Christine and Elle.

Christa A German form of Christina. *Other form*: Chrysta. *Variants*: Crista (Italian); Crysta (Spanish).

Christabel Latin; fair follower of Christ. *Other forms*: Christobel, Chrystabel.

Christelle, Christella Blends of Christa and Ella.

Christian Latin; a Christian. *Other form*: Christiane. (See Gender-neutral names.)

Christina Latin; a Christian. Occasional use from 1900, peaking in 1955. More popular than the alternative spelling Christine in 1900, but declined steadily as Christine rose. However it recovered in 1990, when it was used five times more often than its rival. *Other forms*: Christeena, Christiana, Christiania, Kristina, Krystyna, Tina, Xina. *Variants*: Khrustina (Bulgarian); Krista, Kristina, Kuryska, Tyna (Czech); Kristia, Kristina (Finnish); Christa, Stina (German); Christin, Tina (Greek); Kilikina (Hawaiian); Kriska, Krisztina (Hungarian); Cristiona (Irish Gaelic); Cristina (Italian); Krista (Latvian); Krysta, Krystyna (Polish); Cristina (Portuguese); Khristina, Khristya (Russian); Cairistiona (Scottish Gaelic); Christiana, Cristina (Spanish); Kristina, Kolina (Swedish); Khristina (Ukrainian).

Christine Latin; a Christian. Occasional use from 1900,

rising rapidly from 1935 to a peak of very heavy use in 1950, and then declining into occasional use again by 1970. This has been the favourite form of the name, at its peak more than twenty times as popular as Christina. *Other forms*: Chris, Chrissie, Chrissy, Christee, Christel, Christen, Christene, Christian, Christiane, Christie, Christy, Chrystine, Crissie, Cristene, Cristin, Cristine, Kersti, Kerstin, Kristin, Krista, Kristi, Kristine, Kristyan, Kristy, Tine. *Variants*: Chesten (Cornish); Kirsten, Kristina, Stinne (Danish); Christie (Dutch); Christele, Christiane, Crestienne (French); Christiane, Christelle, Chrystel, Kirsten, Kristel, Tine (German); Cristin (Irish Gaelic); Kristine (Latvian); Kjersti, Kristin, Stina (Norwegian); Krystyn (Polish); Kirsteen, Kirstey, Kirstie, Kirsty (Scottish); Ciorstaidh (Scottish Gaelic); Cristy (Spanish); Kristen, Kristine (Swedish); Cristyn (Welsh).

Ciara Irish Gaelic; dark-haired.

Cindora A blend of Cindy and Dora.

Cindy A form of Cynthia or Lucinda. Occasional use from 1960. *Other forms*: Ciji, Cindee, Cindi, Cynda, Cyndale, Cyndee, Cyndi, Cyndy, Sindie, Syndy.

Cindy-Lou A blend of Cindy and Louise.

Cinnabar Persian; red. Cinnabar (vermilion) is a bright red dye.

Cinnamon Hebrew; from the name of the spice. *Other form*: Cynamon.

Cinta Indonesian; affection. *Other forms*: Centa, Cynta.

Cirine Irish Gaelic; exalted.

Cirra, Cyrra From cirrus, a type of cloud.

Civia Hebrew; deer.

Clair Latin; clear, bright. Occasional use 1970–85.

Claire Latin; clear, bright. This French version is the most popular form of the name, outperforming Clair and Clare by a big margin. Occasional use from 1935, peaking in very heavy use in 1975 and declining into light use by 1990. *Other forms*: Clair, Clairette, Clare, Klaire. *Variants*: Klara (Czech); Clair, Clarette, Clarice (French); Clara, Clarissa, Klara (German); Klarika (Hungarian); Clar (Irish Gaelic); Chiara, Clarissa (Italian); Klara (Polish, Russian); Sorcha (Scottish Gaelic); Clara, Clareta, Clarita (Spanish).

Clairona A blend of Claire and Rona.

Clanis A blend of Clare and Janis.

Clara Latin; clear, bright. This Spanish version of the name was the most popular form in 1900, when it was in light use. However it declined rapidly and fell out of use by 1960. A small revival in 1985 was not sustained. *Other forms*: Claran, Clarina, Clarinda, Claritza, Clarrie, Clary, Klara.

Claranda A blend of Clara and Amanda.

Clarantha A blend of Clara and Samantha.

Clare Latin; clear, bright. Light use from 1925, peaking in 1975.

Clarenda Latin; brightening.

Claribel A blend of Clare and Bella (Isabel).

Clarice Probably Latin; fame. Occasional use from 1900 to 1935.

Clarina A blend of Clare and Marina.

Clarinda Invented by Edmund Spenser for his allegorical poem *The Faerie Queene*.

Clarissa A form of Clarice, a French version of Claire. Popularized by the novel *Clarissa* by Samuel Richardson. *Variant*: Clarisa (Spanish).

Clarity Latin; clearness.

Claudette A French diminutive form of Claudia. Occasional use from 1950 falling out of use in 1970. *Other forms*: Claudeen, Claudelle, Claudetta, Claudina, Claudine.

Claudia Latin; from the Roman name Claudius, meaning lame. In occasional use from 1900, but now in decline probably due to the unfortunate meaning. *Variants*: Claudine (French), Klaudia (German, Polish); Klavdia (Russian); Gladys, Gwladys (Welsh).

Clea A form of Cleopatra. Popularized by the novel *Clea* by Lawrence Durrell.

Cleandra A blend of Clea and Sandra.

Cleantha A blend of Clea and Samantha.

Clem, Clemmie Forms of Clementine. Latin; merciful. *Other forms*: Clemence, Clementina. *Variant*: Klementyna (Polish). (See Gender-neutral names.)

Cleodel Greek; famous place.

Cleome Greek; from the name of the flowering plant.

Cleone Greek; light, clear.

Cleopatra Greek; fame of her father. *Other forms*: Clea, Cleo. *Variant*: Cleta (French).

Cleora A blend of Cleo (Cleopatra) and Dora.

Cliandra A blend of Clio and Sandra.

Cliantha Greek; flower of glory. *Variant*: Cleanthe (French).

Clio Greek; to praise.

Cliona Irish Gaelic; from Cliodhna, the name of a fairy princess in Irish legends. *Other forms*: Cleona.

Clodagh Irish Gaelic; the name of a river in Tipperary.

Clorinda A blend of Cloe (Chloe) and Lorinda.

Cocha Quechua; sea. Mamacocha is the Inca goddess of the sea.

Cochava Hebrew; starlight.

Cocheta Native American; the unknown.

Codie, Codey, Codi Irish Gaelic; riches. (See Gender-neutral names.)

Cohelee Creek; good place for cane.

Coir Scottish Gaelic; kind.

Colby Old English; dark-haired. *Other forms*: Colbi, Colbee. (See Gender-neutral names.)

Colette Latin; victorious. Occasional use from 1950. *Other forms*: Coleta, Collette, Cosetta, Kalotte.

Colina A feminine form of Colin, a version of Nicholas.

Colista Greek; most lovely.

Colleen Irish Gaelic; girl. Occasional use from 1925. *Other forms*: Coleen, Colena, Colene, Colina, Collene.

Collette A form of Colette. Occasional use from 1965.

Columba, Columbia Latin; dove. Also a reference to the columbine plant, so named because its flowers resemble a group of doves. *Other forms*: Columbana, Columbina, Columbine. *Variants*: Colombe (French); Colomba (Spanish).

Connie A form of Constance. Occasional use 1925–55.

Conrada Old German; brave counsel. A feminine form of Conrad. *Other forms*: Conradina, Conradine, Konradine. *Variants*: Koenrada (Dutch); Konrada (German); Corrada, Corradina (Italian); Konradina (Polish).

Constance Latin; steadfast. Light use from 1900, peaking in 1925 and falling out of use in 1965. A modest revival started in 1985. *Other forms*: Connie, Constancy, Constanta, Conte, Custance, Konstance. *Variants*: Konstanze (German); Kosta, Tina (Greek); Constanza,

Costanza (Italian); Kostyusha (Russian); Constancia, Constanza (Spanish).

Coos Pennicook; pine trees.

Cora Greek; maiden. Occasional use from 1900, falling out of use in 1950. *Other forms*: Cohra, Coralie, Corene, Coretta, Cori, Corinna, Corissa, Corita, Cory, Kora. *Variants*: Corrine (French); Corina (Spanish).

Corabel, Corabella Blends of Cora and Belle.

Corabeth A blend of Cora and Elizabeth.

Coral Latin; coral. Occasional use from 1925. *Other forms*: Corral, Koral. *Variant*: Coralie (French).

Coralee A blend of Cora and Lee. *Other forms*: Coralie, Coraleen.

Coralena A blend of Cora and Lena. *Other form*: Coralene.

Coralina A blend of Cora and Lina. *Other forms*: Coralin, Coraline, Coralyn.

Corana Old French; crown.

Coranda A blend of Cora and Amanda.

Corantha A blend of Cora and Samantha.

Corazon Spanish; heart.

Cordelia Celtic; daughter of the sea. *Variants*: Cordelie (French); Kordela, Kordula (German).

Cori, Cory, Corye Irish Gaelic; from the hollow. Occasional use from 1970. *Other forms*: Corie, Corri, Corrie, Corrye. (See Gender-neutral names.)

Coriantha Greek; a feminine form of Coriander, from the name of the herb. *Other forms*: Coryantha, Koriantha, Koryantha.

Corinna A form of Corinne. Occasional use from 1965.

Corinne A form of Cora. Occasional use from 1935 peaking in 1965. *Other forms*: Corin, Corina, Corinda, Corine, Corinna, Corrine, Corynna, Korina, Korinne. *Variant*: Corene (French).

Corinthe A blend of Cora and Ianthe.

Coris, Koris, Corys Greek; from the name of the flowering plant.

Corisanda Greek; singer in a chorus.

Corisande Old French; a name used in medieval French romances.

Corissa A blend of Cora and Larissa.

Corita A blend of Cora and Rita.

Corla Old English; curlew.

Cornelia Latin; horn-coloured. A feminine form of Cornelius. *Variants*: Cornelie (French); Kornelia (German); Nelia (Spanish); Kornelis (Swedish).

Coromel Latin; sweet ruler.

Corona, Korona Latin; crown.

Corrine A form of Corinne. Occasional use from 1970, peaking in 1990.

Cory-Ann, Cori-Ann Blends of Cori and Ann.

Cory-Lee, Cori-Lee Blends of Cori and Lee.

Cosima Greek; world harmony.

Cosma Greek; order, the universe, the cosmic scheme of things.

Coty French; old house. *Other forms*: Coti, Cotye.

Courtney Latin; courtyard. Occasional use from 1965. *Other forms*: Cortney, Courteny, Courtenay, Courtnay, Courtni, Courtny, Kortney, Kortni, Kortny, Kourtney, Kourtni. *Variant*: Courtnee (French). (See Gender-neutral names.)

Creola French; home-bred.

Creona A blend of Creola and Fiona.

Cressida Greek; gold. *Other form*: Cressyda.

Cresta Old French; mountaintop.

Crionna Scottish Gaelic; wise.

Crisann A blend of Christine and Ann.

Cristella, Cristelle Blends of Christine and Ella.

Crystal Greek; clear glass. Occasional use from 1970.
   Other forms: Christal, Christel, Cristal, Cristalle, Cristel,
   Cristella, Crystala, Crystale, Crystalin, Crystall, Crystel,
   Crystelia, Crystle, Crystol, Crystyl, Krystal, Krystol.
   Variants: Krystal (Polish); Criostal (Scottish Gaelic).

Crystonel A modern invention meaning crystal of the
   elves.

Cyan Greek; dark blue. *Other form*: Cian.

Cygna Latin; swan.

Cyma Greek; to grow, flourish.

Cymry Welsh; of Wales. *Other forms*: Cymri, Kymri,
   Kymry. (See Gender-neutral names.)

Cyndora A blend of Cyndy (Cindy) and Dora.

Cynthia Greek; moon goddess. Light use from 1925 until
   it fell out of use in 1990. *Other forms*: Cinda, Cindi,
   Cindy, Cyndy, Cynthea, Cynthiana, Cynthie, Cynthya,
   Cythia, Kynthia, Sindee, Sindy. *Variants*: Kynthia
   (Greek); Cinzia (Italian); Cintia (Portuguese); Cinta
   (Spanish).

Cyrena Greek; from Cyrene in Greece. *Other form*:
   Cyrene.

Cyrille Greek; lord, ruler. A feminine form of Cyril.
   (See Gender-neutral names.)

D

Dacey Irish Gaelic; southerner. *Other forms*: Dacee, Daci, Daycey, Dayci. (See Gender-neutral names.)

Dacia Latin; the far land.

Dae, Daye Old English; day.

Daelynn A blend of Dae and Lynn.

Daeshawna A blend of Dae and Shawna.

Dagomba Dagomba; the name of a tribe in Ghana.

Dahlia From the flower, named after the Swedish botanist Anders Dahl. Occasional use 1935–55. *Other forms*: Daliah, Daylia, Daylea.

Daintry Possibly Old English; hardy Dane.

Daireen A character in the novel *Daireen* by F. F. Moore.

Daisy Old English; from the name of the flower, meaning day's eye. Light use in 1900, but declined until it fell out of use in 1950. A modest revival from 1985 showed a sharp increase in 1990. *Other forms*: Dasia, Daisie, Dasey, Dasy, Daysy.

Dakota Dakota; alliance of friends. From the United States geographical name, derived from the name of the Dakota Native American nation. (See Gender-neutral names.)

Dalila Swahili; gentle.

Dalinda Linda with the *Da-* prefix.

Dalisa Lisa with the *Da-* prefix.

Dallas Irish Gaelic; wise. *Other forms*: Dallys, Dalyce. (See Gender-neutral names.)

Dalta Scottish Gaelic; favourite child.

Dalya A Slavonic form of Delilah.

Damae Mae with the *Da-* prefix.

Damala Mala with the *Da-* prefix.

Damara Greek; taming.

Damarel A modern invention meaning lady elf.

Damaris From the name of the evergreen tree.

Damiana, Damienne Greek; to tame. Feminine forms of Damian.

Damica French; friendly.

Damita Spanish; small noblewoman.

Dana Irish Gaelic; brave, bold. Dana (or Danu) was a mother goddess in Irish mythology. *Variants*: Danka (Czech); Dayna (Scandinavian).

Danae The mother of Perseus in Greek mythology.

Danella, Danelle Blends of Dana and Ella.

Danessa A blend of Danielle and Vanessa.

Dangara Tajik; a place-name in Tajikistan.

Dania Hebrew; God is my judge.

Danica Slavonic; morning star. *Other forms*: Danice, Danika.

Daniela A form of Danielle. Occasional use 1960–75.

Daniella A form of Danielle. Occasional use from 1990.

Danielle Hebrew; God is my judge. A feminine form of Daniel. Light use from 1960, but a steady increase from 1980. *Other forms*: Danae, Daneela, Daneen, Danelle, Danella, Danessia, Danette, Dani, Dania, Daniela, Daniella, Dannii, Danya, Dannye, Donelle, Donniella. *Variants*: Daniell (French); Dania, Danya (Hebrew); Danata, Danza (Hungarian); Daniella (Italian); Danielka (Polish); Danila, Danya (Russian); Daniela (Spanish).

Danii A form of Danielle. *Other forms*: Danni, Dannie, Dannii. (See Gender-neutral names.)

Danuih According to Murry Hope in her book *The Gaia Dialogues* this is the Atlantean name for the earth Goddess, the devic consciousness which regulates and programmes this planet.

Danya A Russian form of Danielle.

Danza A Hungarian form of Danielle.

Daoma, Daomi Blends of Dana and Naomi.

Daphne Greek; the laurel tree. Light use from 1925 until it fell out of use in 1965. *Other forms*: Dafna, Dafne, Dafny, Daphnie.

Dara Irish Gaelic; oak tree. *Other forms*: Darah, Deri.

Daranda A blend of Dara and Amanda.

Darantha A blend of Dara and Samantha.

Darby Irish Gaelic; free. (See Gender-neutral names.)

Darcy Irish Gaelic; dark-haired. *Other forms*: Darcee, Darcey, Darci, Darcie. *Variant*: Darcelle (French). (See Gender-neutral names.)

Darel, Darelle Old English; dear one.

Daria Persian; queenly. *Variants*: Darie, Darina (Czech); Darya, Dasha (Russian).

Darina Irish Gaelic; bountiful.

Darissa A blend of Dara and Larissa.

Darla Middle English; loved one.

Darlene Old English; dearly beloved. Occasional use from 1980. *Other forms*: Darla, Darleen, Darlena, Darlin, Darline, Darlyn.

Darlita Greek; young girl.

Darsha Sanskrit; gift of God.

Daru Hindi; pine tree.

Darvasa Turkmen; a place-name in Turkmenistan.

Daryl A French form of Darlene. *Other forms*: Darielle, Darile. (See Gender-neutral names.)

Daryllyn, Darilin, Darylyn Blends of Daryl and Lyn.

Daryn Greek; gifts.

Dashawna Shawna with the *Da-* prefix.

Dauphine French; princess.

Dava A Slavonic form of Davida.

Davalynn A blend of Davida and Lynn. *Other form*: Davalinda.

Davida Hebrew; beloved by God. A feminine form of David. *Variants*: Tevita (Fijian); Davina, Devina (Scottish); Dava (Slavonic); Davita (Spanish).

Davidene Hebrew; beloved by God. A feminine form of David.

Davina Scottish feminine form of David. Occasional use from 1955. *Other forms*: Dava, Daveen, Daveena, Davena, Davene, Daviana, Davida, Davine, Davinia, Davita, Davona, Devene, Devina, Vida, Veda, Vita. *Variant*: Davita (Spanish).

Davora A blend of Davina and Dora.

Dawn Middle English; daybreak. Light use from 1935 peaking in heavy use in 1965. *Other forms*: Dawana, Dawanna, Dawna, Dawne.

Dawnella, Dawnelle Blends of Dawn and Ella.

Dawnisha A blend of Dawn and Aisha.

Daya Hebrew; bird, hence a free spirit.

Dayala, Dayla Sanskrit; mercy.

Dayle Old English; from the valley. A feminine form of Dale.

Daymer A Cornish name of uncertain meaning.

Dealas Scottish Gaelic; affection.

Deandra A blend of Dee and Andrea.

Deanna A form of Diana. Occasional use from 1950. *Other forms*: Deana, Deann, Deanne, Deeanne, Deena.

Deanisha A blend of Deana and Aisha.

Debbie A form of Deborah. Light use from 1955. *Other forms*: Debbe, Debbee, Debbi, Debby, Debi, Debs.

Debora A form of Deborah. Occasional use in 1965.

Deborah Hebrew; a bee, hence industrious. Light use from 1900 peaking in very heavy use in 1965. Still in occasional use, but now in a steady decline. *Other forms*: Debera, Debora, Debra, Debria, Debrina, Devera, Devora, Devorah, Devra, Dovra. *Variants*: Devora (Bulgarian); Deboran (German); Devora (Greek); Dwora (Hebrew); Deerah (Hungarian); Devora (Russian).

Debra A form of Deborah. Light use from 1955.

Debre Amharic; mountain, hill.

Debrelle A blend of Deborah and Ella.

Dechen Tibetan; great bliss.

Decia Latin; tenth.

Dede Ochi, Ga; first-born daughter.

Dee Welsh; black, dark-haired. *Other form*: DeeDee. (See Gender-neutral names.)

Dee-Ann A blend of Dee and Ann.

Deinol Welsh; attractive, charming.

Deirdre Possibly Irish Gaelic; young girl. Occasional use from 1935. *Other forms*: Dede, Dee, Deedra, Deedre, Deidre, Dierdre.

Deka Somali; pleasing.

Del Welsh; pretty.

Dela A Czech form of Adele.

Delana Old German; noble protector.

Delane, Delaine Elaine with the *De-* prefix.

Delanne A blend of Del and Anne.

Delara Lara with the *De-* prefix.

Delaura Laura with the *De-* prefix.

Delcine Latin; sweet.

Delena Lena with the *De-* prefix.

Delfine Greek; from Delphi. *Other forms*: Delfene, Delfyne.

Delia Latin; from the Greek island of Delos. Occasional use from 1925. *Other forms*: Dee, Dehlia, Del, Delea, Deli, Della, Dellya.

Delicia Latin; delightful.

Delilah Hebrew; alluring, amorous. *Other form*: Dalilah.

Delimara Maltese; from Delimara Point on the island of Malta.

Delina Lina with the *De-* prefix.

Delinda Old German; gentle.

Delise Lise (Lisa) with the *De-* prefix.

Delissa Lissa (Larissa) with the *De-* prefix.

Delita Lita (Lolita) with the *De-* prefix.

Della A form of Adele. Occasional use from 1950. *Other forms*: Del, Delle, Dellie.

Dellen Cornish; petal. *Other forms*: Delen, Delenn, Dellene.

Delmelda Greek; to announce.

Delola Lola with the *De-* prefix.

Delora Latin; seashore.

Delorna Lorna with the *De-* prefix.

Delpha Greek; dolphin.

Delphine Greek; woman from Delphi. Occasional use from 1900 to 1925, then falling out of use. A small revival in 1970 was not sustained. *Other forms*: Delfine, Delphi, Delphia, Delvina.

Delshay A blend of Del and Shayla.

Delta Greek; fourth.

Delwen Welsh; pretty.

Delynda, Delyn Lynda with the *De-* prefix.

Delyth Welsh; pretty.

Dema, Demelda Greek; to proclaim.

Dembe Luganda; peace.

Demelza From the Cornish place-name which may mean hill fort of Maeldaf.

Demetria Greek; earth mother, surface covering of the earth. Demeter was the Greek goddess of the harvest.

Demi A form of Demetria. Occasional use from 1995.

Dena Native American; valley.

Denia Greek; of Dionysus, god of wine. *Other form*: Denica.

Denise French; from Dionysus, the Greek god of wine. A feminine form of Dennis. Light use from 1925 peaking in 1960. *Other forms*: Dency, Denice, Deneice, Denese, Deniese, Denize, Denyse, Dinny, Dione, Dionetta, Dionise, Dionycia, Dionysia. *Variant*: Denisa (Spanish).

Deolinda Latin; beautiful goddess.

Derenda A blend of Deri (Derry) and Brenda.

Derora Hebrew; flowing stream.

Derowen Cornish; oak tree.

Derry, Deri Irish Gaelic; red-haired. (See Gender-neutral names.)

Derryth Celtic; oak grove.

Derwena Welsh; oak tree.

Deryn Welsh; bird, hence a free spirit. *Other forms*: Derene, Derren, Derrine.

Deshawna Shawna with the *De-* prefix.

Deshieka Shieka (Rashieka) with the *De-* prefix.

Desiree Old French; desired one.

Desma Greek; bond.

Desna A form of Desdemona, a character in Shakespeare's *Othello*. The name is Greek and probably means ill-starred.

Dessa Greek; wanderer.

Desta Amharic; happiness. Or Oromo; happy.

Destina Latin/Spanish; fate, destiny. *Other forms*: Desty, Destyne. *Variant*: Destine (French).

Destiney, Destinie, Destiny Latin; fate, destiny.

Desya A form of the Russian name Modest. Latin; moderate, modest.

Deva Sanskrit; angel, shining one, being of light. *Other forms*: Daeva, Dayva, Deeva, Diva.

Devadatta Sanskrit; given by God.

Deverie Old English; river bank. *Other form*: Deverelle.

Deverne Verna with the *De-* prefix.

Devina, Devinda Celtic; poet. Feminine forms of Devin.

Devita Vita with the *De-* prefix.

Devona, Devonna Old English; dweller in the deep valley.

Dexy Latin; right-handed, hence skilful.

Deya Hebrew; bird, hence a free spirit.

Dhanie Sanskrit; wealthy.

Diadora A blend of Diana and Dora.

Diamanda A blend of Diamond and Amanda.

Diamanta, Diamantha Greek; unconquerable.

Diamond Greek; from the name of the precious stone.

Dian Scottish Gaelic; strong.

Diana Latin; divine. Light use from 1925. *Other forms*: Dayana, Deana, Deanna, Deann, Deanne, Dee, Dena, Di, Dian, Diandra, Dianna, Dianne, Dianys, Didi, Dina, Dyana, Dyane, Dyanna, Dayanne. *Variants*: Diane (French); Dianora (Italian); Dione, Dionne (Portuguese); Dyanna (Russian).

Diandra Greek; flower with two stamens.

Diane A French form of Diana. Light use from 1935, peaking in heavy use in 1965 and now in decline. Since 1950 this has been the most popular form of the name. *Other forms*: Dianne, Diann.

Dianne A form of Diana. Occasional use 1935–75.

Dianora Latin; divine.

Diantha Greek; divine flower.

Diella Latin; holy girl.

Dieudonnee French; given by God. *Variants*: Deodata (Italian); Devadatta (Sanskrit).

Dillys Welsh; genuine, sincere. *Other form*: Dilys.

Dilwen Welsh; honeycomb.

Dinah Hebrew; judgement, hence vindicated. Occasional use from 1900. *Other forms*: Deena, Dina, Dynah.

Dinka Dinka; people. From the name of the Sudanese tribe.

Diola Diola; the name of a tribe in Senegal.

Dione A Greek form of Diana. Occasional use from 1965. *Other forms*: Deona, Deondra, Deonna, Deonne, Dion,

Diona, Dionara, Dionella, Dionetta, Dionna, Dionne.

Dionne Greek; divine queen. The mother of Aphrodite in Greek mythology.

Dior, Diore French; golden.

Diorella A blend of Dionne and Morella.

Diretta Italian; to direct, control.

Disa Norwegian; active spirit.

Dixie Old Norse; sprite. Also associated with those States which formed the Southern Confederacy during the American Civil War.

Diya Arabic; brightness.

Diza Hebrew; joy.

Doanna Celtic; sand dunes. *Other form*: Doanne.

Dolinda A blend of Dora and Linda.

Dolisa A blend of Dora and Lisa.

Dolita A blend of Dora and Lita (Lolita).

Dolly, Dollie Forms of Dolores. (See Gender-neutral names.)

Dolores Spanish; strong woman. Occasional use from 1935 until it fell out of use in 1960. *Other forms*: Delora, Delores, Deloris, Delorita, Lo, Lola, Lolita. *Variants*: Dolore (Hawaiian); Dolours (Irish Gaelic); Dores (Portuguese); Delores, Lola, Lolita (Spanish).

Dominique A French feminine form of Dominic. Occasional use from 1970. *Other forms*: Domanique, Domenica, Domenique, Domineka, Domini, Domique, Dominika, Domino, Domonika, Domonique. *Variants*: Doma (Czech); Domonique (French); Dominika (German); Domenica (Italian); Niki (Polish); Dominika, Domka, Mika (Russian); Dominga (Spanish). (See Gender-neutral names.)

Domino French; masquerade cloak and mask.

Dona Welsh; the name of the Celtic goddess linked to the river Danube. *Other form*: Donah.

Donella, Donelle Blends of Donna and Ella.

Donna Italian; lady. Light use from 1950 peaking in 1975. *Other forms*: Donnella, Donnelle, Donnita, Donnay, Donnica, Donnie, Donnisha, Dontia, Donya. *Variant*: Dona (Spanish).

Donnie A form of Donna. *Other forms*: Donnee, Donney, Donni. (See Gender-neutral names.)

Donoma Omaha; the first or last sunshine of the day.

Donwenna Welsh; holy, fair.

Donya A blend of Dora and Sonya.

Dora A form of Dorothy. Light use from 1900, declining until it fell out of use in 1955. There was a small revival in 1990. *Other forms*: Doralie, Dorella, Doressa, Doretta, Dorinda.

Doral Greek; goldfish.

Doralynn, Doralin Blends of Dora and Lynn.

Doranda A blend of Dora and Amanda.

Dorann A blend of Dora and Ann.

Dorantha A blend of Dora and Samantha.

Dorcas Greek; gazelle. Occasional use from 1925 until it fell out of use in 1970. *Other forms*: Dorcia, Dorkas.

Dorea Greek; gift.

Doreen A form of Dorothy. In heavy use 1925–35. It then declined rapidly, falling out of use in 1985. *Other forms*: Dorena, Dorina, Dorine.

Dorella, Dorelle Blends of Dora and Ella.

Dorena Greek; bountiful.

Doria Greek; from Doris in central Greece.

Dorianne Greek; gift.

Dorina Hebrew; perfection.

Dorinda A blend of Dora and Linda. *Other form*: Dorenda.

Doris Greek; sea. The wife of Nereus in Greek mythology and the mother of the sea nymphs Nereids. In heavy use 1900–25, and then began to decline steadily until it fell out of use in 1975. *Other forms*: Dorea, Doria, Dorisa, Dorita, Dorris, Dory, Rinda. *Variants*: Dorika, Dorka (Czech); Dorisa (Hawaiian); Dorit (Hebrew); Dorita (Spanish).

Dorna A blend of Dora and Lorna.

Dorona A blend of Dora and Rona.

Dorothea Greek; gift of God. The original form of Dorothy. Occasional use 1900–35. *Other forms*: Doretta, Dorota.

Dorothy Greek; gift of God. Heavy use from 1900, peaking in very heavy use in 1925 and then declining. Only occasional use since 1965. *Other forms*: Dasha, Dasya, Dede, Dodie, Dolly, Dora, Doralane, Doralene, Doralia, Doreen, Dorene, Doretta, Dorinda, Dorita, Dory, Dorothea, Dot, Dottie, Tigo, Tottie. *Variants*: Dora, Dorota (Czech); Dorothea (Danish); Dorothee, Doretta (French); Dore, Dorlisa, Dorothea, Thea (German); Theadora (Greek); Doreen, Dorrit (Irish); Tarati (Maori); Dorte (Norwegian); Dorota (Polish); Tarita (Polynesian); Daisha, Darja, Dasha, Dorinda, Doroteya (Russian); Diorbhail (Scottish Gaelic); Dasya (Slavonic); Dorotea, Teodora (Spanish); Lolotea (Zuni).

Drew Old Norse; lover, sweetheart. (See Gender-neutral names.)

Drisana Sanskrit; daughter of the sun.

Drucella Latin; the strong one. From the Roman family

name Drusus. *Other form*: Drusilla.

Druella Old German; elfin vision.

Duana Celtic; song.

Dulcie Latin; charming, sweet. Occasional use from 1900 until it fell out of use in 1960. *Other forms*: Delcina, Delcine, Dulcea, Dulcia, Dulciana, Dulcine. *Variants*: Delcine (French); Dulcina (Italian); Dulcinea (Spanish).

Duma Hebrew; quiet, gentle woman. *Other form*: Dunia.

Duretta Spanish; little steadfast one.

Durga Sanskrit; inaccessible. The name of a goddess in Hindu mythology.

Dusha Russian; soul, sweetheart. *Other forms*: Duscha, Dushenka.

Dusty Old English; brownstone quarry. A feminine form of Dustin. Used only as a feminine name in UK. *Other forms*: Dustee, Dustey, Dusti, Dustine, Dustyne. (See Gender-neutral names.)

Duvessa Irish Gaelic; dark beauty.

Dyan Native American; deer. *Other forms*: Dyane, Dyani.

Dyana Sanskrit; meditation.

Dyota Sanskrit; light.

Dyshawna Shawna with the *Dy-* prefix.

Dysis Greek; sunset.

E

Ebba Old German; strong.

Ebony Greek; hard, dark wood. *Other forms*: Ebonee, Eboni, Ebonie.

Ebrel Cornish; April. *Other form*: Ebrelle.

Ecola Chinook; whale.

Eda Old English; blessed.

Edana Irish Gaelic; little fiery one. *Other form*: Edda.

Eden Hebrew; delightful, pleasant. Or Babylonian; a plain. (See Gender-neutral names.)

Edie Old Norse; whirlpool.

Edina Old English; rich friend.

Edith Old English; prosperous war. Very heavy use in 1900, but then declined rapidly till it fell out of use in 1970. A small revival in 1985 was not sustained. *Other forms*: Ardith, Eady, Eda, Edie, Edita, Edythe, Eydie. *Variants*: Dita, Edita (Czech); Editha (German); Edi (Hawaiian); Duci (Hungarian); Edetta, Edita (Italian); Edda, Ita (Polish); Dita (Spanish).

Edlyn Old English; happy brook.

Edna Hebrew; delight, desired. Light use from 1900, peaking in 1925 and declining until it fell out of use in 1975. *Other forms*: Adena, Adina, Edana, Ednah. *Variants*: Edena (Hawaiian); Eithne (Irish Gaelic).

Edwina Old English; prosperous friend. A feminine form of Edwin. Occasional use from 1925 until it fell out of use in 1965. *Other forms*: Eddie, Edina, Edwyna. *Variant*: Edina (Scottish).

Effia Gurma; born on Friday.

Effie A modern form of Iphigenia. Greek; famed and fair. Princess Iphigenia was the daughter of King Agamemnon. *Variant*: Oighrig (Scottish Gaelic).

Efrona Hebrew; sweet-singing bird.

Eia A Celtic saint's name of uncertain meaning.

Eileen An Irish form of Helen. Popular from 1900, peaking in heavy use in 1925 and then declining and falling out of use in 1975. A small revival in 1985 was not sustained. *Other forms*: Aileen, Ayleen, Elaine,

Elane, Elayne, Ellie, Ilene. *Variants*: Elaine (French); Aileen (Irish); Aibhilin, Eibhlin (Irish Gaelic).

Eira Welsh; snow.

Eirene Old Norse; peace.

Eirian Welsh; silver.

Eirlys Welsh; snowdrop.

Eirwen Welsh; white as snow.

Ekata Sanskrit; unity.

Elaila A blend of Elaine and Leila.

Elain Welsh; fawn (young deer).

Elaine A French form of Helen. Light use from 1900, peaking in heavy usage in 1955, but then steadily declining. *Other forms*: Elain, Elayne, Laina.

Elamara A blend of Ella and Mary.

Elan French; grace, style. (See Gender-neutral names.)

Elana Hebrew; tree. *Other form*: Elani.

Elandra A blend of Elana and Sandra.

Elantha A blend of Elana and Samantha.

Elara The granddaughter of Zeus in Greek mythology.

Eldora Spanish; golden.

Eleanor An Old French form of Helen. Occasional use from 1900. It has dipped down into fairly rare usage three times, but always recovered, and is now showing signs of serious revival into light use. *Other forms*: Alianora, Alienor, Elea, Eleana, Eleanora, Elen, Elenor, Eleonora, Eli, Elianora, Elin, Elinor, Elinore, Ellen, Ellenor, Ellie, Ellon, Ellyn, Elnora, Elyn, Heleanor, Leanor, Lenorea, Leonora, Leora, Nelda, Nellie, Nora, Norah, Noreen, Norene, Norine, Nureen. *Variants*: Leonora, Elena (Czech); Eleanore, Eleonore (French); Elenore (German); Nora, Norah (Irish); Eileanoir,

Eileanora (Irish Gaelic); Elenora, Eleonora (Italian); Lenore (Russian); Leonor (Spanish); Elin (Welsh).

Elektra Greek; brilliant. *Other form*: Electra.

Elele Hawaiian; angel.

Elena Greek; light. Occasional use from 1955. *Other forms*: Eleana, Eleena, Elene, Eleni, Elina, Ellena, Elyna.

Elenda A blend of Elena and Brenda.

Elenya According to Tolkien, the first day of the week in the Elven calendar, meaning star's day.

Eleri From a Welsh river name.

Elestren Cornish; iris.

Elfed Welsh; autumn.

Elfen Welsh; element.

Elfreda Old English; elf strength. Occasional use 1925–35.

Elfyna Welsh; brow of hill.

Eliana Hebrew; God has answered me.

Elinor A form of Eleanor. Occasional use from 1900.

Eliora Hebrew; God is my light.

Elisabeth A form of Elizabeth. Occasional use from 1925.

Elise A French form of Elizabeth. *Variants*: Ilise, Liese (German).

Elisena From the name of the flowering plant.

Elisha Hebrew; God is my salvation. (See Gender-neutral names.)

Elita French; chosen.

Eliza A form of Elizabeth. Light use in 1900, declining and falling out of use several times until a revival in 1985. *Other forms*: Elisa, Elize, Elyza, Liza, Lyza. *Variant*: Elize (French).

Elizabeth Hebrew; God's oath. Very heavy use at its
peak in 1900, but then declining into light use by 1975.
This is a name of great resilience; it declined a little in
the 1980s but now shows signs of making a strong
recovery. *Other forms*: Babette, Bella, Belita, Bess, Bessie,
Beth, Betsie, Bette, Betty, Elisa, Elisabeth, Elise, Elissa,
Eliza, Else, Elspeth, Elysa, Elyssa, Helsa, Ilise, Ilse,
Isabel, Letha, Letty, Libby, Lili, Lilibet, Lisa, Lisbeth,
Lisette, Liza, Lizbeth, Lizette, Lizzy, Lysbeth, Tetty,
Tibby, Ysabel. *Variants*: Yeghisapet (Armenian); Elisa,
Elizabete (Basque); Elisveta (Bulgarian); Eppow
(Cornish); Alzbeta, Betuska, Bozena, Eliska (Czech);
Elisabet, Helsa, Lisbet (Danish); Els, Liesje (Dutch);
Betti, Elsbet, Liisa (Estonian); Elli, Elisa, Liisa (Finnish);
Babette, Bettine, Elisabeth, Elise, Lise, Lisette (French);
Bettina, Elsa, Elschen, Elsbeth, Ilse, Lisa, Lieschen,
Liese, Liesel (German); Elisavet (Greek); Elikapeka
(Hawaiian); Erzebet, Liza, Zizi (Hungarian); Eilis (Irish
Gaelic); Bettina, Elisa, Elisabetta, Elissa, Isabetta
(Italian); Elizabete, Lizina (Latvian); Elzbieta, Elzbute
(Lithuanian); Elise, Ellisif, Lise (Norwegian); Ela, Elka,
Elzbieta, Elzunia (Polish); Elzira, Isabela, Izabel
(Portuguese); Elisabeta (Romanian); Elisaveta, Lisenka,
Liza, Lizka, Yelizaveta (Russian); Elsbeth, Elsie, Elspet,
Elspeth (Scottish); Ealasaid (Scottish Gaelic); Elisia,
Elissa, Lisavetta, Veta (Slavonic); Belicia, Belita, Elisa,
Isabel, Isabella, Liseta, Ysabel (Spanish); Elisabet, Elsa,
Lisa (Swedish); Lisaveta, Yelysaveta (Ukrainian); Beti,
Betsan (Welsh).

Elke, Elkie German forms of Alice. *Other forms*: Elga,
Elka.

Ella Old German; all, entirely. Occasional use from 1935.
Other forms: Ala, Ela, Elle, Hela, Hele.

Ellana A blend of Ellen and Lana.

Ellen A form of Helen. Heavy use in 1900, but then steadily declined until 1970. In 1975 began a modest revival. *Other forms*: Elen, Eleny, Elin, Elina, Ellena, Ellie, Ellin, Ellon, Ellyn, Elyn. *Variants*: Elene, Elaine (French); Elina, Elita (Spanish); Elna, Elina (Swedish).

Ellendea Greek; God's light.

Ellie A form of Ellen. Occasional use from 1995.

Elma Greek; pleasant, fair.

Elmira A blend of Elma and Mira (Myra).

Elnora A blend of Ella and Nora.

Elodie Greek; fragile flower.

Eloise A form of Heloise, a French name of Germanic origin and uncertain meaning. Occasional use from 1965. *Variants*: Heloise (French); Aloysa, Aloysia (German); Eloisa (Italian).

Elola A blend of Ella and Lola.

Elora Greek; happy.

Elouisa A blend of Eloise and Louisa.

Elowen Cornish; elm tree.

Elphine Welsh; brow of hill.

Elra Old German; elfin wisdom.

Elsa A German form of Elizabeth.

Elsena A blend of Elora and Cynthia.

Elsie A form of Elspeth. Very heavy use in 1900, but rapidly declined and fell out of use in 1960. A small revival in 1975 was not sustained. *Other forms*: Elcie, Elsi, Elsy.

Eluned Welsh; idol.

Elva Old English; elfin, good.

Elvina Old English; noble/elf friend.

Elvira Probably from the Spanish place-name. *Variants*: Elvire (French); Wira (Polish).

Elysia Greek; ideal happiness. *Other forms*: Elyse, Elyssa, Ilyse. *Variant*: Ilyse (French).

Emer Possibly Irish Gaelic; twin. In Irish legend Emer was the wife of Cuchulainn. *Other form*: Emir. *Variants*: Eamair, Eimear (Irish Gaelic); Eamhair, Eimhear (Scottish Gaelic). (See Gender-neutral names.)

Emerald Greek; from the name of the precious stone. *Variants*: Meraud (Cornish); Emeraude (French); Esmeralda (Spanish).

Emi Japanese; smile.

Emily Old German; industrious. Heavy use in 1900 but then declined until it fell out of use in 1955. In 1960 it had started to revive, and there was steady growth towards heavy use again by 1990. *Other forms*: Amelia, Emaline, Emele, Emeline, Emilia, Emiline, Emma, Emmy, Imma, Millie, Milly, Ymma. *Variants*: Emilia, Melia (Armenian); Milia (Basque); Emiliia (Bulgarian); Ema, Emilie, Milka (Czech); Emilia (Dutch); Amalie, Emilie, Emmaline (French); Amalie, Emilie, Emmi (German); Aimilios (Greek); Emele (Hawaiian); Amalia (Hungarian); Emmali (Iranian); Eimile (Irish Gaelic); Emilia (Italian); Amalija (Latvian); Emilija (Lithuanian); Emere (Maori); Emilia (Polish, Portuguese, Romanian); Amalija (Russian); Aimil (Scottish Gaelic); Emmilene (Slavonic); Amelita, Emilia, Mema, Neneca, Nuela (Spanish); Amalia, Emilia (Swedish); Emilya (Ukrainian).

Emilyann A blend of Emily and Ann.

Emma Greek; grandmother. Light use from 1900 until it fell out of use in 1955. Revived in 1965 and peaked in very heavy use in 1980. Now declining slightly, but still a popular choice. *Other forms*: Em, Ema, Emm, Emmie, Emmy, Imma, Irma, Ymma. *Variants*: Emeline (French); Erma, Irma (German); Ema (Spanish and Hawaiian).

Emma-Jayne A blend of Emma and Jane. Occasional use from 1970. *Other forms*: Emma-Jane, Emmajane, Emmajayne.

Emmalee A blend of Emma and Lee.

Emma-Louise A blend of Emma and Louise. Occasional use from 1975. *Other forms*: Emmalou, Emmylou, Emylou.

Emmalynn A blend of Emma and Lynn.

Emmanuelle Hebrew; God with us. A feminine form of Emmanuel. *Other form*: Immanuelle. (See Gender-neutral names.)

Emmeline A French form of Emma. Occasional use from 1900. *Other forms*: Emaline, Emelina, Emeline, Emmaline, Emmeline.

Emuna Arabic; faith.

Ena A form of Eithne. Occasional use from 1900 until it fell out of use in 1960. *Other forms*: Aine, Ina.

Encina Spanish; live oak tree.

Endora Old German; noble.

Enfys Welsh; rainbow.

Enid Welsh; soul, life. Light use from 1900, peaking in 1925 and falling out of use in 1960. *Other forms*: Enyd, Ynid.

Enola A Native American name of uncertain meaning.

Enora Greek; light.

Enya A form of Eithne.

Eola Greek; dawn. *Other form*: Eolande.

Eos Greek; dawn. Eos was the goddess of dawn in Greek mythology.

Eowyn Welsh; fair, golden.

Erantha Greek; from the flower name Eranthis. *Other forms*: Erana, Eranthe.

Erda Old German; child of the Earth.

Erelah Hebrew; angel.

Erianthe Greek; sweet as a field of flowers.

Erica German; honourable ruler. Light use from 1935. *Other forms*: Arica, Eryka, Rica. *Variant*: Erika (Swedish).

Erika A Swedish form of Erica. Occasional use from 1965.

Erina Irish Gaelic; western island, hence Ireland. Occasional use from 1980. *Other forms*: Arin, Erana, Eren, Erena, Erene, Erina, Erine, Erinn, Erinna, Eryn, Erynne. (See Gender-neutral names.)

Erlina Old English; little elf. *Other form*: Erline.

Erlinda Hebrew; lively.

Ertha Irish Gaelic; strong of faith. *Other form*: Eartha, Earthra.

Eryl Welsh; watcher. (See Gender-neutral names.)

Esma French; to esteem. *Other forms*: Esme, Esmee.

Esmeralda Spanish; emerald. *Variant*: Esme (French).

Esperanza Spanish; hope. *Variant*: Speranza (Italian).

Estella An Italian form of Estelle. Occasional use from 1925 to 1970.

Estelle Latin; star. Occasional use from 1955. *Other forms*: Estella, Estrella, Stella, Stelle. *Variants*: Estella (Italian); Estelar, Estrelle, Estrellita, Trella (Spanish).

Esther Persian; star, the planet Venus. Light use from

1900. *Other forms*: Essa, Esta, Estella, Ester, Ettie, Heddy, Hedy, Heidi, Heiki, Hester, Hesther, Hettie, Hetty, Trella. *Variants*: Hester (Dutch); Eszter (Hungarian); Eister, Eistir (Irish Gaelic); Ester (Italian); Estralita, Estrella (Spanish); Ester (Swedish).

Eswen Welsh; strength.

Etain Irish Gaelic; shining. The name of a beautiful woman in Irish legend. *Other forms*: Etaine, Etayne.

Etana Hebrew; strong.

Etandra A blend of Etana and Sandra.

Etelka Slavonic; noble.

Etenia Native American; wealth.

Ethana Hebrew; strong, firm. A feminine form of Ethan.

Ethel Old English; noble. Heavy use in 1900 but declined sharply and fell out of use in 1940. A small revival in 1965 was not sustained. *Other forms*: Adal, Edel, Ethelda, Etheline, Ethelyn.

Ethena A blend of Ethel and Lena.

Ethne Irish Gaelic; little fire. *Other forms*: Eithne, Ethna.

Etta Old German; little.

Ettare Greek; steadfast.

Eulalia Greek; well spoken. *Variants*: Eulalie (French); Ula (Spanish).

Eunice Greek; victorious. Occasional use from 1900 until it fell out of use in 1965. *Other forms*: Niki, Nikki, Unice.

Eurwen Welsh; fair, golden.

Eva A German and Italian form of Eve. Light use in 1900 but then declined rapidly and fell out of use in 1950. It revived in 1990. *Variant*: Ava (Greek).

Evadne Possibly Greek; good fortune.

Evania Greek; tranquil.

Evanthe Greek; flower.

Evara A blend of Eva and Sara.

Eve Hebrew; life. Although much used in previous centuries, this name had no popular appeal between 1900 and 1975, when it came back into occasional use. *Other forms*: Eeve, Eva, Evadne, Evaline, Evie, Eviene, Evita, Evy, Yeva. *Variants*: Eva (Cornish); Evinka, Evka, Evuska (Czech); Eeva (Finnish); Evaine (French); Eva, Evy (German); Evathia (Greek); Chava (Hebrew); Evi, Vica (Hungarian); Evaleen, Eveleen (Irish); Aiofe, Aioffe, Eabha (Irish Gaelic); Eva (Italian); Ewa, Ina (Polish); Yeva, Yevka (Russian); Eubha (Scottish Gaelic); Evuska (Slavonic); Evita (Spanish).

Evelia A blend of Eve and Delia.

Eveline A form of Evelyn. Occasional use from its peak in 1900 to 1975.

Evelyn Celtic; pleasant. Light use from 1900, peaking in 1925 and falling out of use in 1990. *Other forms*: Avelina, Aveline, Avelyn, Evalina, Eveleen, Eveline, Evie, Eviene, Evy. *Variants*: Evaline (French); Ewa, Ewalina (Hawaiian). (See Gender-neutral names.)

Evinda A blend of Eve and Linda.

F

Fabana Zulu; leader.

Fabia Probably Latin; bean farmer.

Fabrice Latin; skilled craftswoman.

Faine Old English; joyful. *Other form*: Fayne.

Faith Latin; to trust. *Other forms*: Faithe, Fayeth.

Fala Choctaw; clever crow.

Fallon Irish Gaelic; grandchild of the ruler. Popularized by the television series *Dynasty*. (See Gender-neutral names.)

Fanny A form of Frances. Occasional use from its peak in 1900 to 1925, falling out of use in 1935. There were two small revivals (in 1960 and 1985) but it seems unlikely that it will revive again due to the slang uses of the word fanny. These uses arose after 1900 and they have made a respectable name virtually unusable, as two out of the four entries in the *Concise Oxford Dictionary* amply demonstrate.

Farah Persian; joy.

Faranda Breton; spinning. Linked to the *farandole*, a fast dance with a spinning movement.

Farica Old German; peace-loving ruler.

Farida Arabic; precious jewel.

Faron A blend of Farah and Sharon.

Farrah Arabic; wild ass.

Fawne Latin; young deer. *Other form*: Fawn.

Fay A form of Faye. Occasional use from 1925.

Faye Old French; fidelity. Occasional use from 1955, and a sudden rise into light use in 1990. *Other forms*: Fae, Fay, Fayette, Fayina, Feya.

Fayola Yoruba; lucky.

Fedora Greek; divine gift.

Feena Irish Gaelic; little deer. *Variant*: Fiadhnait (Irish Gaelic).

Felantha A blend of Felina and Samantha.

Felda Old German; the field.

Felicity Latin; happiness. Occasional use from 1950, with a steady increase since 1985. *Other forms*: Felcia, Felica, Felice, Felicia, Felise, Felisha, Felisse, Felita, Fliss.

Variants: Felice, Felicite, Felise (French); Felizia (German); Phylicia (Greek); Felicia, Felicita (Italian); Felka (Polish); Felicidade (Portuguese); Felica, Feliciana, Felicidad (Spanish).

Felina Latin; cat-like. *Other forms*: Felene, Felyna.

Fenella Irish Gaelic; white shoulder. Occasional use from 1955. *Variants*: Finola (Irish); Fionnghuala, Fionnuala (Irish Gaelic); Finella (Scottish); Fionnghal (Scottish Gaelic).

Fern Old German; from the plant name. Light use from 1990. *Other form*: Ferne.

Fernley Old English; clearing with ferns. *Other forms*: Fernlea, Fernleigh, Fernly. (See Gender-neutral names.)

Ffion Welsh; foxglove.

Fiala Czech; violet flower.

Fidelma A blend of Fidel and Mary.

Finesse French; subtle and elegant skill.

Fiona Scottish Gaelic; white, fair. Light use from 1950, peaking in 1965. *Other forms*: Fee, Finella, Fionia, Fionna, Fionnuala, Nuala. *Variant*: Ffiona (Welsh).

Fiorella Italian; little flower.

Fiorina A blend of Fiona and Rina.

Flair Latin; style, instinct for excellence.

Flavia Latin; yellow-haired. From the Roman clan name Flavius. *Variant*: Flavien (French). (See Gender-neutral names.)

Fleur French; flower. Occasional use from 1955. *Variant*: Fflyr (Welsh).

Flora Latin; flower. Light use from 1900, but had fallen out of use by 1950. Small revival in 1970. *Other forms*: Fiora, Fleur, Flo, Florella, Floretta, Floria, Florida,

Florie, Floris, Flory, Flossie. *Variants*: Floria (Basque); Kveta (Czech); Fleur, Fleurette, Flore (French); Fiora, Fiorentina, Fiorenza (Italian); Lorca (Russian); Florrie (Scottish); Floraidh (Scottish Gaelic); Flor, Florida, Florita (Spanish); Fflyr (Welsh).

Florence Latin; blooming, prosperous. Very heavy use at its peak in 1900 but then went into a decline, falling out of use in 1960. There were small revivals (not sustained) in 1970 and 1985. *Other forms*: Flo, Flonda, Florance, Florina, Florinda, Florrie, Flory, Floryn, Flossie. *Variants*: Floris (Dutch); Florentia, Florenz (German); Florenza (Italian); Florenti (Russian); Florencia, Florentina (Spanish).

Floriane A blend of Flora and Diane. *Other forms*: Floriana, Florianne, Floryane.

Florida From the name of the American State. Spanish; flowery.

Florimel Latin; honey flower.

Florinda A blend of Flora and Linda.

Fola Yoruba; honourable.

Fonda Spanish; profound.

Fondra French; to melt. *Other form*: Foneda.

Fontara A blend of Fontayne and Tara.

Fontayne Old English; spring water. *Other forms*: Fontaene, Fontaine.

Fotina Old German; free.

Francelle, Francella Blends of Frances and Ella.

Frances Latin; free. Steady light use from its peak in 1900, but there has been a gradual decline since then. *Other forms*: Fanchette, Fancy, Fran, Francesca, Francine, Francoise, Francyne, Franja, Fronia. *Variants*: Franca (Czech); Fanchette; Francene, Francoise

(French); Franziska (German); Fotina (Greek); Franci (Hungarian); Proinseas (Irish Gaelic); Francesca (Italian); Franciska (Polish); Francise (Romanian); Fedora (Russian); Frangag (Scottish Gaelic); Francisca, Frasquita, Paca, Paquita, Quita (Spanish).

Francesca An Italian form of Frances. Occasional use from 1965, increasing rapidly to light use in 1990. *Other forms*: Chesca, Cheska, Francella, Franceska, Francetta, Franchelle, Franchesca, Francheska, Francisca, Franciska, Frantiska. *Variants*: Frantiska (Czech); Francoise (French); Franziska (German); Franciszka (Polish); Proinseas (Irish Gaelic); Frangag (Scottish Gaelic); Francisca, Frasquita (Spanish).

Francine A French form of Frances. Occasional use from 1960. *Other forms*: Francene. *Variant*: Franci (Hungarian).

Frankie A form of Frances. (See Gender-neutral names.)

Freda Old German; peace. Light use from 1900, peaking in 1925 and falling out of use in 1965. *Other forms*: Fredda, Freida, Frieda, Frida, Frederica, Rica, Rikki. *Variants*: Frederique (French); Frida, Friederike, Fritze, Fritzi (German); Federica (Italian); Fredricka (Norwegian); Fryderyka (Polish).

Frenelle A blend of Freda and Donelle.

Freya Old Norse; the Norse goddess of love and beauty.

Fritha Old English; woodland. *Other form*: Frytha.

Frysa Frisian; curly-haired.

G

Gabriella Hebrew; God is my strength. Occasional use from 1965. *Other forms*: Gabby, Gabi, Gabriela, Gabriell, Gabrielle, Gaby, Gavra. *Variants*: Gabrielle (French);

Gabi, Gabriel (German); Gavriella (Hebrew); Gabriela (Italian, Polish); Gavrila (Russian).

Gabrielle A form of Gabriella. Occasional use from 1965.

Gael, Gaelle Celtic; Gaelic speaker. *Other forms*: Gaela, Gaella.

Gaetana From Gaeta in southern Italy.

Gaia Greek; spirit of planet earth. The earth Goddess or devic consciousness which regulates and programmes this planet. James Lovelock's book *Gaia: A New Look at Life on Earth* gave this name new relevance within the context of ecology. (See also Danuih.)

Gaiane Greek; child of the earth. *Other form*: Gayane.

Gail A form of Abigail. Light use from 1950, peaking in 1965. *Other forms*: Gaila, Gale, Gayla, Gayle.

Gala Arabic; festive gathering.

Galantha Greek; snowdrop.

Galatea Greek; milky white. In Greek legend the sculptor Pygmalion carved from a white stone the statue of a beautiful woman, which Aphrodite turned into a real woman.

Galaxie Greek; star system.

Gale A form of Abigail. Occasional use from 1955 to 1965.

Galena Greek; tranquil, healer.

Galia Hebrew; God has redeemed. *Variants*: Galenka, Galya (Russian).

Galiena Old German; tall.

Galilah Hebrew; redemption of God. *Other form*: Galilea.

Galina Greek; peace. *Other form*: Gallina.

Galway Irish Gaelic; Scotsman in Ireland.

Galya Hebrew; God has redeemed.

Gana Hebrew; garden.

Ganya Zulu; clever.

Garnet From the jewel name. *Other forms*: Garnetta, Garnette. (See Gender-neutral names.)

Gavra Hebrew; the Lord is my foundation.

Gay Middle English; merry. Occasional use 1950–75. Since the adoption of the word gay in quite a different context this name has fallen out of use. *Other forms*: Gae, Gai, Gaye, Gayla.

Gayle A form of Abigail. Occasional use from 1965 to 1975.

Gaynor A form of Guinevere. Occasional use from 1950, peaking in 1965. *Other forms*: Gaenor, Gaynore. *Variants*: Guanor (Scottish Gaelic); Gaenor (Welsh).

Gayora Hebrew; valley of light.

Gazara Arabic; sparkling silk.

Geela Hebrew; joyful.

Gelya Russian; angelic.

Gemara Arabic; completion.

Gemelle Latin; jewel.

Gemma Latin; jewel. Light use from 1965, rising to a peak of very heavy use in 1985. *Other forms*: Gem, Gemelle, Ghemma, Jemma.

Geneth Welsh; girl.

Genevra Latin; juniper berry. *Other forms*: Geneva, Genevia.

Genevieve Celtic; white wave. *Other forms*: Geneveve, Genna. *Variants*: Genovefa (German); Ginevra (Italian); Genevra (Welsh).

Genista Latin; the broom plant.

Georgia Greek; farmer. A feminine form of George.

Occasional use from 1955. *Other forms*: Georgea, Georgeana, Georgette, Georgie, Georgiana, Georgina, Georgine, Georgy. *Variants*: Jirina (Czech); Georgette, Georgine (French); Georgina (German); Gruzia (Hungarian); Giorgia (Italian); Gina (Russian); Gerda (Scandinavian); Jorgina, Yoya (Spanish).

Georgina A German form of Georgia. Light use from 1900 peaking in 1990. *Variants*: Gena (French); Gina (Italian).

Georgy A form of Georgia. (See Gender-neutral names.)

Geraldine Old German; spear ruler. A feminine form of Gerald, invented by the sixteenth-century poet, the Earl of Surrey. Light use from 1925, peaking in 1950 and falling out of use in 1990. *Other forms*: Deena, Drina, Geralda, Geraldene, Gerardine, Geri, Gerrie, Jeralee, Jeri, Jerri, Jerrie. *Variants*: Geraudene (French); Geralde, Gerhardine (German); Giralda (Italian).

Geralyn A blend of Geraldine and Lyn.

Germaine Latin; bud or sprout. Occasional use from 1935. *Other forms*: Germayne, Jermaine, Jermayne. *Variant*: Germana (Italian).

Gertrude Old German; adored warrior. Light use at its peak in 1900, but then declined rapidly and fell out of use by 1950. *Other forms*: Gertie, Trudy, Trula. *Variants*: Gertraud, Gertrud (German); Gertruda (Italian); Gerda (Scandinavian); Jara (Slavonic); Gertrudis (Spanish).

Geva Hebrew; hill.

Gevira Hebrew; lady, queen.

Gianina Hebrew; God's grace.

Gila Hebrew; joy.

Gilana Hebrew; exultation.

Gilberte A French feminine form of Gilbert. *Variant*: Gigi (French); Giselberta (German).

Gilda Celtic; servant of God.

Gillian Probably Greek; soft-haired. A feminine form of Julian. Heavy use at its peak in 1955 and now in a sharp decline into occasional use. *Other forms*: Gill, Jill. *Variants*: Juliette (French); Giula, Giuletta (Italian).

Gina A form of Georgina. Occasional use from 1935.

Ginette A diminutive of Gina. (See Gender-neutral names.)

Ginger A form of Virginia, or a reference to ginger-coloured hair.

Giselle Old English; bright pledge. *Variants*: Gizela (Czech); Gisele (French); Gisa (German); Gizike (Hungarian); Gisella (Italian); Gisela (Spanish).

Gita Sanskrit; song. *Other forms*: Geeta, Gitta.

Gitana Spanish; gypsy, wanderer.

Githa Old Norse; war.

Gizane Basque; like Christ.

Gladys Possibly Welsh; ruler. Heavy use at its peak in 1900 but then declined rapidly falling out of use in 1960. *Other forms*: Glad, Gladis, Gleda. *Variants*: Gladez (Breton); Gwladuse (Cornish); Gwladys (Welsh).

Glain Welsh; jewel. *Other forms*: Glaine, Glayne.

Gleda Icelandic; make happy.

Glenda Welsh; fair and good. Light use from 1950 until it fell out of use in 1975.

Glendora A blend of Glenys and Dora.

Glenis A form of Glenys. Occasional use 1925–60.

Glenna Celtic; secluded wooded valley. *Other form*: Glen.

Glenys Welsh; holy, fair. Occasional use from 1925 until it fell out of use in 1970. *Other forms*: Glenice, Glenis.

Glinda A blend of Glenys and Linda.

Gloria Latin; glory. Light use from 1925 until it fell out of use in 1965. *Other forms*: Glora, Glori, Gloriana, Glorianna, Gloriette.

Glynis Welsh; little valley. Light use from 1950 until it fell out of use in 1975. *Other forms*: Glinis, Glyn, Glynnis.

Golda Old English; gold. *Other form*: Goldie.

Goma Swahili; joyful dance.

Gonza Rutooro; love.

Grace Latin; grace. Declined from a peak of light use in 1900 until 1985 when it started to revive. *Other forms*: Gracie, Grania, Grayce, Grazina. *Variants*: Grazielle (French); Gratia (German); Arete (Greek); Grazia, Graziosa (Italian); Graca (Portuguese); Giorsal (Scottish Gaelic); Engracia, Gracia, Graciana (Spanish).

Grania, Grainne Irish Gaelic; love. *Variant*: Graidhne (Irish Gaelic).

Grazyna Polish; grace.

Greer Greek; guardian, watchful.

Greta A German form of Margaret. Occasional use from 1935 until it fell out of use in 1960. *Other forms*: Gretchen, Gretel. *Variants*: Greet (Dutch); Grete, Gretchen (German).

Guatay Diegueno; large, tall.

Guinevere Celtic; white wave. *Other forms*: Gayna, Genevieve, Guinivere, Gwen, Gwenevere, Gwynnevere, Jennifer. *Variants*: Jenifer, Jennifer, Jenniver, Wenna (Cornish); Ginevra (Italian); Vanora (Scottish); Gwenhwyfar (Welsh).

Gwen A form of Guinevere. Occasional use 1955–65. *Variant*: Wenna (Cornish).

Gwendolen Welsh; white or fair circle; a reference to the moon and hence the moon goddess. Occasional use from 1900 until it fell out of use in 1965. *Other forms*: Gwen, Gwenda, Gwendoline, Gwendolyn, Wyn, Wynette, Wynne. *Variant*: Guendalina (Spanish).

Gwendoline A form of Gwendolen. Occasional use from 1900, peaking in light use in 1925 and falling out of use in 1965.

Gwendolyn A form of Gwendolen. Occasional use 1900–55.

Gwenlyn Welsh; white valley.

Gwylan Welsh; seagull.

Gwyneth A feminine form of Gwynedd, the name of a region in North Wales. Occasional use from 1925 until it fell out of use in 1970. *Other forms*: Gweneth, Gwenith, Gwen, Gwenn, Gwenyth, Gwyn, Gwynne, Gwynneth, Wynne. *Variants*: Aouregwenn (Breton); Ado, Gunoda (Cornish).

Gwynfa Welsh; good lady.

Gwynneth A form of Gwyneth. Occasional use from 1925 to 1950.

Gypsy Old English; an Egyptian.

Gytha Old English; warrior.

H

Habiba Arabic; beloved.

Hadara Hebrew; adorn with beauty.

Hadiya Arabic; guide to righteousness. Or Swahili; gift.

Hafina Welsh; summer.

Haidee, Haydee Greek; modest.

Hainey Old English; fenced land.

Hala Arabic; halo around the moon.

Halcyone Greek; kingfisher. In Greek mythology Alcyone was a demi-goddess who, mourning her dead husband, flung herself into the sea to die, but was turned by Aphrodite into a kingfisher.

Halene, Haleen Blends of Haley and Eileen.

Haley Old Norse; hero. *Other forms*: Hally, Hayley.

Halima Arabic; kind, gentle. *Other form*: Halimah.

Halona Native American; happy fortune.

Hamida, Hamidah Arabic; praiseworthy.

Hana Arabic; happiness.

Hanata Semitic; evening star.

Hania Hebrew; resting place.

Hanifa, Hanifah Arabic; true believer.

Hanita A blend of Hannah and Anita.

Hannah Hebrew; gracious, merciful. Light use in 1900 but declined rapidly and fell out of use by 1930. Revived in 1965 and had shown a steady rise into heavy use by 1990. *Other forms*: Chana, Chanah, Hana, Hanita, Hanna, Hannie, Nana. *Variants*: Anezka, Hana (Czech); Annalie (Finnish); Hanna, Hanni (German); Anci, Aniko, Annuska, Nina (Hungarian); Ania, Anka, Hania (Polish); Anouska (Russian); Ana, Hanita (Spanish); Anneka (Swedish).

Hanu Hawaiian; natural breath of the spirit; people.

Happy Middle English; lucky, glad. (See Gender-neutral names.)

Hareta Japanese; serene.

Harika Turkish; most beautiful.

Harmonie Greek; concord. *Other form*: Harmony.

Harper Old English; harp player. (See Gender-neutral names.)

Harriet Old German; home ruler. A feminine form of Harry. Light use in 1900, declining until it fell out of use in 1955. A small revival in 1980 had risen into light use by 1990. *Other forms*: Enrica, Etty, Jarri, Hattie, Hatty, Henka, Henrietta, Hetty, Minette, Yetty. *Variants*: Jindraska (Czech); Henriette (French); Henia, Henrieta (Polish); Enrieta (Romanian); Enriqueta, Queta (Spanish); Arriet (Swedish).

Haru Japanese; spring.

Hasana Swahili; she arrived first. A name often given to a first-born twin daughter.

Hasia Hebrew; protected by God. *Other form*: Hassie.

Hasina Hebrew; strong.

Hasita Sanskrit; laughing.

Hasna Arabic; beautiful.

Hateya Moquelumnan; footprints.

Hauora Maori; lively, spirit of life.

Haviva Hebrew; beloved. *Other form*: Hava.

Hawa Hebrew; breath of life. Or Swahili; longed for.

Haya Haya; the name of a tribe in Tanzania.

Hayfa Arabic; slender.

Hayley Old Norse; hero. Light use from 1965, rising to a peak of heavy use in 1985.

Hayze Origin uncertain; mist, haze. *Other forms*: Haeze, Haze.

Hazara Arabic; nightingale.

Hazel Old English; hazel tree. Light use from 1900, peaking in 1935 and now in decline. *Other forms*: Hazelle, Hazle. *Variant*: Aveline (French).

Hazelbelle A blend of Hazel and Bella (Isabel).

Hazena Middle English; harbour. *Other forms*: Hazeen, Hazine.

Hazira A blend of Hazel and Mira.

Heather Middle English; from the name of the healthland scrub, said to have lucky and protective attributes. Light use peaking in 1955 and having declined a little now seems to be holding steady in light usage. *Variant*: Kekessa (Cornish).

Hebe Greek; youth.

Hedda Greek; warrior. *Variants*: Hedviga (Czech); Edda, Hedy (German); Edda (Italian); Eda (Spanish).

Heddwen Welsh; white (or fair) peace.

Hedera Latin; ivy.

Hedli Old English; hiding place in a meadow.

Hedy Greek; delightful, sweet.

Heera Sanskrit; diamond.

Heidi A German form of Adelaide. Light use from 1965.

Heini Welsh; active, sprightly.

Heiwa Native American; peace.

Helaine, Helayne Blends of Helen and Elaine.

Helandra A blend of Helen and Sandra.

Helantha A blend of Helen and Samantha.

Helayne A blend of Helen and Elaine.

Helen Greek; torch, light (hence bright, shining, brilliant). Light use from 1900, peaking in heavy use in 1965. Although now in decline this is still a widely used name. *Other forms*: Eileen, Elaia, Elaine, Eleanor, Elena, Ellen, Elyn, Helayne, Helene, Helina, Leonora, Liolya, Nella. *Variants*: Heghine (Armenian); Nora

(Basque); Elena (Bulgarian); Helena, Elenka, Jelena, Lenka (Czech); Ellen, Elna (Danish); Elly, Lena (Dutch); Aili, Helli, Laina (Finnish); Elaine, Helene, Helenore, Leonore (French); Helena, Lena, Leni (German); Elena, Eleni, Elleni, Helena, Lena (Greek); Elionora, Helena, Helina, Onella (Hawaiian); Chaim, Eliora (Hebrew); Ileana, Ilka, Ilona (Hungarian); Aileen, Ayleen, Eileen (Irish); Lean (Irish Gaelic); Elena, Eleonora, Leonora, Lina (Italian); Helena (Latvian); Ale, Aliute, Elena (Lithuanian); Eli, Lene (Norwegian); Haliana, Helena (Polish); Ailinn, Helena (Portuguese); Elena (Romanian); Alena, Elena, Halina, Halinka, Lelya, Lenka, Yelena (Russian); Eilidh (Scottish Gaelic); Ilena (Slavonic); Elena, Eleonor (Spanish); Elna, Helena (Swedish); Galena, Olena (Ukrainian); Elen (Welsh).

Helena A German form of Helen. Steady light use from 1900.

Helene A French form of Helen. Occasional use 1965–75.

Helenor A blend of Helen and Eleanor.

Helga Old English; holly.

Heliantha Greek; sunflower.

Helinda A blend of Helen and Linda.

Helissa A blend of Helen and Larissa.

Helita A blend of Helen and Lita (Lolita).

Helma Old English; helm.

Helora A blend of Helen and Lora (Laura).

Hema Sanskrit; golden.

Henrietta Old German; home ruler. A French feminine form of Henry. Occasional use from 1900. *Other forms*: Etta, Harriet, Hattie, Hatty, Henriette, Hetty. *Variants*: Hendrika (Dutch); Henriette (French); Heinrike (German); Enrichetta (Italian); Eiric (Scottish Gaelic);

Enrica, Enriquetta, Quetta (Spanish); Henrika (Swedish).

Hera Greek; queen of heaven. The wife of Zeus in Greek mythology.

Herma Latin; signpost.

Hermione Greek; derived from Hermes, the messenger of the gods. *Other form*: Hermia.

Hermosa Spanish; beautiful.

Hesper Greek; evening star.

Hestia Persian; star. The Greek goddess of the hearth.

Heulwen Welsh; sunshine.

Heulyn Welsh; ray of the sun.

Hila, Hillela Hebrew; praise.

Hilana A blend of Hila and Lana.

Hilanda A blend of Hila and Amanda.

Hilantha A blend of Hila and Samantha.

Hilary Latin; cheerful. Light use from 1925, peaking in 1950. *Other forms*: Hilaire, Hilarie, Hillary. *Variants*: Alair, Hilaire (French); Hilaria (German); Hiolair (Irish Gaelic); Ilaria (Italian); Ilari (Russian); Hilaria (Spanish); Ilar (Welsh).

Hilda Old German; warrior. Heavy use at its peak in 1900, but then declined until it fell out of use in 1970. *Other forms*: Hilde, Hildy, Hylda. *Variant*: Hilde (Irish).

Hildegarde Old German; warrior. *Variant*: Ildegarda (Italian).

Hildelith, Hildelyth Blends of Hilda and Delyth.

Hillela Hebrew; praised.

Hiloka Creek; gum tree.

Hilora Hebrew/Maori; praise to life.

Hina Tahitian; maiden. The name of the Tahitian moon goddess.

Hirondel, Hirondelle French; a swallow.

Hoa Vietnamese; flower.

Hoku Hawaiian; star.

Hokulani Hawaiian; star in the heavens.

Holliday Old English; holy day.

Hollie A form of Holly. Occasional use from 1985.

Holly Old English; holly tree. Occasional use from 1900 until it fell out of use in 1930. A strong revival started in 1975. *Other forms*: Holli, Hollie, Hollye.

Hollyann A blend of Holly and Ann.

Honey Old Norse; sweetness, excellence.

Hononah Miwok; bear.

Honor Latin; honour, beauty. *Variants*: Inira, Ynyra (Irish Gaelic).

Honovi Hopi; strong deer.

Hope Old English; optimism, hope. Light use from 1990.

Hopi Hopi; peaceful ones. The name of a Native American nation.

Hoshi Japanese; star.

Hua Hawaiian; idea, concept, flowing out.

Huahine Tahitian; beautiful girl.

Huela Old German; bright in mind. A feminine form of Hugh.

Hula Hebrew; to make music. Or Hawaiian; woman's dance.

Hulah Probably Osage; eagle.

Hulani Hawaiian; rise to heaven; praise.

Hulda, Huldah Old German; gracious. *Other form*: Hulandah.

Humayra A name of uncertain meaning given by the Prophet Muhammad to his wife Aisha.

Huso Ovimbundu; the feigned sadness of the bride.

Huyana Miwok; rain falling.

Hyacinth Greek; the flower name meaning blue gem or sapphire. *Other forms*: Hiacinth, Hyacynth. *Variants*: Hyacinthe (French); Hyacinthie (German); Giacinta (Italian); Jacinta (Spanish).

Hyacynta, Hyacinta Blends of Hyacinth and Cinta.

Hye Korean; graceful.

Hyldara A blend of Hylda (Hilda) and Dara.

Hyone Greek; sea dream.

Hyonella A blend of Hyone and Ella.

I

Ianthe, Iantha Greek; violet flower.

Ida Possibly Old German; youthful. Occasional use from 1900 to 1935. *Variants*: Iuska (Czech); Ide (French); Idetta, Idette (German); Ita (Hebrew); Aida, Idalia (Italian); Itka (Polish); Idelle (Welsh).

Idalia, Idalya Spanish; sunny.

Idana A blend of Ida and Ana (Ann).

Idelia Old German; noble.

Idena A blend of Ida and Dena. *Other forms*: Idina, Idyna.

Idoma Idoma; the name of a tribe in Nigeria.

Idonea Old Norse; from Idhuna, the Norse goddess of spring.

Idylla Greek; perfection.

Iesha Arabic; alive, healthy.

Ila Aramaic; the best.

Ilana Hebrew; tree.

Ileana Greek; from Troy. *Other form*: Ileane.

Ilena A Slavonic form of Helen.

Ilka Old German; light. Or Scottish Gaelic; of the same kind or clan, hence kinswoman.

Ilona A Hungarian form of Helen.

Ilora A blend of Ilona and Lora.

Ilva Old English; elfin.

Imala Native American; strong-minded.

Iman Arabic; faith, belief.

Imelda Old German; all-embracing battle.

Imma Akkadian; water pouring from a jug (associated with the sign of Aquarius).

Imogen Latin; innocent. Occasional use from 1965. *Other forms*: Emogene, Immy, Imogene, Imojean.

Ina Latin; mother.

Inanna From the name of the Sumerian goddess of love and war.

Inaret Welsh; much loved.

India Hindi; from India. Light use from 1990. *Other forms*: Indie, Indy, Indya.

Indica Latin; to make known.

Indira Hindi; splendid. The god of heaven in Hindu mythology.

Indra Possibly Sanskrit; raindrop. The god of sky and rain in Hindu mythology).

Inga Old Norse; protection of Ing (the god of peace in Norse mythology).

Ingeborg Old Norse; fortification of Ing (the god of peace in Norse mythology). *Other form*: Inge.

Ingrid A Scandinavian form of Inga, with an added element meaning fair, beautiful. *Variants*: Inge (Danish); Ingeborg (German); Inga, Inger (Swedish).

Innes Scottish Gaelic; island.

Inola Probably Cherokee; black fox.

Iola Greek; dawn cloud.

Iolana, Iolani Hawaiian; soaring like a hawk.

Iona Greek; purple-coloured jewel. Also associated with the island in the Inner Hebrides rich in Christian and Celtic history. Light use from 1990. *Other forms*: Ione, Ionia.

Ionia Greek; wanderer, rover.

Iora Latin; gold.

Iorwen Welsh; beautiful.

Irene Greek; peace. The goddess of peace in Greek mythology. Light use from 1900, peaking at a heavy level in 1925 but then declining and falling out of use by 1985. *Other forms*: Erena, Irena, Irina, Reena, Rena, Rene, Renie, Rina. *Variants*: Irenka (Czech); Ereni, Rena (Greek); Hiraani (Hawaiian); Irenka (Hungarian); Irisha (Latvian); Irena (Polish); Irini (Romanian); Arina, Irina, Jereni, Orina, Orya, Yarina (Russian); Erena, Irana, Irissa (Slavonic); Irenea (Spanish); Iryna (Ukrainian).

Iris Greek; play of colours, rainbow. Light use from 1900, peaking in 1925 and then declining and falling out of use in 1965. *Other forms*: Irisa, Irita, Irys. *Variant*: Irisha (Russian).

Irma Old German; whole, universal.

Irona A character in the novel *Dancing on the Volcano* by Anne Gay.

Iryl A blend of Iris and Beryl.

Isabel A Spanish form of Elizabeth. Light use from 1900, declining in the 1960s but reviving strongly in 1990. *Other forms*: Bel, Belicia, Belita, Bella, Belle, Ibby, Isabelle, Isobel, Issy, Sabella, Tibby. *Variants*: Belle, Isabeau (French); Ilsa, Isabelle (German); Bella (Hungarian); Isibeal, Sibeal (Irish Gaelic); Isabella (Italian); Izabella (Russian); Isa, Ishbel, Isobel (Scottish); Iseabail (Scottish Gaelic); Belicia, Belita, Chava, Isabelita, Ysabel (Spanish).

Isabella An Italian form of Isabel. Light use at its peak in 1900, when it was three times as popular as Isabel. This form of the name was overtaken by Isabel in 1950, though by then reduced to occasional usage.

Isabelle A form of Isabel. Occasional use from 1925.

Isadora Greek; gift of Isis.

Isalee A blend of Isabel and Lee.

Isla Scottish Gaelic; a phonetic form of the Scottish river and island name Islay. Or Salinian; the hollyleaf cherry bush. Occasional use from 1960.

Islien Celtic; sweet voiced. *Other form*: Isleen.

Ismay Possibly Old German; bright.

Isobel A Scottish form of Isabel. Occasional use from 1900, but a strong revival in 1990 makes it almost as popular as Isabel.

Isolda Celtic; the fair one. *Variants*: Yseult (French); Isolde (German).

Issara A blend of Isabel and Sara.

Istana Malay; palace.

Ita Irish Gaelic; thirst.

Ivanna Hebrew; God's gracious gift. *Other forms*: Iva, Ivah, Ivana.

Ivena Hebrew; grace of the Lord.

Iverna Latin; Ireland.

Ivy Middle English; clinging vine. Heavy use in 1925, but then declined and had fallen out of use by 1985.

Iwona Scandinavian; archer.

Izarra Basque; star.

Izora Arabic; dawn.

J

Jaala Hebrew; wild she-goat.

Jacada A blend of Jacinta and Ada.

Jacana Tupi-Guarani; bird who walks on water.

Jacanda A blend of Jacinta and Amanda.

Jacantha A blend of Jacinta and Samantha.

Jacinda A blend of Jacinta and Linda.

Jacinta Greek; sapphire. *Other forms*: Jacinth, Jacintha, Jaquinda. *Variants*: Hyacinthe (German); Giacinta (Italian).

Jackie A form of Jacqueline. Occasional use from 1950. *Other forms*: Jacky, Jacqui, Jaqui. (See Gender-neutral names.)

Jaclyn A form of Jacqueline. Occasional use 1980–5.

Jacqueline A French feminine form of James. Steady light use from 1925, peaking in very heavy use in 1965. Now in decline into light use again. *Other forms*: Jackelyn, Jacki, Jackie, Jaclyn, Jacoba, Jacquelyn, Jacquenetta, Jacquetta, Jacqui, Jakolina, Jaqueline, Jaquetta. *Variants*: Jacqui, Jae (French); Jakoba (German); Jacquetta, Jaoquina, Quetta (Spanish).

Jacquelyn A form of Jacqueline. Occasional use 1955–70.

Jacquetta An Italian feminine form of James. *Other forms*:

Jacquette, Jaquetta. *Variant*: Jaquet (Cornish).

Jada Hebrew; wise.

Jade Spanish; from the name of the precious stone. Light use from 1975, with a very rapid rise into heavy use in 1990. *Other forms*: Jaide, Jayde. *Variant*: Ijada (Spanish).

Jadeen, Jadene Blends of Jade and Doreen.

Jaella Hebrew; mountain goat. *Other forms*: Jael, Jaelle. (See Gender-neutral names.)

Jagoda Serbo-Croatian; strawberry.

Jahlia A blend of Jane and Dahlia.

Jahola Hebrew; dove.

Jai Sanskrit; hail, praise, victory.

Jaime A form of Jamie. Occasional use since 1980. *Other forms*: Jamie, Jaomi. (See Gender-neutral names.)

Jairia Hebrew; enlightened by God.

Jakinda Spanish; hyacinth.

Jala Arabic; clarity.

Jaleesa Leesa (Lisa) with the *Ja-* prefix. Popularized by the television series *A Different World*. *Other form*: Jalisa.

Jalena, Jalene Blends of Jane and Lena. *Other form*: Jalyna.

Jalila Arabic; glory, greatness. *Other form*: Galila.

Jamie Hebrew; a supplanter. A feminine form of James. Light use from 1960, rising rapidly into heavy use in 1990. *Other forms*: Jaimi, Jaimy, Jamee, Jami, Jayme, Jaymee, Jaymi. (See Gender-neutral names.)

Jamila Arabic; beautiful. *Other forms*: Jameela, Jamelah, Jamella, Jamelle, Jamyla, Yamila. *Variant*: Djamila (French).

Jamilynn A blend of Jami and Lynn. *Other forms*: Jamielyn, Jamiline, Jamilyn, Jamylin.

Jan A form of Janet. Occasional use from 1900. *Variant*: Janna (German). (See Gender-neutral names.)

Jana A Hungarian form of Jane. *Other forms*: Jaana, Jannah.

Janan Arabic; heart, soul.

Janay A blend of Jane and Fay (Faye). *Other form*: Janae.

Jances A blend of Jane and Frances.

Jancis A character in the novel *Precious Bane* by Mary Webb.

Janda A blend of Jane and Amanda.

Jandora A blend of Jane and Dora.

Jandy A blend of Jane and Mandy.

Jane Hebrew; God is gracious. A feminine form of John. Popular from 1900, peaking in heavy use in 1925 and 1965. Now in decline but still in light use. *Other forms*: Jain, Janella, Janessa, Janet, Janice, Janine, Janita, Jantina, Janyce, Jayne, Jean, Jenine, Jennie, Jenny, Jessie, Joan, Joanna, Juanita, Sheena, Vania, Zaneta. *Variants*: Ohana (Armenian); Jone, Yoana (Basque); Jana, Jenna (Cornish); Hana, Jahna, Jannine, Janica, Jenka (Czech); Johanna (Danish); Jantje, Jansje (Dutch); Janne (Finnish); Janine, Jeanne, Jeanette (French); Hanna, Johanna (German); Ioanna (Greek); Ioana (Hawaiian); Janka, Zsanett (Hungarian); Shavon, Shavonne, Sheena, Shivon (Irish); Sine, Siobhan (Irish Gaelic); Gianna, Giovanna, Jovanna (Italian); Jana, Janina, Zanna (Latvian); Janina, Janyte (Lithuanian); Jana, Janay, Janina, Jasia, Jayna, Joanka (Polish); Joana (Portuguese); Ioana, Jenica (Romanian); Ivana, Ivanna (Russian); Jean, Jeanie (Scottish); Sine, Seonaid, Siubhan (Scottish Gaelic); Iva, Ivana (Slavonic); Juana, Juanita, Nita, Zaneta (Spanish); Johanna (Swedish);

135

Ioanna, Ivanna (Ukrainian); Shan, Shana, Shanay, Sian (Welsh).

Janeese A blend of Jane and Elise.

Janella, Janelle Blends of Jane and Ella.

Janet A diminutive of Jane. Light use from 1900, peaking in heavy use in 1955, and then declining and falling out of use by 1985. *Other forms*: Jan, Janessa, Janeta, Janette, Janita, Jessie, Nettie. *Variants*: Sinead (Irish Gaelic); Gianetta (Italian); Jessie (Scottish); Seonaid (Scottish Gaelic); Sioned (Welsh).

Janette A form of Janet. Occasional use from 1925 to 1985, peaking in 1960.

Janice A form of Jane. Light use from 1935 peaking in 1950. *Other forms*: Janis, Janys.

Janine A diminutive of Jane. Light use from 1935, peaking in 1965. *Other forms*: Geneen, Janeen, Janene, Janina, Janyne.

Janis A form of Janice. Occasional use 1950–65, peaking in 1955.

Jannine A form of Janine. Occasional use from 1990.

Janora A blend of Jane and Nora.

Jantha A blend of Jane and Samantha.

Janthea A blend of Jane and Anthea.

Jaomi A form of Jamie. (See Gender-neutral names.)

Jaqueline A form of Jacqueline. Occasional use from 1935 to 1980.

Jarawa Andamanese; the name of a tribe in the Andaman Islands.

Jardena, Jardenia Hebrew; flowing down.

Jarita Sanskrit; motherly bird.

Jarrah From the name of the broadleaved tree.

Jarrahlee A blend of Jarrah and Lee.

Jasa A blend of James and Sara.

Jasmine Persian; from the flower name. Occasional use from 1960. *Other forms*: Jasmeen, Jasmin, Jasmina, Jazmine, Jazzmin, Jesamine, Jesmond, Jess, Jessamine, Jessamy, Jessie, Yasmin, Yasmine, Yasmyne. *Variants*: Yasmin (Arabic); Jasmuheen (Egyptian); Jessamine (French); Jasmin (German); Yasmine (Hindi); Gelsomina (Italian).

Jatara A blend of Jane and Tara.

Javana Malay; from Java.

Jaya Sanskrit; victory.

Jaycee A combination of the initials J and C. *Other forms*: Jaci, Jayci. (See Gender-neutral names.)

Jaydee A blend of Jaye and Dee.

Jaye A feminine form of Jay. Latin; from the name of the bird. (See Gender-neutral names.)

Jayelle A blend of Jaye and Ella.

Jayla Jaye with the *La-* suffix.

Jaylene A blend of Jane and Helene.

Jaylynn A blend of Jaye and Lynn.

Jayme, Jaymie Forms of Jamesina, a feminine version of James.

Jayne A form of Jane. Light use from 1950 peaking in 1965.

Jazlyn A blend of Jazmine (Jasmine) and Lyn.

Jean A Scottish form of Jane. Heavy use from 1925, peaking in very heavy use in 1935, but then declining steadily and falling out of use in 1990. *Other forms*: Genna, Jeane, Jeanette, Jeanice, Jeanine, Jeanne, Jeannette, Jenica, Jenni, Jennie, Jenny, Jinnie, Nettie. *Variants*: Jannine, Jeanne (French); Kini (Hawaiian); Jena (Polish); Sine (Scottish Gaelic).

Jeanelle A blend of Jean and Ella.

Jeanette A dimunitive of Jean. Light use from 1935 peaking in 1965. *Other form*: Jeanetta. *Variant*: Jennet (Scottish).

Jeanne A blend of Jean and Anne. Occasional use 1935–55.

Jeannette A dimunitive of Jean. Occasional use 1935–65.

Jelena Greek; light. *Other forms*: Jalina, Jelina.

Jelita Indonesian; beautiful.

Jemima Hebrew; dove. Occasional use from 1900. *Variant*: Simeag (Scottish Gaelic).

Jemira A blend of Jemima and Mira (Myra).

Jemma A form of Gemma. Light use from 1975, peaking in 1985.

Jenalyn A blend of Jennifer and Lynda.

Jenariel A blend of Jena (Jean) and Ariel.

Jenavee Jena (Jean) with the *-vee* suffix.

Jendaya Shona and Tonga; thankful.

Jenelle A blend of Jennifer and Ella.

Jenifer A form of Jennifer. Occasional use 1935–85.

Jenilee, Jennilee Blends of Jennifer and Lee.

Jenna A Welsh form of Jennifer. Light use from 1975 peaking in 1985.

Jennie A form of Jennifer. Light use from 1900.

Jennifer A Cornish form of Guinevere. Steady light use from 1925, peaking in very heavy use in 1950. After that it declined a little, but rose again in the 1980s and continued in light use. *Other forms*: Gaynor, Ginevra, Guinevere, Gwyneth, Jen, Jenifer, Jenna, Jennie, Jenny, Jenyth, Jinny, Vanora. *Variants*: Gweniver, Jenifer, Jenniver (Cornish); Jennieka (Czech); Jena (Hungarian);

Gwenifer, Jenna (Welsh).

Jennilynn A blend of Jennifer and Lynn.

Jenny A form of Jennifer. Light use from 1900.

Jeony A blend of Jean and Bryony.

Jerilynn A blend of Jerri (Geraldine) and Lynn.

Jermaine A form of Germaine. Occasional use from 1980.

Jerrica A blend of Jessie and Erica.

Jervaise Old German; spear. *Other forms*: Jervaese, Jervayse. (See Gender-neutral names.)

Jeska Hebrew; she who looks out.

Jessalyn A blend of Jessica and Lyn.

Jessamy, Jessamie Blends of Jessie and Amy.

Jessamyn A blend of Jessie and Lynda.

Jessica Hebrew; God's grace. Light use from 1900 until it fell out of use in 1975. When it revived again in 1980 it started rising rapidly, and had reached heavy use by 1990. *Other forms*: Jesica, Jessika. *Variants*: Janka (Hungarian); Gessica (Italian).

Jessie A form of Jessica. Light use in 1900 then declining and falling out of use in 1970. Revived again in 1990. *Other form*: Jessey. *Variant*: Seasaidh (Scottish Gaelic). (See Gender-neutral names.)

Jetta, Jette Old English; jet black gemstone.

Jevera Hebrew; life.

Jevette A blend of Jean and Yvette.

Jewel, Jewelle Old French; gemstone.

Jill A form of Gillian. Light use from 1925 peaking in 1960. *Other forms*: Jil, Jilly.

Jillian A form of Gillian. Light use from 1935 until it fell out of use in 1975. *Variant*: Jilleen (Irish).

Jinna Arabic; genie, spirit of air or fire.

Jivanta Hindi; giver of life.

Jo A form of Joanna. (See Gender-neutral names.)

Joan A form of Jane. Very heavy use at its peak in 1900, but then declined rapidly and fell out of use in 1975. There was a small revival in 1990. *Other forms*: Joann, Joanna, Joanne, Johanna, Joni, Jonie, Jovana, Juana, Nita, Zaneta. *Variants*: Jeanne (French); Janna, Johana (German); Wanika (Hawaiian); Siobhan (Irish Gaelic); Giann, Giovanna (Italian); Joaquina (Portuguese); Ioana, Oana (Romanian); Yana (Russian); Jean, Sheena, Shona (Scottish); Seonag (Scottish Gaelic); Jonnika (Slavonic); Juana, Juanita (Spanish); Sian, Siwan (Welsh).

Jo-Ann A form of Joanna. Occasional use from 1965 to 1975.

Joanna A form of Joan. Light use from 1935, peaking in the 1980s. *Other forms*: Joanne, Johanna, Johanne, Jontaya, Jontel, Jontelle, Jontila. *Variants*: Jowna (Cornish); Joanne (French); Johanna (German); Giovanna (Italian); Joana (Romanian).

Joanne A French form of Joanna. Light use from 1950 until it rose into heavy use in 1965. It increased to very heavy use in 1970, before declining into light use again by 1990. *Other forms*: Joann, Jo-ann, Jo-anne.

Jo-Anne A form of Joanne. Occasional use from 1960.

Jobeth A blend of Joan and Elizabeth.

Jocasta Greek; a name of uncertain meaning borne in Greek mythology by the mother of Oedipus, King of Thebes.

Jocelyn Old German; descendant of the Goths. Occasional use from 1925. *Other forms*: Jocelin, Joceline, Jocelyne, Joscelyn, Josette, Josie, Joslin, Joslyn, Joss.

Variant: Jocinta (Spanish). (See Gender-neutral names.)

Jodiann A blend of Jodie and Ann.

Jodie A form of Judith. Occasional use from 1970, rising steadily to light use in 1990. This is the favourite form of the name, ten times more popular than Jodi, and five times more widely used than Jody. (See Gender-neutral names.)

Joely, Joella, Joelle Hebrew; God is willing. Feminine forms of Joel. (See Gender-neutral names.)

Johanna A form of Joanna. Occasional use from 1900, peaking in 1975.

Johanne A form of Joanna. Occasional use from 1965 to 1980. *Variant*: Janne (Danish).

Jola A blend of Joanna and Lola.

Jolaine, Jolayne Blends of Joseph and Elaine.

Jolan Greek; violet flower.

Jolanta Greek; violet blossom. *Other form*: Jola.

Jolantha A blend of Joanna and Samantha.

Jolene A form of Jolie. Occasional use from 1970.

Joletta Latin; violet.

Jolie Middle English; high spirits.

Jolinda, Jolynda Blends of Joanna and Linda.

Jolisa A blend of Joanna and Lisa.

Jolynn A blend of Joanna and Lynn.

Jomanda A blend of Joanna and Amanda.

Jonatha Hebrew; God has given. A feminine form of Jonathan. *Other forms*: Jonathelle, Jonetha, Jonathene.

Jonella, Jonelle Blends of Joan and Ella.

Joni Hebrew; God is gracious. A feminine form of John.

Jonina Hebrew; dove.

Jonquil Spanish; from the flower name.

Jora Hebrew; autumn rain. The Hebrew term for the sign Scorpio.

Jordan Hebrew; to flow down. (See Gender-neutral names.)

Jordana A form of Jordan. Occasional use from 1980. *Other forms*: Joree, Jorey, Jori, Jorie, Jorina, Jorita, Jory. *Variants*: Yordana (Basque); Jordane (French); Giordana, Jiordana (Italian).

Jorelle A blend of Joyce and Ella.

Joren Scandinavian; love of the chief. *Variant*: Jorunn (Norwegian).

Joriann A blend of Jori (Jordana) and Ann.

Josephine A French feminine form of Joseph. Light use from 1900 peaking in 1950. *Other forms*: Fifi, Fifine, Josepha, Josette, Josie, Yosepha. *Variants*: Fifi, Josee, Josephe (French); Josefa, Josepha (German); Seosaimhin (Irish Gaelic); Giuseppina, Peppina (Italian); Josefina, Pepita (Spanish).

Josie A form of Josephine. Occasional use from 1950.

Jovita Latin; of Jupiter (the supreme god in Roman mythology).

Joy Latin; gladness, delight. Light use from 1925 peaking in 1955. *Other forms*: Joia, Joye, Joyla.

Joya Spanish; treasure. *Other form*: Joyaa.

Joyann, Joyanne Blends of Joy and Ann.

Joyce Breton; champion. Very heavy use in 1925, but then declined rapidly and fell out of use in 1985. *Other forms*: Jocey, Jocosa, Joice, Joisse, Jolia, Joycia. *Variant*: Joisse (French).

Joyella, Joyelle Blends of Joy and Ella.

Joylene A blend of Joy and Helene.

Joylyn A blend of Joy and Lynn. *Other form*: Joylin.

Juanita A Spanish form of Joan. Occasional use from 1935. *Other form*: Juana. *Variants*: Wanika (Hawaiian); Kwanita (Zuni).

Juba African; lion's mane.

Jude A form of Judith. (See Gender-neutral names.)

Judith Hebrew; praise. Light use from 1900, peaking in 1960 and now in decline. *Other forms*: Judi, Judie, Judy, Yuta. *Variants*: Judithe (French); Juditha (German); Ioudith (Greek); Judit (Hungarian); Iule (Irish Gaelic); Guiditta, Giulia (Italian); Judite (Portuguese); Judita (Lithuanian); Yudita (Russian); Siubhan (Scottish Gaelic); Juditha (Swedish).

Judy A form of Judith. Light use from 1935. *Other forms*: Judi, Judie. *Variant*: Jud (Hungarian).

Judyann A blend of Judy and Ann.

Julantha A blend of Julie and Samantha.

Julene Latin; youthful.

Julia Probably Greek; soft-haired. A feminine form of Julian. Light use from 1900 peaking in 1965. *Other forms*: Juliana, Julianne, Julie, Julienne, Juliet, Juliette. *Variants*: Yulia (Armenian); Julene, Yulene (Basque); Judita, Julie, Julka (Czech); Juliana (Dutch); Julie, Julienne, Juliet, Juliette (French); Julie (German); Iola, Ioulia (Greek); Iulia (Hawaiian); Juli, Juliana, Juliska (Hungarian); Sile (Irish Gaelic); Giulia, Giulietta (Italian); Iuliya, Julija (Latvian); Iulija (Lithuanian); Jula, Julita (Polish); Iulia (Romanian); Yulia, Yuliya, Yulya (Russian); Sileas (Scottish Gaelic); Jahlia (Slavonic); Julieta, Julita (Spanish); Ulyana, Yulia (Ukrainian).

Julie A French form of Julia. Light use from 1935 but rose rapidly to a peak of very heavy use in 1965. It was twice as popular as Julia in 1955 and by 1965 had

143

outpaced that name by more than four to one. However Julie had declined back to light use again by 1990. *Other forms*: Juley, Juli.

Julie-Mae A blend of Julie and Mae (May).

Juliet A French diminutive of Julia. Light use from 1955. *Other forms*: Julietta, Juliette. *Variants*: Juliette (French); Julietta (Italian); Julieta (Spanish).

Juliette A form of Juliet. Occasional use from 1925 to 1975.

June Latin; from the name of the month. Light use from 1925, peaking in 1935, and then declining and falling out of use in 1990.

Juniper Latin; from the plant name. (See Gender-neutral names.)

Juno Latin; queen of heaven. The name of the wife of Jupiter in Roman mythology.

Jurisa Slavonic; storm.

Justina A Spanish form of Justine. Occasional use from 1970.

Justine Latin; fair, just. A feminine form of Justin. Popularized by the novel *Justine* by Lawrence Durrell. Light use from 1950, peaking in 1970. *Other forms*: Justina, Justyna. *Variants*: Giustina (Italian); Justina (Spanish); Jestina (Welsh).

K

Kabira Arabic; powerful.

Kacey Irish Gaelic; brave. *Other forms*: Casey, Kacie, Kacy, Kasey, Kaycee, Kayci. (See Gender-neutral names.)

Kachina Shoshone; sacred dancer.

Kady Irish Gaelic; first child. *Other forms*: Kaydi, Kaydy.

Kaela, Kaella Forms of Kalila. *Other forms*: Kae, Keyla.

Kaelyn A blend of Kaela and Lynn.

Kagami Japanese; mirror.

Kahlia, Kahlya Blends of Kathy and Dahlia.

Kahu Hawaiian; to make a fire, guardian, provider.

Kahuna, Huna Hawaiian; craft, art, profession, way of life.

Kai Hawaiian; sea. Or Hopi; willow tree. (See Gender-neutral names.)

Kaila Hebrew; crown.

Kaili The name of the Hawaiian water goddess.

Kaimana Hawaiian; diamond.

Kaira Irish Gaelic; sheep.

Kairos Greek; the name of the last child of Zeus.

Kaitara A blend of Kaitlin (Caitlin) and Tara.

Kaiya A form of Keya.

Kaka Papago; clearing.

Kala Hawaiian; sun. Or Sinhala; the name of a river in Sri Lanka.

Kalama Hawaiian; flaming torch.

Kalanda A blend of Kaley (Kayley) and Amanda.

Kalani Hawaiian; sky.

Kalantha A blend of Kaley (Kayley) and Samantha.

Kalare Latin; bright, clear.

Kaldora A blend of Kaley (Kayley) and Dora.

Kalea Hawaiian; bright.

Kalena Hawaiian; pure.

Kalila Arabic; beloved, sweetheart.

Kalina Slavonic; flower. *Variant*: Kalinka (Russian).

Kalinda Sanskrit; sun.

Kalisa A blend of Kate and Lisa.

Kaliska Miwok; coyote chasing deer.

Kaluwa Usenga; never-forgotten spirit.

Kalwa Finnish; heroic.

Kalya Sanskrit; healthy.

Kalyana Sanskrit; virtuous one.

Kama Sanskrit; love, desire.

Kamahina Hawaiian; strong or powerful girl. The name of the Hawaiian moon goddess.

Kamala Sanskrit; lotus flower. Or Arabic; perfection.

Kamali Polynesian; princess. Or Mahona; spirit guide, protector.

Kamani Sranan; the name of a river in Suriname.

Kamaria African; like the lioness.

Kamba Kamba; the name of a tribe in Kenya.

Kamea Hawaiian; precious one.

Kamele Hawaiian; song, melody.

Kami Japanese; divine aura.

Kamila, Kamilah Arabic; complete, perfect.

Kamla Mashona; spirit.

Kana Welsh; beautiful.

Kanani Hawaiian; a beauty.

Kanchana A blend of Kana and Chana.

Kanda Native American; magical power.

Kandora A blend of Kandy (Candace) and Dora.

Kandra Sanskrit; bright, lovely.

Kanielle Arabic; bright spear.

Kanika Mwera; black cloth.

Kannitha Cambodian; angel.

Kanoa Polynesian; free. Or Hawaiian; key, hidden meaning. (See Gender-neutral names.)

Kanta Sanskrit; beautiful, desired.

Kanya Thai; young lady. Or the Hindi term for the sign Virgo.

Kara A Danish form of Katherine. Occasional use from 1970. *Variant*: Karielle (French).

Karalynn A blend of Kara and Lynn.

Karamanda A blend of Kara and Amanda.

Karana Sanskrit; crown.

Karanda A country in the *Malloreon* cycle of novels by David Eddings.

Karantha A blend of Kara and Samantha.

Karella, Karelle Blends of Kara and Ella.

Karen A Danish form of Katherine. Light use from 1950, rising to a peak of very heavy use in 1960 and has now declined to light use again. *Other forms*: Caron, Karin, Karon, Karrin, Karyn. *Variants*: Caryn (Danish); Kaarina (Finnish); Kalana, Kalaena (Hawaiian); Karina, Karyna (Russian); Karena, Karin (Scandinavian); Caryn (Slavonic); Carina (Swedish); Carey (Welsh).

Karena A blend of Karen and Karina.

Karenza, Kerenza Cornish; love, affection.

Kari Sanskrit; doer.

Kariba Shona; from the name of the lake on the Zambesi River.

Karilynn A blend of Kari and Lynn.

Karima Arabic; generous, noble. *Other forms*: Kareema, Karime.

Karin A Swedish form of Katherine. Occasional use 1950–85.

Karina A Norwegian form of Katherine. Occasional use from 1955. *Variant*: Karna (Swedish).

Karla Old English; womanly. A feminine form of Karl. Occasional use from 1975. *Other forms*: Karleen, Karlene, Karli, Karly.

Karly A form of Karla. Occasional use from 1980.

Karon A form of Caron. Occasional use 1960–70.

Karona A blend of Karen and Rona.

Karuna Sanskrit; compassion.

Karyn A form of Karen. Occasional use from 1955, falling out of use in 1965 but reviving in 1990.

Kasey A form of Casey. (See Gender-neutral names.)

Kashawna Shawna with the *Ka-* prefix.

Kashima Shima with the *Ka-* prefix.

Kasi Laotian; from the place-name in Laos.

Kasia Polish; pure. *Other form*: Kazia.

Kasinda Umbundu; our last baby.

Kasmira Slavonic; commander of peace. *Other form*: Kasmyra.

Kasota Native American; clear sky.

Kasumi Japanese; haze, mist.

Katana A blend of Kate and Tanya.

Katanga Hausa; buildings. *Other form*: Karanga.

Katara Kirundi; a place-name in Burundi.

Katarinda A blend of Katherine and Linda.

Kate A form of Katherine. Light use from 1900, falling out of use in 1935 and reviving in 1955. It peaked in 1980 and is now declining again. *Other forms*: Kati, Katie, Katy. *Variants*: Kata, Katica (Czech); Kati (Estonian); Cait, Kait (Irish); Katka, Katya (Russian).

Katharine A form of Katherine. Occasional use from 1900, peaking in 1990.

Katherine Greek; pure. Light use from 1900, declining in the 1930s but reviving in 1950. A steady increase in use since 1980, peaking in 1990. This spelling is four times as popular as Katharine. *Other forms*: Cassie, Catherine, Cathleen, Kate, Katharine, Kathleen, Kathrine, Kathryn, Kathy, Katie, Katy, Kitty. *Variants*: Garine (Armenian); Katalin (Basque); Katerina (Bulgarian); Katarina, Katka, Katuska (Czech); Kara, Karen, Kasen (Danish); Kaatje, Katrien, Tryn (Dutch); Katharina, Rina (Estonian); Kaarina, Kaisa, Karita, Katrie (Finnish); Catharine, Catherine (French); Kaethe, Katerine, Katharina, Katia, Katja, Katrine, Trina (German); Katrina; Kolina (Greek); Kakalina, Kalena (Hawaiian); Katalin, Katarina, Kati (Hungarian); Katrin (Icelandic); Caitlin, Caitrin, Cathleen, Kathleen (Irish); Caitriona (Irish Gaelic); Catarina, Caterina, Catia (Italian); Kathryn, Trina (Latvian); Katerina, Kofryna (Lithuanian); Karen, Karena, Karin, Karina, Katrine (Norwegian); Kasane, Kasani, Kasia, Kassia, Kataryzna, Kisani (Polish); Catarina, Catia (Portuguese); Caterina, Ecaterina (Romanian); Ekaterina, Katerina, Katinka, Katja, Katrushka, Katryna, Katya, Katyana, Kiska, Olena, Yekaterina (Russian); Catrina, Catryna, Katrina, Katrine (Scottish); Catriona (Scottish Gaelic); Kassia, Katina, Katrinka, Kaysha (Slavonic); Catalina (Spanish); Karin, Katarina, Kolina (Swedish); Karina, Katerina (Ukrainian); Cadi, Catrin (Welsh).

Kathleen An Irish form of Katherine. Heavy use at its peak in 1925, but then declined slowly into its present light usage. *Other forms*: Cathleen, Cathy, Kathy.

Kathlyn A blend of Kathleen and Lynda.

Kathrine A form of Katherine. Occasional use 1955–65.

Kathryn A form of Katherine. Steady light use from 1950. Seven times as popular as Katherine in 1950, it was overtaken by the rise of that name in 1975. *Other forms*: Cathryn, Kathrin.

Kathy A form of Katherine. Occasional use from 1965 to 1980.

Kathymanda A blend of Kathy and Amanda.

Katie A form of Katherine. Occasional use from 1900, falling out of use in 1935 but reviving in 1960. Steady growth from 1970 into heavy use at its peak in 1985. *Other forms*: Katey, Katy.

Katinka A Russian form of Katherine.

Katriel Hebrew; God is my crown.

Katrina A German form of Katherine. Light use from 1950. *Other forms*: Katrena, Katryna.

Katura Babudja; feeling better.

Katy A form of Katherine. Occasional use from 1965 peaking in 1985.

Kaula Polynesian; prophet.

Kaulana Hawaiian; famous.

Kava Maori; bitter. The name of a shrub whose powdered root is made into an intoxicating drink throughout Polynesia.

Kavinda A blend of Kavita and Linda.

Kavindra Hindi; poet.

Kavita Sanskrit; poetry.

Kawa Japanese; river. Or Osage; horse.

Kawena Hawaiian; glow, hence glowing, radiant.

Kay A form of Katherine. Light use from 1935 peaking in 1960.

Kaya Hopi; wise child, elder sister. Or Nyika; hilltop village.

Kaye A form of Kay. Occasional use from 1955 to 1985.

Kayla Irish Gaelic; comely. Or Hebrew; crown. Popularized by the television series *Days of Our Lives*.

Kayle Hebrew; faithful. (See Gender-neutral names.)

Kaylea A form of Kayley. Occasional use from 1985.

Kaylee A form of Kayley. Occasional use from 1980.

Kayleigh A form of Kayley. Occasional use from 1985, peaking in 1990.

Kayley Irish Gaelic; slender. Occasional use from 1980. *Other forms*: Kaileigh, Kaley, Kaylea, Kaylee, Kayleigh, Kaylie.

Kaylie A form of Kayley. Occasional use from 1985.

Kaylin Irish Gaelic; slender and fair. *Other forms*: Kaylyn, Kaylynn, Keelan.

Kayna Cornish; beautiful.

Kaysa Greek; pure.

Keala Hawaiian; path.

Kealoha Hawaiian; loved one.

Keara Irish Gaelic; dark-haired.

Keatchie Caddoan; panther.

Kedi Turkish; cat.

Keela, Keelah Irish Gaelic; so beautiful that only poets can describe her. *Other forms*: Kayleigh, Keeley, Keely, Kyla.

Keeley A form of Keela. Light use from 1960, peaking in 1975. *Other forms*: Keeli, Keelie, Keely.

Keely A form of Keeley. Occasional use from 1960.

Keena, Keenah Celtic; ancient (hence wise) one.

Keesha A blend of Keeyah (Keya) and Lakesha.

Kefirah Hebrew; young lioness.

Keilani Hawaiian; glorious chief.

Keira Irish Gaelic; black, dark-haired. A feminine form of Keiran.

Keisha African; favourite. *Other forms*: Keesha, Keysha.

Kekona Hawaiian; second-born child.

Kelai Maldivian; the name of an island in the Maldives.

Kelana A character in the novel *Isle of Illusion* by Carol Severance.

Kelanda A blend of Keela and Amanda.

Kelantha A blend of Keela and Samantha.

Kelcey Old English; victory at sea. Light use from 1985. *Other forms*: Kelcie, Kelsie. (See Gender-neutral names.)

Kelda Scandinavian; fresh mountain.

Kelila Hebrew; crown.

Kelin Irish Gaelic; slender and fair.

Kelinda A blend of Kelly and Linda.

Kellie A form of Kelly. Occasional use from 1970.

Kelly Irish Gaelic; brave warrior. Light use from 1960, peaking in heavy use in 1980. *Other forms*: Kaley, Kellee, Kelley, Kelli, Kellie. (See Gender-neutral names.)

Kellyn A blend of Kelly and Lynn.

Kemba Old English; Saxon ruler.

Kemuelle Probably Arabic; high or great angel. Kemuelle (or Kemu-el) is a great angel of the order of Seraphim.

Kenda Old English; water child. Or Dakota; magical power.

Kendall Celtic; ruler of the valley. *Other forms*: Kendelle, Kendyll, Kyndall. (See Gender-neutral names.)

Keneisha A blend of Kenna and Aisha.

Kenna, Kendra Old English; woman of knowledge, wise woman.

Kensa Cornish; first daughter. (See also Nessa and Tressa).

Kenya African; antelope. Also linked with the African State.

Kenyangi Rukiga; white egret.

Keola Hawaiian; life. *Other form*: Keoma.

Kerani Todas; sacred bells.

Kerella A blend of Keren and Ella.

Keren Hebrew; horn of antimony.

Keretta Hebrew; settlement.

Kerenza, Kerensa Cornish; love, affection.

Keri A form of Kerry. Occasional use from 1965.

Kerra Cornish; dearer.

Kerri A form of Kerry. Occasional use from 1975.

Kerrie A form of Kerry. Occasional use from 1960.

Kerry Irish Gaelic; the place of Ciar's people. Light use from 1960, peaking in 1980. *Other forms*: Kerree, Kerrey, Kerri, Kerrie, Keryn. (See Gender-neutral names.)

Keshena Native American; swift.

Keshet Hebrew; rainbow.

Keshi Sanskrit; beautiful hair.

Keshia Aramaic; an elder. *Other forms*: Kesha, Keshya.

Kesia, Kesya African; favourite one.

Kesira A character in the novel *The Jade Demons Quarter* by Robert Vardeman.

Kessie Ashanti; chubby baby.

Ketana Sanskrit; home.

Ketty, Keta Blends of Kitty (Katherine) and Betty.

Ketura, Keturah Hebrew; fragrance.

Keva Irish Gaelic; handsome at birth.

Keya Scottish Gaelic; daughter of the fiery one. *Other forms*: Kaiya, Keeyah.

Keyne Possibly Cornish; knowing, wise.

Keziah Hebrew; fragrant powdered bark. *Other forms*: Kezia, Ketzia.

Khadija Swahili; born prematurely.

Khalida Arabic; immortal. *Other form*: Khalidah.

Khanya Zulu; beautiful.

Kia, Kiah, Kyah African; season's beginning.

Kiana Anna with the *Ki-* prefix.

Kiara From Kiaran, an Irish saint's name of uncertain meaning.

Kiba Possibly Cornish; charioteer.

Kichi Japanese; fortunate.

Kiera Irish Gaelic; dark, black. *Other form*: Kierra.

Kiersten Swedish; anointed one.

Kijai Ateso; first girl born in the family.

Kilohana Hawaiian; apex, hence high aspiration.

Kim A form of Kimberley. Occasional use from 1950, peaking in light use in 1960. *Other forms*: Kym, Kymbal. (See Gender-neutral names.)

Kimana Shoshone; butterfly.

Kimberley Old English; land belonging to Cyneburg. Light use from 1955, peaking in 1985. *Other forms*: Kim, Kimberlie, Kimberly, Kimble, Kym, Kymberley, Kymberly, Kymble.

Kimberly A form of Kimberley. Occasional use from 1955, peaking in 1990.

154

Kimberlyn A blend of Kimberley and Lyn.

Kimi Japanese; the best. *Variants*: Kimiko, Kimiyo (Japanese).

Kimshew Maidu; little stream.

Kina, Kinetta Greek; to move.

Kinta Choctaw; beaver.

Kintla Kootenai; bag, sack.

Kinu Japanese; silk.

Kiokee Muskogean; waterfall.

Kiona Native American; brown hills.

Kiowa From the name of the Native American nation.

Kira, Kirah Persian; sun.

Kirby Old English; church farm. *Other forms*: Kirbee, Kirbey, Kirbi. (See Gender-neutral names.)

Kireen Old English; church.

Kirelle A character in the novel *That Way Lies Camelot* by Janny Wurts.

Kiri Maori; fair. *Other form*: Kirima.

Kirima Eskimo; hill.

Kirin Japanese; unicorn.

Kirsi Dravidian; the unfading amarinth flower.

Kirsten A Scandinavian form of Christine. Light use from 1970. *Other forms*: Kersten, Kirsteen, Kirstene, Kirstin, Kirstyn.

Kirstie A form of Kirsty. Occasional use from 1970.

Kirsty A form of Kirsten. Light use from 1970 steadily increasing to 1990. *Other forms*: Kirsti, Kirstie.

Kisha Russian; pure.

Kishi Japanese; long and happy life.

Kismet, Kysmet Arabic; fate, destiny.

Kita Maori; bright colours.

Kitaura A blend of Kita and Aura.

Kitena, Ketena Blends of Kitty (Katherine) and Tena (Tayna).

Kitra Hebrew; crown.

Kivu Rwanda; from Lake Kivu in Rwanda.

Kiyo Japanese; happiness in our family.

Kizzy A form of Keziah. The name of a character in the novel *Roots* by Alex Haley. Occasional use from 1980.

Koa Hebrew; princess.

Koha Maori; gift, respect. *Other form*: Kolha.

Kohana Sioux; swift. (See Gender-neutral names.)

Kohanda Japanese; little flower.

Kolina Greek; pure.

Komala Sanskrit; charming.

Komati Swazi; the name of a river in Swaziland.

Kona Hawaiian; lady.

Konocti Probably Pomo; mountain woman.

Konowa Seminole; string of beads.

Koo Maori; girl. *Other form*: Kohaia.

Kooskia Nez Perce; clear water.

Kora Greek; maiden. *Other form*: Cora. *Variants*: Koressa, Koretta (Spanish).

Koranda A blend of Kora and Amanda.

Korantha A blend of Kora and Samantha.

Kore Greek; maiden. One name of the Greek goddess Persephone.

Korella, Korelle Blends of Kora and Ella.

Koren Greek; beautiful maiden. *Other form*: Kore. *Variant*: Korenza (Italian).

Kori Maori; to play. *Other forms*: Koree, Korie. (See Gender-neutral names.)

Korianda Greek; from the herb name Coriander.

Korinda, Korynda Blends of Kori and Linda.

Korintha, Koryntha Blends of Kori and Cynthia.

Koruna Czech; crown.

Koshka Russian; cat. *Other form*: Koya.

Kotari Hiri Motu; a place-name in Papua New Guinea.

Koya Koya; the name of a tribe in India.

Kris A form of Kristine. *Other forms*: Kriss, Krissie, Krissy. (See Gender-neutral names.)

Krisha A blend of Kris and Trisha (Patricia).

Kristian Latin; a Christian. A feminine version of the Danish form of the name Christian. *Other form*: Kristiane. (See Gender-neutral names.)

Kristina A Swedish form of Christine. Occasional use from 1970. *Other forms*: Kristie, Kristy. *Variant*: Krystyna (Polish).

Kristy A form of Kirsten, Kristen, Kristina etc. Occasional use from 1980.

Krystal A form of Crystal. *Other form*: Krystle.

Krystalee A blend of Krystal and Lee.

Krystalynn A blend of Krystal and Lynn.

Krystle A form of Krystal. Popularized by the television series *Dynasty*.

Kula Zulu; an Indian or East Indian. Or Dzongkha; the name of a mountain in Bhutan.

Kulwa Zaramo; first-born of twins.

Kuma Japanese; bear.

Kumari Sanskrit; girl, princess.

Kuni Japanese; country born.

Kupala Slavonic; to bathe (in the water of life). The name of the Slavonic goddess of water and healing.

Kura Maori; darling.

Kushuma Sanskrit; always be happy.

Kyla Irish Gaelic; so beautiful that only poets can describe her. *Other forms*: Keela, Kylah, Kylee.

Kylanda A blend of Kyla and Amanda.

Kylie Aborigine; curved stick, boomerang. Popularized by the television series *Neighbours*, in which Charlene was played by Kylie Minogue. Occasional use from 1980.

Kylinda, Kylynda Blends of Kylie and Linda.

Kylora, Kylore Blends of Kylie and Lora (Laura).

Kyna Scottish Gaelic; great wisdom. Or Irish Gaelic; champion, best.

Kyra Greek; lady, ruler.

L

Lacara Cara with the *La-* prefix.

Lacey Norman French; from the place-name Lassy in Calvados. Occasional use from 1985. *Other forms*: Lacie, Lacy.

Lachana Chana with the *La-* prefix.

Lachandra Chandra with the *La-* prefix.

Lachelle Chelle (Michelle) with the *La-* prefix.

Lacole Cole (Nicole) with the *La-* prefix.

Lada The goddess of beauty in Slavonic mythology.

Ladaisha Daisha (Dorothy) with the *La-* prefix. *Other form*: Ladasha.

Ladena, Ladene Dena with the *La-* prefix.

Ladina Spanish; wise, crafty.

Ladonna Donna with the *La-* prefix.

Ladonya Donya with the *La-* prefix.

Laina Greek; light.

Lajuana Juana (Juanita) with the *La-* prefix.

Laka The Hawaiian goddess of the hula.

Lakaiya Kaiya (Keya) with the *La-* prefix.

Lakecia Kecia (Keziah) with the *La-* prefix.

Lakeisha Keisha with the *La-* prefix.

Lakendra Kendra (Kenna) with the *La-* prefix.

Lakesha Kesha (Keshia) with the *La-* prefix.

Lakisha Kisha with the *La-* prefix.

Lakita Kita with the *La-* prefix. *Other form*: Laketa.

Lakotah Sioux; friend to us. The name given to the Teton branch of the Sioux Native American nation. (See Gender-neutral names.)

Lakshana Shana (Shan) with the *La-* prefix.

Lala Slavonic; tulip flower.

Lalaka Sanskrit; caressing.

Lalana Sanskrit; woman. *Other form*: Lala.

Lalita Sanskrit; darling. *Other form*: Lali.

Lalla, Lally Greek; to talk, prattle. *Other form*: Laleh.

Lamar French: lake. (See Gender-neutral names.)

Lamorna Middle English; morning.

Lamya Arabic; dark lips.

Lana Latin; wool. Occasional use from 1960.

Lanakila Polynesian; victory.

Lanata Nata (Natalie) with the *La-* prefix.

Landa A blend of Lana and Wanda. *Other form*: Landra.

Landora, Landore Blends of Lana and Dora.

Laneisha Neisha (Nessa) with the *La-* prefix. *Other form*: Lanetta.

Lanette French; from the little lane.

Lani, Lanie Hawaiian; sky.

Lanisha Nisha with the *La-* prefix.

Lanora Nora with the *La-* prefix.

Lantana From the name of the flowering shrub.

Lantha A blend of Lana and Samantha.

Lanza Spanish; lance, spear (hence sharpness, intelligence).

Laquana Quana with the *La-* prefix.

Laquetta Quetta with the *La-* prefix. *Other form*: Laquela.

Laquinda Quinda with the *La-* prefix. *Other form*: Laquinta.

Lara A Russian form of Larissa. Occasional use from 1970.

Laraine Latin; seagull.

Laralyn A blend of Laura and Lyn.

Lareina, Lareine Spanish; the queen. *Other form*: Larena.

Larella, Larelle Blends of Lara and Ella.

Laresha Resha (Rashida) with the *La-* prefix.

Laria A character in the novel *Lyon's Pride* by Anne McCaffrey.

Larina Latin; seagull.

Larissa Latin; cheerful. *Other forms*: Larisa, Larise. *Variants*: Lara, Larisa, Laryssa (Russian).

Larita Rita with the *La-* prefix.

Lashana Shana (Shan) with the *La-* prefix. *Other form*: Lashanda.

Lashauna Shauna with the *La-* prefix.

Lashawna Shawna with the *La-* prefix.

Lashea Shea with the *La-* prefix. *Other form*: Lashay.

Lasheba Sheba with the *La-* prefix.

Lashieka Shieka (Rashieka) with the *La-* prefix. *Other forms*: Lashayka, Lasheka.

Lashona Shona with the *La-* prefix. *Other form*: Lashonda.

Lasonda Sonda with the *La-* prefix.

Lasonya Sonya with the *La-* prefix.

Lataisha Taisha with the *La-* prefix.

Latania Tania with the *La-* prefix.

Latanya Tanya with the *La-* prefix.

Latara Tara with the *La-* prefix.

Latasha Tasha with the *La-* prefix. *Other forms*: Lateisha, Latesha.

Latashia Tashia (Tasha) with the *La-* prefix.

Lateefah, Lateefa Arabic; gentle, pleasant.

Latona The Roman name for Leto, the mother of Apollo and Artemis.

Latonia Tonia with the *La-* prefix. *Other forms*: LaTonia, Latonya, LaTonya.

Latoya A form of Latonya. *Other forms*: LaToy, LaToya, Latoyah.

Laulani Hawaiian; heavenly branch, hence descendant.

Laura Latin; laurel tree. Light use from 1900, declining in the 1950s, but then rising steadily into heavy use by 1980, and continuing to increase by 1990. *Other forms*: Laraine, Larinda, Laureen, Laurel, Lauren, Lauretta, Laurie, Laurinda, Lawrie, Lora, Loraine, Lorann, Lorayne, Loreen, Loren, Lorena, Lorene, Loretta, Lori, Lorinda, Lorita, Lorrie, Loura, Lorana. *Variants*: Lora (Bulgarian); Laure, Laurette, Lorette (French); Lola (Hawaiian); Lauretta, Lora, Lorenza (Italian); Laurka (Polish); Laurinda (Portuguese); Lavra (Russian); Laureana, Lorena (Spanish); Lora, Lowri (Welsh).

Laurana, Lauranne Blends of Laura and Anne.

Lauranda A blend of Laura and Amanda.

Laurantha A blend of Laura and Samantha.

Laurel Latin; laurel tree. Occasional use from 1900, falling out of use in 1950 but reviving in 1990.

Laurella, Laurelle Blends of Laurel and Ella.

Lauren A form of Laura. Light use from 1960, falling out of use in 1970 but reviving to peak in heavy use by 1990. *Other forms*: Lauryn, Lori, Lorien, Lorienne, Lorin, Loryn, Lorynne.

Laurie A form of Laura. Occasional use from 1950. (See Gender-neutral names.)

Laurina Latin; woman from Laurentium. *Other forms*: Laureen, Laurena, Laurene, Laurine, Lorina, Lorine.

Laverne Latin; spring-like, verdant.

Lavinia Latin; woman of Rome. Occasional use from 1900, falling out of use in 1970 but reviving modestly in 1990. *Other forms*: Lavena, Vina, Vinny.

Lavonne Yvonne with the *La-* prefix. *Other forms*: Lavon, Lavonna, Lavonya.

Layana Sanskrit; repose. *Other forms*: Layna, Layne.

Layla Arabic; born at night.

Lazetta Zetta with the *La-* prefix.

Lea A form of Leah. Occasional use 1900–85.

Leaf Old English; the plant term used as a name. (See Gender-neutral names.)

Leah Hebrew; to be weary. Occasional use from 1925. *Other forms*: Lea, Leia. *Variants*: Lia (French, Italian); Lea (Swedish).

Leala Middle English; loyal. *Other form*: Liala.

Leanda Greek; lion woman. *Other forms*: Le-An, Le-Ann.

Leandra A blend of Leah and Sandra.

Leanne A blend of Leah and Anne. Light use from 1965, peaking in 1985. *Other forms*: Leanna, Leane.

Leanora A blend of Leah and Nora.

Leantha A blend of Leah and Samantha. *Other form*: Leanza.

Lebca A name formed from the initials of the Loving Essence of Being and Consciousness, a modern definition of God.

Leda From the name of the Spartan queen.

Lee Old English; wood, clearing. This has only so far been popular as a girl's name in the USA. In the UK usage has been dominated by its popularity as a boy's name. *Other form*: Leigh. (See Gender-neutral names.)

Leeann, Leanne Blends of Lee and Ann.

Leena Sanskrit; devoted.

Lei Hawaiian; flower wreath, child.

Leigh Old English; wood, clearing. Light use from 1955, peaking in the 1970s. (See Gender-neutral names.)

Leigh-Ann A blend of Leigh and Ann. Occasional use from 1980. *Other forms*: Leighann, Leighanne, Leigh-Anne.

Leighanne A blend of Leigh and Anne. Occasional use in 1980.

Leigh-Anne A blend of Leigh and Anne. Occasional use from 1980.

Leihina Hawaiian; wreath around the moon.

Leila Arabic; dark beauty. Occasional use from 1925, until it fell out of use in 1985. *Other forms*: Layla, Leyla.

Leilani Hawaiian; heavenly flower. *Other forms*: Leilane, Lelani, Leelee, LeeLee.

Leinani Hawaiian; beautiful flower.

Leisha A blend of Leila and Aisha.

Lelia From the Roman clan name Laelius.

Lelina Lina with the *Le-* prefix.

Lelita Lita (Lolita) with the *Le-* prefix.

Lemarr, Lamar Latin; of the sea.

Lena A German form of Helen. Occasional use from 1900 until it fell out of use in 1985. *Other forms*: Layna, Lenea, Leyna, Lina. *Variant*: Liene (Latvian).

Leneisha Neisha (Nessa) with the *Le-* prefix.

Leola Native American; prairie flower. *Other form*: Leolie.

Leolani Hawaiian; heavenly voice.

Leolina Welsh; little lion.

Leoma Old English; radiant light.

Leona Latin; lioness. A feminine form of Leon. Occasional use from 1925. *Other forms*: Leoma, Leone, Leonie, Leonora, Leontyne. *Variant*: Leonie (French).

Leonie A French form of Leona. Occasional use from 1960 rising rapidly into light use in 1990. *Other form*: Leone.

Leontice From the name of the flowering plant.

Leontine Greek; like a lion.

Leora Hebrew; my light. *Other form*: Liora.

Leoti Native American; prairie wildflower.

Leshieka Shieka (Rashieka) with the *Le-* prefix.

Lesley Old French; meadowlands. Light use from 1900 rising to a peak of heavy use in 1960. *Other forms*: Leslee, Lesli, Leslie, Lesly. (See Gender-neutral names.)

Leslie A form of Lesley. (See Gender-neutral names.)

Leticia Latin; joy. *Other forms*: Laetitia, Latisha, Letice, Letty, Tisha. *Variants*: Lece, Leetice (French); Latitia (German); Letizia (Italian); Letisha, Letycia (Polish).

Levana Hebrew; moon.

Levani Fijian; anointed with oil.

Levanna Latin; sunrise.

Levina Old English; shining. *Other forms*: Levona, Levonne.

Leya Tamil; born during Leo.

Leyla Turkish; night. *Other form*: Leyea.

Lia A form of Evangelia. Greek; bringer of good news.

Lian Chinese; graceful willow.

Liane French; to bind, hence loyalty, trust. Occasional use from 1960. *Other forms*: Leana, Liana, Liane, Lianne.

Lianne A form of Liane. Occasional use from 1970 peaking in 1980.

Lila Sanskrit; playful. Occasional use from 1955.

Lilac Arabic; lilac tree. Or Persian; bluish.

Lilananda Sanskrit; blissful play.

Lilantha A blend of Lily and Samantha.

Lilian Latin; lily. Heavy use in 1900 but then declined until it fell out of use in 1975. There was a small revival in 1990. *Other forms*: Lili, Liliane, Lilli, Lillian, Lillie, Lilly, Lily, Lilyan. *Variants*: Lilli (Estonian); Lis (French); Liesel, Lili, Lilli (German); Lilika (Greek); Liliana (Hawaiian); Lilika, Lilike (Hungarian); Lile (Irish Gaelic); Lilana (Latvian); Lelya, Olena (Russian); Lileas (Scottish Gaelic); Liljana (Serbo-Croatian); Lilia (Spanish).

Lilika Latin; lily flower.

Lilina A blend of Lily and Nina.

Lilita A blend of Lily and Lita (Lolita).

Lillian A form of Lilian. Occasional use from its peak in 1900 to 1970.

Lily A form of Lilian. Heavy use in 1900 but then declined and fell out of use by 1965. Revived in 1985 and in 1990 was used ten times more often than Lilian.

Lilyann A blend of Lily and Ann.

Lin Chinese; beautiful jade (associated by the Chinese with virtue and wisdom).

Lina Arabic; tender.

Linara A blend of Linda and Cara.

Linda Old German; wise. Light use from 1900 peaking in very heavy use in 1950 and then declining into light use again. *Other forms*: Lindie, Lynda, Lyndie, Lindy.

Linden Old German; lime tree. (See Gender-neutral names.)

Lindsay Old English; linden trees near the water. Occasional use from 1900 peaking in 1980. This is the original and most popular spelling of the name although Lindsey has overtaken it several times. In comparison Linsey is seldom used, as is Lyndsay. However Lyndsey is almost as widely used as the original form of the name. *Other forms*: Lindsey, Linsay,

Linsey, Linzi, Lyndsay, Lyndsey, Lynsay, Lynsey, Lynzee, Lynzi. (See Gender-neutral names.)

Lindsey A form of Lindsay. Occasional use from 1955, peaking in 1985. (See Gender-neutral names.)

Linette Old French; flax, hence flaxen-haired.

Lingala Lingala; the name of a tribe in the Congo.

Linita A blend of Linda and Rita.

Linnea, Lynneya Old Norse; lime blossom.

Linora A blend of Linda and Nora.

Linsey A form of Lindsay. Occasional use 1970–85. (See Gender-neutral names.)

Linya A phonetic form of the Irish name Loinnir, meaning ray of sunshine through dark clouds.

Liria Greek; musical, lyrical.

Lirona, Lirone Hebrew; my song.

Lisa A form of Elizabeth. Light use from 1955 peaking in heavy use in 1970. *Other forms*: Leesa, Lysa. *Variants*: Liesje (Dutch); Lisette (French); Liesa, Lise (German); Lisenka (Slavonic).

Lisha Arabic; darkness before midnight.

Litonya Native American; darting hummingbird.

Livana Hebrew; moon.

Livona Hebrew; incense.

Liwa Twana; inlet.

Liza A form of Elizabeth. Occasional use from 1965.

Lois Greek; good, desirable. Occasional use from 1900.

Lola A form of Dolores. Occasional use in the 1950s.

Lolana A blend of Lola and Nana.

Lolora From the Indian place-name.

Loma Loma; the name of a tribe in Liberia.

Lomasi Native American; pretty flower.

Lona A form of Maelona. Welsh; princess.

Londa A blend of Lona and Wanda.

Loraine A form of Lorraine. Occasional use from 1950 to 1970.

Lorana A blend of Lora (Laura) and Ana (Ann).

Loredana A character in a novel by Luciano Zuccoli.

Lorelle Latin; little one.

Loren A form of Lauren. Occasional use from 1980. *Other forms*: Lorena, Lorene. (See Gender-neutral names.)

Loretha A blend of Loretta and Aretha.

Loreto From the name of the Italian centre of pilgrimage. *Other form*: Loretto.

Loretta A form of Lauretta. Occasional use from 1950.

Lorien, Lorian, Loriane, Lorienne Names influenced by Lorien, an elven kingdom in Tolkien's trilogy *The Lord of the Rings*.

Lorimer Latin; slender vine branch.

Lorinda A blend of Lorina (Laura) and Linda.

Lorna Scottish Gaelic; from the Scottish place-name Lorn. Popularized by the novel *Lorna Doone* by R.D. Blackmore. Occasional use from 1900, peaking in 1990.

Lorraine Latin; from the French province of Lorraine. Light use from 1950 peaking in 1965. *Other forms*: Loraine, Lorrayne.

Lou A form of Louise. (See Gender-neutral names.)

Louann, Louanne Blends of Louise and Ann.

Louella, Louelle Blends of Louise and Ella. *Other form*: Luella.

Louisa Old German; famous in battle. A feminine form of Louis. Light use from 1900.

Louise A French feminine form of Louis. Although a very minor name compared to Louisa in 1900, this spelling steadily gained ground from 1950, peaking in heavy use in 1980. Though it has now fallen back into light use again, it is still used six times more often than Louisa. *Variants*: Aloyse, Heloise, Lisette (French); Aloisa, Aloysia, Luise (German); Eloisa (Greek); Labhaoise (Irish Gaelic); Eloisa, Lodovica, Luisa (Italian); Lovisa (Norwegian); Lilka (Polish); Louisa (Romanian); Luiza (Russian); Eloisa, Eloise, Lucita (Spanish).

Louisiane A blend of Louise and Anne.

Lourana A blend of Louise and Rana.

Loveday A Cornish name based on the custom of calling a community together on a 'loveday' to see if they could settle a quarrel.

Lovina Latin; woman of Rome.

Lovinda A blend of Lovina and Amanda.

Lowenna Cornish; joy. *Other form*: Lowena.

Luana Hawaiian; to be at leisure; enjoyment.

Lucia Latin; feminine form of the Roman name Lucius, meaning light. Occasional use from 1955.

Lucie A form of Lucy. Occasional use from 1965 peaking in 1985.

Lucienne A French form of Lucian, sometimes used as a feminine name. (See Gender-neutral names.)

Lucille A French form of Lucy. Occasional use from 1950, falling out of use in 1975. *Other forms*: Lucila, Lucile, Luzine.

Lucina Latin; a grove.

Lucinda A Spanish form of Lucy. Occasional use from 1960. *Other forms*: Cindi, Cindy, Lucinder, Lucynda.

Lucy Latin; light. Light use from 1900, declining in the 1950s but then reviving again into heavy use by 1990. *Other forms*: Cindi, Cindie, Cindy, Lucette, Lucie, Lucienne, Lucile, Lucina, Lucinda, Lucine, Lucita, Lucky, Luzine. *Variants*: Lucia, Lusia (Armenian); Lukene (Basque); Lucine (Bulgarian); Lucia, Lucie (Czech); Lucie (Dutch); Lucie, Lucienne, Lucille (French); Lucie, Luzi, Luzia (German); Lucia (Greek); Luke (Hawaiian); Luca, Lucia, Lucza (Hungarian); Luighseach (Irish Gaelic); Lucia, Luciana, Lucina (Italian); Lucija (Latvian); Lucya, Lujca (Polish); Lucia (Portuguese, Romanian); Luzija (Russian); Liusaidh (Scottish Gaelic); Luci, Lucika (Slavonic); Luciana, Lucila, Lucilita, Lucinda, Lucita, Luz (Spanish); Lucia (Swedish).

Luella A blend of Louise and Ella.

Luksa Chickasaw; terrapin.

Lulani Polynesian; highest point of heaven.

Lulu Swahili; pearl. *Variant*: Lali (Spanish).

Lumna Arabic; lightness of spirit.

Luna Latin; moon.

Lurene, Lureen French; to invite, lure.

Lusita Spanish; bringer of light.

Lutanza A blend of Lucy and Tanza (Tansy).

Lutricia A blend of Lucy and Patricia.

Lydia Greek; woman from Lydia in Asia Minor. Occasional use from 1900, declining and falling out of use from 1935 to 1955, but showing a steady revival by 1985. *Other forms*: Lidia, Lydie. *Variants*: Lidka (Czech); Lydie (French); Lidi (Hungarian); Lidka (Polish); Lida, Lidiya (Russian).

Lylana Lana with the *Ly-* prefix.

Lylara Lara with the *Ly-* prefix.

Lyn A form of Lynda. Occasional use from 1950 to 1970.

Lynda A form of Linda. Occasional use from 1925, peaking in light use in 1955 and then declining and falling out of use in 1985.

Lyndora, Lyndore Blends of Lynda and Dora.

Lyndsay A form of Lindsay. Occasional use from 1960 to 1985. (See Gender-neutral names.)

Lyndsey A form of Lindsay. Light use from 1960, peaking in 1985 when it briefly overtook Lindsay in usage. *Other form*: Lynsey. (See Gender-neutral names.)

Lynette Celtic; pool, waterfall. Occasional use from 1950. *Other forms*: Linet, Linetta, Lynella, Lynelle, Lynita, Lynnette.

Lynira A blend of Lynda and Mira (Myra).

Lynn A form of Lynda. Light use from 1950, peaking in 1955 and falling out of use in 1990. *Other forms*: Lin, Linne, Lyn, Lynelle, Lynne. *Variants*: Lynette (French); Lina (Spanish).

Lynne A form of Lynda. Light use from 1950, peaking in 1955 and falling out of use in 1985.

Lynora A blend of Lynda and Nora.

Lynwen Welsh; fair image.

Lyra Greek; lyre.

Lyrica Greek; musical, lyrical.

Lysandra Greek; free.

Lyssa A Slavonic form of Alice.

Lystra A Hebrew place-name of uncertain meaning.

Lythanda A character in a short story by Marion Zimmer Bradley.

Lythinda A blend of Lyssa and Lucinda.

M

Maaia Maori; courage.

Maaruu Maori; gentle.

Mabel French; my beautiful one. Light use from 1900 to
   1935. *Other forms*: Mabeline, Mable, Maeb, Maybel,
   Maybelle, Mayble. *Variants*: Mabelle (French); Maible
   (Irish Gaelic); Moibeal (Scottish Gaelic); Mabli (Welsh).

Macawi Dakota; generous, motherly.

Macinda, Macynda Blends of Mabel and Lucinda.

Macintha, Macyntha Blends of Mabel and Cynthia.

Mackenzie Scottish Gaelic; daughter of the wise ruler.
   (See Gender-neutral names.)

Macy French; hill, range of hills. *Other form*: Macey. (See
   Gender-neutral names.)

Madelaine A form of Madeleine. Occasional use from
   1955 to 1985.

Madeleine Hebrew; woman from Magdala, a village on
   Lake Galilee. A name associated with Mary Magdalene.
   Occasional use from 1900. *Other forms*: Dalenna, Leli,
   Lena, Lina, Mada, Madalena, Madelayne, Madeline,
   Maddie, Maddy, Madeena, Madel, Madelaine, Madelia,
   Madeline, Madella, Madelon, Madelyn, Madge,
   Magdala, Magdalen, Magdalene, Mai, Mali, Manda,
   Marla, Marlena, Marlo, Marlys. *Variants*: Magda,
   Magdalena (Czech); Magdelone (Danish); Madelaine,
   Madelon (French); Madlen, Mady, Marla, Marlene,
   Lena (German); Malia (Hawaiian); Magdolna
   (Hungarian); Madailein (Irish Gaelic); Maddalena,
   Maddelena (Italian); Lena, Magda (Polish); Madelina,
   Madlena, Magda, Magdalina (Russian); Madalena,

Magdalena, Magola (Spanish); Malena (Swedish, Danish); Malen, Modlen (Welsh).

Madihah Arabic; praiseworthy.

Madison Old English; fortunate, good. Popularized by a character in the film *Splash*. (See Gender-neutral names.)

Madra Spanish; mother. *Variants*: Madonna (Italian); Madrona (Spanish).

Maegan A blend of Mae (May) and Megan.

Maeko Japanese; honest child.

Maelona Welsh; princess. *Other form*: Lona.

Maeve Irish Gaelic; intoxicating. *Other forms*: Mave, Meave. *Variant*: Meadhbh (Irish Gaelic).

Magdala Hebrew; high tower. A village on the west side of Lake Galilee.

Magena Native American; the coming moon.

Magenta Italian; bright magenta-coloured dye.

Magnolia From the tree named after the French botanist Pierre Magnol.

Mahalia, Mahala Hebrew; tenderness.

Mahica Algonquian; clan of the wolf.

Mahila Sanskrit; woman.

Mahina Hawaiian; moon.

Mahira Hebrew; industrious. *Other forms*: Mahina, Mahra.

Mahlah Hebrew; mildness, gentleness.

Mai A Welsh form of May. Or Japanese; brightness.

Maia Greek; mother. The mother of Hermes in Greek mythology. *Variants*: Maija (Finnish); Maja (German).

Maidie, Maida Middle English; maiden.

Mairi A Scottish Gaelic form of Mary. *Variants*: Mair, Maire (Irish Gaelic).

Mairona A blend of Mairi and Rona.

Mairwen Welsh; blessed. *Other form*: Meirwen.

Maise Scottish Gaelic; beauty.

Maisie A form of Margaret. Occasional use from 1925 until it fell out of use in 1950. There was a small revival in 1985.

Maiya Sanskrit; an aspect of the Goddess (Gaia).

Majella From the name of Saint Gerard Majella. *Other form*: Majel.

Makadisa Baduma; she knows what she wants.

Makala Hawaiian; myrtle tree.

Makalani Mwera; the writer.

Makana Hawaiian; gift.

Makani Hawaiian; wind.

Makara Hindi; born during Capricorn.

Makeda Amharic; the name of the Queen of Sheba.

Makeesha Kesha (Keshia) with the *Ma-* prefix.

Makira Solomonese; an island, also called San Cristobal, in the Solomon Islands.

Makoa Hawaiian; brave.

Makoti Manda; earth-lodge, home.

Mala Sanskrit; prayer beads.

Malaka Palauan; from Malakal, the name of an island in the Palau group.

Malama Hawaiian; torchlight.

Malana Hawaiian; buoyant, light.

Malandra A blend of Mala and Sandra.

Malantha A blend of Mala and Samantha.

Malawi Chichewa; flames, hence fiery one. Linked to the name of the African state.

Malca Old German; active.

Malda Scottish Gaelic; sweet.

Mali Thai; jasmine flower.

Malibu Chumash; a village name of uncertain meaning.

Malika Hungarian; industrious. *Other form*: Mallika.

Malila Salish; salmon swimming fast through rippling waters.

Malina Hebrew; tower.

Malita Native American; salmon.

Mallalai Pashto; beautiful.

Mallory Old German; army counsellor. Popularized by a character in the television series *Family Ties*.

Malu Hawaiian; peace.

Malulani Hawaiian; heavenly calm.

Malva Greek; tender.

Malvina Scottish Gaelic; smooth brow. Invented by the poet James Macpherson. *Variants*: Malwina (German); Malmhin (Scottish Gaelic).

Malvinda A blend of Malvina and Linda.

Manasa Sanskrit; mind, intelligence.

Manda, Mandeana Aramaic; knowing.

Mandala Sanskrit; circular pattern symbolizing the universe, hence completeness, unity.

Mandara Hindi; calm. The mythical mandara tree which makes worries vanish.

Mandella Native American; ceremonial shield.

Mandisa Xhosa; sweet.

Mandora A blend of Mandy and Dora.

Mandy A form of Amanda. Light use from 1955 peaking in 1965. *Other forms*: Mandi, Mandie.

Manenda A blend of Manon and Brenda.

Mangeni Musamia; fish, hence a child at home in the water.

Manita Algonquian; spirit.

Manon Welsh; queen. Or Sanskrit; imagination. Or a French form of Marie.

Manuelle Hebrew; God with us. A Spanish feminine form of Immanuel.

Manuka Polynesian; dove.

Mara, Marah Hebrew; bitter. *Other form*: Marala.

Maralee A blend of Mara and Lee.

Marama Maori; moon.

Maranda A blend of Mara and Miranda.

Marantha A blend of Mara and Samantha.

Maraya A blend of Mara and Maya.

Marcella A French feminine form of Marcellus, a diminutive of the Roman name Marcus. *Other forms*: Marcelle, Marcelinda, Marceline, Marcelyn. *Variants*: Marcelle (French); Mairsile (Irish Gaelic); Marcelina (Italian); Marcela (Spanish).

Marcia Latin; from the Roman name Marcius, linked to Mars, god of war. Occasional use from 1925 until it fell out of use in 1975. *Other forms*: Marci, Marcie, Marcy, Marsha. *Variants*: Marcie (French); Marquita (Spanish).

Marcilynn A blend of Marcia and Lynn.

Mardella, Mardie Old English; meadow near the water.

Mardi French; Tuesday.

Maredella, Maridel Blends of Mary and Della.

Mareetha, Maretha, Maritha Blends of Mary and Aretha.

Marella, Marelle Blends of Mary and Ella.

Margaret Greek; pearl. Heavy use from 1900, peaking in very heavy use in 1935 and then declining to occasional use by 1990. *Other forms*: Gita, Greta, Gretal, Madge, Mady, Mae, Maggie, Maidie, Maiga, Maisie, Mamie, Margareta, Margaretha, Margarinda, Margarita, Margery, Marghanita, Margita, Margot, Marguerite, Marjorie, Marjory, Marles, Meg, Megan, Molly, Peg, Peggy, Polly, Reta, Rita. *Variants*: Margarid, Markarid (Armenian); Errita, Irta, Margarita (Basque); Megane (Breton); Marketa (Bulgarian); Maija (Cornish); Gita, Gitka, Margita, Margareta, Marka (Czech); Grette, Margareta, Margrethe, Mette (Danish); Greta, Grietje, Margaretha (Dutch); Marga, Margarete (Estonian); Marjana, Marjatta (Finnish); Margaux, Margo, Margot, Marguerite (French); Gretel, Gretchen, Grethel, Margarete, Margarethe, Margit, Margret, Meta (German); Gryta, Margaro (Greek); Makaleka (Hawaiian); Margit, Margita, Pera (Hungarian); Pegeen (Irish); Mairead, Muiread (Irish Gaelic); Ghita, Margharita, Margherita (Italian); Grieta, Margarita, Margrieta (Latvian); Margarita (Lithuanian); Margaid (Manx Gaelic); Marete, Margit, Margreta (Norwegian); Gita, Malgorzata, Margarita, Margita, Rita (Polish); Guidinha, Margarida (Portuguese); Margareta (Romanian); Margarete, Margosha (Russian); Mairead, Mairghead, Marghrad (Scottish Gaelic); Perla (Slavonic); Marga, Margara, Margarita, Marghanita, Rita (Spanish); Margareta, Margit, Margita, Margrete (Swedish); Margaryta (Ukrainian); Marged, Margiad, Megan, Meghan, Mererid (Welsh).

Margaris, Margarise Possibly Breton; stallion.

Margery A form of Margaret. Occasional use from 1900 to 1950, peaking in 1925.

Margot A French form of Margaret. Occasional use from 1935 to 1960. *Other form*: Margo.

Margolaine A blend of Margo (Margot) and Elaine.

Marguerite French; a daisy. Occasional use from 1900 to 1935. *Variants*: Margarita, Marguerita (Spanish).

Maria An Italian form of Mary. Light use from 1900, peaking in 1965. *Variant*: Marya (Slavonic).

Mariam A blend of Mary and Miriam.

Marian A form of Marion. Occasional use 1900–70, peaking in 1935.

Marianne A form of Marion. Occasional use 1950–85.

Maribelle A blend of Mary and Belle (Isabel).

Maribeth A blend of Mary and Elizabeth.

Marie A French form of Mary. Light use from 1900 peaking in 1975. *Variant*: Marietta (Italian).

Marigold Middle English; from the flower name.

Mari-Jo A blend of Mary and Joanna.

Mariko Japanese; circle.

Marilaine, Marilane Blends of Mary and Elaine.

Marilee A blend of Mary and Lee.

Marilou, Marylu Blends of Mary and Louise.

Marilyn A blend of Mary and Lynda. Light use from 1935, peaking in 1950 and falling out of use in 1985. *Other forms*: Maralyn, Marilee, Marilin, Marilynn, Marylyn.

Marina Latin; the sea. Light but declining use from 1935. *Other forms*: Marena, Marni, Marnina. *Variants*: Marenka (Slavonic); Marna (Swedish).

Marinda A blend of Mary and Linda.

Marini Swahili; pretty.

Marintha A blend of Mary and Cynthia.

Marion A form of Marie. Light use from 1900, peaking in 1950 and falling out of use in 1985. *Other forms*: Marian, Marianne. *Variants*: Manetta, Manette (French); Marianne (German); Marianna (Italian); Mariana (Spanish).

Marisa, Marise Mary influenced by the Dutch form Maryse. *Variants*: Maritza (German); Mariza (Russian); Marita (Spanish).

Marissa Latin; the sea. Occasional use from 1975 to 1980. *Other form*: Maris. *Variants*: Marisha, Mariska (Russian).

Marita A blend of Mary and Rita.

Marjalena A blend of Marjorie and Lena.

Marjana A blend of Marjorie and Jana (Jane).

Marjani Swahili; coral.

Marjolaine, Marjolayne French; the herb marjoram.

Marjorie Latin; the herb marjoram. Light use from 1900, peaking in heavy use in 1925 and falling out of use in 1975. *Other forms*: Majorie, Marja, Marji, Marjory. *Variants*: Meadhbh (Irish Gaelic); Macail, Marsali (Scottish Gaelic).

Marjory A form of Marjorie. Occasional use from 1900 to 1935.

Marlene A German form of Madeleine. Occasional use from 1935. *Other forms* Marlana, Marlanna, Marlee. *Variant*: Marlena (German).

Marlin A form of Marlene. (See Gender-neutral names.)

Marlise A blend of Mary and Lisa. *Other forms*: Marlis, Marlyssa.

Marlo Latin; the sea. *Other forms*: Marli, Marly.

Marmora Greek; radiant, shining. Or Sardinian; a mountain on the island of Sardinia. *Other form*: Marmara.

Marni Hebrew; to rejoice. *Other forms*: Marnie, Marney, Marny.

Maroa A form of Tamaroa, a Native American tribal name.

Marola Latin; the sea.

Marosa A blend of Mary and Rosa.

Marquise French; marchioness.

Marsala From the Italian place-name.

Marsha A form of Marcia. Occasional use from 1975.

Martha Aramaic; lady of the house. Light use from its peak in 1900, falling out of use from time to time but reviving again in 1990. *Other forms*: Mardi, Marta, Martelle, Marthe, Marthena, Martie, Martita, Marty, Matty, Merta. *Variants*: Marticka (Czech); Marthe (French); Martuska (Hungarian); Marta (Italian); Moirragh (Manx Gaelic); Masia (Polish); Marutha (Slavonic); Martina, Martita (Spanish).

Martina An Italian feminine form of Martin. Occasional use from 1955. *Other forms*: Martine, Martyna, Martyne. *Variant*: Martine (French).

Martine A French form of Martina. Occasional use 1955–85.

Maru Maori; gentle.

Marva Hebrew; the herb sage. *Other forms*: Marvella, Marvelle.

Mary Hebrew; wished-for child. Very heavy use from 1900 to its peak in 1925, but then in a slow decline into its present occasional use. *Other forms*: Mae, Maire, Malia, Mamie, Manette, Manon, Manya, Mara, Mari,

Maria, Mariah, Mariamne, Marian, Marie, Mariel,
Mariene, Mariessa, Marietta, Marika, Marion, Marita,
Marya, Maureen, Maura, May, Merriah, Mimi, Minnie,
Mira, Miriam, Mirjana, Mitzi, Moira, Mollie, Molly,
Morine, Moya, Muire, Polly. *Variants*: Maro, Meroom
(Armenian); Mari, Miren, Molara (Basque); Melle
(Breton); Marya (Cornish); Mara, Maren, Marenka,
Mariska (Czech); Marieke, Marika, Marisa, Maryk,
Maryse, Mies (Dutch); Amara (Esperanto); Marye
(Estonian); Maija, Maikki, Marja (Finnish); Manette,
Manon, Marie, Mariette, Marja, Merane (French);
Maike, Maja, Maria, Mariel, Mia, Mitzi (German);
Marika, Maroula (Greek); Malia, Mela, Mele
(Hawaiian); Miriam, Mirit (Hebrew); Mara, Marcsa,
Marika, Mariska, Maritza, Mirena (Hungarian); Maura,
Maureen, Moira, Moya (Irish); Mairi, Mairin, Meari,
Mhairi, Muire (Irish Gaelic); Mara, Maria, Marietta
(Italian); Mare (Latvian); Marija (Lithuanian); Maren,
Mirjam (Norwegian); Macia, Maryla, Maryna, Marysia,
Morla (Polish); Maricar, Maricara (Romanian); Marya,
Marinka, Marisha, Mariya, Maruska, Masha, Mashka,
Mura (Russian); Moira, Moire, Moyra (Scottish);
Maireag, Mairi, Moireach, Muire (Scottish Gaelic);
Maressa, Marija, Marika, Marissa, Marja, Mayra
(Slavonic); Mari, Maria, Marita, Mariquita, Maruja
(Spanish); Marja, Mia (Swedish); Marynia, Maryska
(Ukrainian); Mair, Mari (Welsh); Meli (Zuni).

Marya Arabic; purity.

Maryam A blend of Mary and Miriam.

Maryann A blend of Mary and Ann.

Marybeth A blend of Mary and Elizabeth.

Maryellen A blend of Mary and Ellen.

Maryjo A blend of Mary and Joanna.

Marylou, Marylu Blends of Mary and Louise.

Marylyn, Marylin Blends of Mary and Lynda.

Masika Swahili; born in the rain.

Matana Hebrew; gift.

Matay Kazakh; a place-name in Kazakhstan.

Mathena A French blend of Marie and Therese.

Matilda Old German; mighty in battle. Occasional use from 1900. *Other forms*: Matelda, Mathilda, Mattie, Matty, Matya, Maud, Maude, Metilda, Patty, Tilda, Tillie, Tilly. *Variants*: Matylda, Tylda (Czech); Matilde (French); Maddy, Mathilde (German); Maitilde (Irish); Maitilde, Matelda (Italian); Macia, Mala, Tila (Polish); Majalda (Portuguese); Matya (Slavonic); Matilde, Matusha, Matuxa (Spanish); Mallt (Welsh).

Mau Hawaiian; endurance, eternal.

Maud A form of Matilda. Occasional use from 1900 until 1935, then falling out of use until it showed a modest revival in 1990. *Other forms*: Maude, Maudie, Maudine. *Variant*: Mada (Irish).

Maureen An Irish form of Mary. Light use from 1925, peaking in heavy use in 1935 and then declining. *Other forms*: Mauraine, Maurayne, Maurene, Mauri, Morina, Morine, Moryne. *Variants*: Moirin (Irish Gaelic); Maurizia (Italian); Morena (Spanish).

Maurelle French; dark, elfin.

Maurila Latin; woman who sympathizes. *Other form*: Maurilia.

Maurise French; dark. A feminine form of Maurice.

Maurita A blend of Maureen and Rita.

Mavis Old French; song thrush. Occasional use from 1900, peaking in light use in 1935 and falling out of use in 1985. *Other forms*: Maeve, Mavys.

Mavorna Irish Gaelic; my little darling. *Other forms*: Mavourna, Mavourneen.

Maxi, Maxie Forms of Maxine. (See Gender-neutral names.)

Maxine Latin; greatest. Occasional use from 1950 peaking in 1965. *Other forms*: Maxene, Maxi, Maxie, Maxima, Maxy. *Variant*: Maxime (French).

May A form of Margaret or Mary. Heavy use in 1900, but then declining rapidly and falling out of use in 1985. *Other forms*: Mae, Mei, Maye. *Variants*: Mae, Mai (French, German); Mai (Welsh).

Maya Mayan; my people, our people.

Mayda Old English; maiden.

Maylea Hawaiian; wild flower.

Maylyn A blend of May and Lynn.

Mayoree Thai; beautiful.

Maysa Arabic; walk gracefully.

Mayu Japanese; true reason.

Mazala Hebrew; star. *Other forms*: Mazal, Mazana.

Mazara Sicilian; from Mazara del Vallo on the island of Sicily.

Mazella Hebrew; lucky. *Other forms*: Mazarella, Mazel, Mazerina.

Mazonne A blend of Mazella and Yvonne.

Meade Greek; honey wine.

Meadow Old English; grassland.

Meara Irish Gaelic; laughter, mirth.

Meda Native American; prophet, priestess.

Medina Arabic; city, the name of an Islamic sacred city.

Medora Old English; patient wife.

Medwin, Medwyn Possibly Welsh; fair-mannered, courteous.

Meera Sanskrit; saintly woman.

Megan A Welsh form of Margaret. Occasional use from 1925, peaking in light use in 1990. *Other forms*: Meagan, Megen, Meghann. *Variant*: Meghan, Meghana (Welsh).

Megara Greek; first. The first wife of Hercules in Greek mythology.

Mehira Hebrew; energetic.

Meira Hebrew; light.

Meironwen Welsh; dairymaid. *Other forms*: Meirion, Merion.

Meita Burmese, affectionate.

Mela A Polish form of Melanie. *Other form*: Malia.

Melah Latin; honey. *Other form*: Mella.

Melaina, Melaine, Melane Blends of Melanie and Elaine.

Melana A blend of Mela and Lana.

Melanda A blend of Mela and Amanda.

Melandra A blend of Mela and Sandra.

Melanie Greek; dark-skinned. Light use from 1950 peaking in 1975. *Other forms*: Mel, Mela, Melaina, Melaine, Melane, Melania, Melany, Melayne, Melloney, Melonie, Meloney, Milena. *Variants*: Melloney (Cornish); Melania (French, German, Italian); Mera (Hungarian); Emela, Mela, Melka (Polish); Melana, Melanya, Melasya, Milena (Russian).

Melantha Greek; dark flower. A character in Dryden's play *Marriage à la Mode*.

Melara A blend of Mela and Lara.

Melcena The name of an island in the *Malloreon* cycle of novels by David Eddings.

Mele Hawaiian; song, poem.

Meleta A blend of Mela and Rita.

Melina Greek; honey.

Melinda A blend of Melina and Linda. Occasional use from 1955. *Other forms:* Mellinda, Melynda, Mindy.

Melinka A blend of Melina and Katinka.

Melintha A blend of Melina and Samantha.

Meliora Latin; better.

Melissa Greek; bee, hence industrious. Occasional use from 1965 peaking in light use in 1990. *Other forms*: Lissa, Lissie, Malissa, Mel, Melisa, Melisande, Melise, Melita, Misha, Missy. *Variant*: Melisande (French).

Melita Greek; little honey flower.

Melody Greek; song, choral singing. Occasional use from 1950. *Other forms*: Melodee, Melodie.

Melola A blend of Mela and Lola.

Melora Greek; golden apple.

Melosa Spanish; like honey.

Melvina Old English; friendly counsellor.

Melwyn Cornish; fair as honey.

Melyn, Melyna Blends of Mela and Lynda.

Melys Welsh; sweet.

Mentha Latin; mint.

Merari Hebrew; girl of sadness.

Meraud Cornish; little one of the sea.

Mercedes Spanish; grace, mercy. The cars produced by Daimler-Benz are named after Mercedes, the daughter of one of the firm's founders. *Variants*: Mercedas

(Dutch); Mercille (French); Mercedalia (Greek); Mercede (Italian).

Mercia From the name of the Anglo-Saxon kingdom.

Meredith, Meredyth Welsh; defender of the sea. *Other form*: Meredithe. (See Gender-neutral names.)

Merelyn, Merelina Blends of Meryl and Lina.

Meri Finnish; the sea.

Meribeth A blend of Meryl and Elizabeth.

Meriel A Welsh form of Muriel. Occasional use from 1955 to 1965.

Merilyn A blend of Merrie and Lyn.

Merina Malagasy; elevated people, dwellers on the plateau.

Merissa A blend of Meryl and Clarissa.

Merita A blend of Meryl and Rita.

Merlain, Merlaine, Merlayne, Merlane Welsh; sea fort. Feminine forms of Merlin.

Merle French; blackbird. Occasional use in the 1930s. *Other forms*: Merla, Merlina, Merline, Merola, Meryl, Morrel.

Merlyn, Merline, Merlene Welsh; sea fort. Feminine forms of Merlin. (See Gender-neutral names.)

Merna Scottish Gaelic; beloved.

Meronel A modern invention meaning lake of the elves.

Merridee A blend of Merrie and Dee.

Merrie Old English; joyful, pleasant. *Other forms*: Merita, Meryn.

Meru Meru; the name of a tribe in Kenya.

Meryl A form of Meriel.

Meryna A Cornish name of uncertain meaning.

Mesha Hindi; born under the sign of Aries.

Metea Greek; gentle.

Metlaka Tsimshian; from a Native American village name.

Metra Persian; moon. Metra was the Persian moon goddess.

Metta, Meta Pali; love for all, unconditional love.

Mhina Swahili; delightful.

Mia A Scandinavian form of Mary.

Michaela Hebrew; who is like God. A feminine form of Michael. Light use from 1955 peaking in 1965. *Other forms*: Mia, Mica, Michaella, Michal, Mikelina. *Variants*: Meka (Czech); Michelle (French); Mici, Michaella (Italian); Misha (Russian); Miguela (Spanish).

Michaella An Italian form of Michaela. Occasional use from 1980.

Michal Hebrew; brook. (See Gender-neutral names.)

Michele A form of Michelle. Occasional use 1950–80, peaking in 1965.

Michelle A French feminine form of Michael. Light use from 1950 peaking in heavy use in 1970. *Other forms*: Chelle, Me'shell, Michele, Micheline, Mychelle. *Variants*: Michele (French); Michaelle (Italian); Misha (Russian); Michal (Slavonic); Miguela, Miguelita (Spanish); Mikaela, Mikaila (Swedish).

Michi Japanese; the righteous way.

Michiko Japanese; beauty and wisdom.

Midori Japanese; green.

Mieko Japanese; prosperous.

Miette French; small sweet things.

187

Migina Omaha; new moon.

Mignon French; delicate, graceful.

Mika Japanese; new moon.

Mikaela A Swedish form of Michelle. *Other form*: Mika.

Miki Japanese; beautiful tree.

Mila, Milah Slavonic; loved by the people.

Milana Italian; woman from the city of Milan.

Mildred Old English; mild, gentle. Light use from 1900, but then declining rapidly and falling out of use by 1960. *Other forms*: Milda, Millie, Milly, Mindy. *Variants*: Mila, Milah (Hungarian).

Milena Old German; mild, peaceful.

Miliani Hawaiian; caress.

Millicent Old German; noble strength. *Other forms*: Millie, Milly. *Variants*: Melisande (French); Melisenda (Spanish).

Millie, Milly Forms of Millicent. Occasional use from 1925. *Other forms*: Mili, Millee.

Milora A blend of Millicent and Lora (Laura).

Mima Burmese; woman.

Mimi An Italian form of Maria. Popularized by Puccini's opera *La Boheme*.

Mimosa From the flower name.

Minna A character in *The Pirate* by Sir Walter Scott.

Minnie A diminutive of Wilhelmina. *Other forms*: Min, Minni. *Variant*: Minka (Slavonic).

Minoa Greek; from the island of Minos.

Minowa Native American; singer.

Minya Osage; older sister.

Mio Japanese; waterway.

Mirabel Latin; wonderful. *Other form*: Mirabelle. *Variant*: Mirabai (Hawaiian).

Mirago A blend of Mira (Myra) and Margo (Margot).

Miranda Latin; admirable. Invented by Shakespeare for the heroine of *The Tempest*. Occasional use from 1925. *Other forms*: Marenda, Mirada, Myrada, Myradene.

Mirari Basque; miracle.

Miraya, Miraye French; miracle.

Mirella, Mirelle Blends of Mira and Ella.

Mirembe Luganda; peace.

Mirena A blend of Mira and Irene.

Miri Romany; mine.

Miriam Hebrew; wished-for child. Occasional use from 1900. *Other forms*: Myriam, Myrian. *Variants*: Mirjam (Finnish); Mimi, Miryam (French); Mitzi (German); Maroula (Greek); Miliama (Hawaiian); Macia (Polish); Maruska (Russian); Maruca (Spanish).

Mirielle A blend of Miriam and Elle.

Mirola A blend of Mira and Lola.

Miromel A blend of Mira and Mela.

Mistral French; cool Mediterranean wind.

Misty Old English; mysterious, misty. Occasional use in 1975. *Other forms*: Mistie, Mysty.

Mitena Ojibwa; born under a new moon. Given to a child born on a night between the new and full moon.

Mitsu Japanese; light.

Mitzi A German form of Mary.

Miwa Japanese; far-seeing.

Miya Japanese; temple.

Miyo Japanese; beautiful child. *Other form*: Miya.

Moana Hawaiian and Maori; ocean.

Moani Hawaiian; fragrance.

Mocara Scottish Gaelic; my friend.

Mohala Hawaiian; flowers in bloom.

Moina Celtic; gentle.

Moira A phonetic form of the Irish Gaelic version of Mary. Occasional use from 1925 peaking in 1950. *Other forms*: Moya, Moyra.

Molanda A blend of Molly and Amanda.

Molantha A blend of Molly and Samantha.

Molinda A blend of Molly and Linda.

Mollie A form of Molly. Occasional use 1925–35.

Molly A form of Mary. Occasional use from 1900 peaking in 1935. *Other forms*: Molley, Mollie. *Variant*: Maili (Scottish Gaelic).

Mona Irish Gaelic; noble.

Mondiale French; the world.

Monica Probably Latin; to advise, counsel. Occasional use from 1925 peaking in 1950. *Other forms*: Monise, Monnica, Monika, Monnie, Monya. *Variants*: Monique (French); Mona, Monika (German); Monca, Moncha (Irish Gaelic).

Monona Fox, Sauk; a semi-divine being in Native American mythology.

Montana From the name of the American State. Latin; mountain.

Montina Latin; mountain.

Mora Spanish; blueberry.

Morag Scottish Gaelic; great.

Moranda A blend of Morag and Amanda.

Morantha A blend of Morag and Samantha.

Morasha Hebrew; inheritance.

Morela, Morella, Morelle Polish; apricot.

Morena Spanish; brown.

Morenwyn Cornish; fair maiden.

Moretta Possibly Hebrew; teacher.

Morgan Welsh; great, bright. *Other forms*: Morgana, Morgane, Morganetta, Morgann, Morgen, Morgyn. (See Gender-neutral names.)

Moria, Moriah, Mariah Hebrew; God is my teacher.

Moriana A character in the *War of Powers* series of novels by Robert E. Vardeman and Victor Milan.

Morita A blend of Morag and Rita.

Moritha A blend of Morag and Tabitha.

Morleena A character in the novel *Nicholas Nickleby* by Charles Dickens.

Morna Scottish Gaelic; beloved, gentle.

Morowa Akan; queen.

Morrigan Celtic; great war queen. In Celtic mythology, Morrigan was a powerful goddess.

Morva Cornish; mermaid.

Morven Scottish Gaelic; big mountain peak.

Morvenne Irish Gaelic; tall blonde.

Morwen, Morwenna Welsh; sea maiden, mermaid. *Variant*: Morvoren (Cornish).

Moswen, Moswena Tswana; white.

Motya A Russian form of Matrona, a Latin name meaning lady.

Moya An Irish form of Mary.

Moyenna A blend of Moya and Anna.

Mugisha Rukiga; lucky.

Muna Maori; darling.

Munira, Munirah Arabic; illuminating.

Mura Japanese; village.

Muriel Irish Gaelic; sea-bright. Occasional use from 1900, peaking in light use in 1925 and falling out of use in 1965. *Other forms*: Meriel, Meryl, Meryle, Miriel, Murial. *Variants*: Muirgheal (Irish Gaelic); Moirreach, Muireall (Scottish Gaelic); Meriel (Welsh).

Murphy Irish Gaelic; sea warrior. Popularized by the television series *Murphy Brown*. (See Gender-neutral names.)

Mya Burmese; emerald.

Myanna A blend of Mya and Anna.

Myfanwy Welsh; my fine one. *Other forms*: Myfi, Myfina.

Myla Old English; compassionate, gentle.

Mylene Greek; dark.

Myra Latin; wonderful. A place-name in southwest Asia Minor. Occasional use from 1900. *Other form*: Mira.

Myrica From the name of the flowering shrub.

Myrna Scottish Gaelic; beloved.

Myrtle Latin; from the name of the flowering shrub. Occasional use from 1900 to 1935. *Other form*: Myrza. *Variant*: Makala (Hawaiian).

N

Naava Hebrew; beautiful.

Nabihah Arabic; clever.

Nabila Arabic; noble.

Nachusa Winnebago; fair or white-haired.

Nacienne Old French; iridescent.

Nada Arabic; generosity.

Nadia Slavonic; hope. Occasional use from 1980. *Other forms*: Nada, Nadine, Nadya. *Variants*: Nadja (Hungarian); Nadina (Latvian); Nata (Polish); Nada, Nadina, Nadiya, Nadya (Russian); Nadja (Scandinavian).

Nadine A Russian form of Nadia. Occasional use from 1955 peaking in 1980.

Nadira Arabic; precious, rare.

Nadya Arabic; moist with dew.

Nahimana Sioux; mystic.

Nahla Arabic; a drink of water, something valued in desert countries.

Naia, Naiia Greek; to flow. Naiad was a water nymph in Greek mythology.

Najina Arabic; benevolent.

Nakeisha Keisha with the *Na-* prefix.

Nakita A Russian form of Nicola. *Other forms*: Nakia, Nakeita, Naquita.

Nakotah Probably Sioux; friend to all. The name of one of the three branches of the Sioux Native American nation. (See Gender-neutral names.)

Nalani Hawaiian; calmness of the heavens.

Nalina Sanskrit; lotus flower.

Namah Hebrew; pleasant. *Other forms*: Naama, Naamah.

Namaste An ancient Sanskrit salutation and blessing, meaning 'I honour the essence of God within you, a place of love, truth and peace. When you are in that place, and I am in that place, there is only one of us.'

Nami, Namiko Japanese; wave.

Namida Chippewa; star dancer.

Nana Hawaiian; spring. Or a form of Nancy.

Nancy Probably a form of Ann. Light use from 1900, peaking in 1925 and falling out of use in 1990. *Other forms*: Nan, Nana, Nance, Nanci, Nancie, Nannie. *Variants*: Nanette (French); Nainsi (Irish Gaelic).

Nanda Sanskrit; joy. *Other forms*: Nandi, Nandie, Nandy. (See Gender-neutral names.)

Nanumea Tuvaluan; one of the nine Islands of Tuvalu.

Naomi Hebrew; delight. Occasional use from 1900, peaking in light use in 1990. *Other forms*: Naoma, Naome, Noemi. *Variants*: Neoma, Neomi (Spanish).

Naoni A blend of Naomi and Noni (Nona).

Nara Celtic; happy.

Narda Greek; aromatic ointment.

Narelle Australian; woman from the sea. *Other forms*: Narel, Narella.

Nari, Nariko Japanese; thunder.

Narinda Malagasy; the name of a bay in Madagascar.

Narissa A blend of Nara and Larissa.

Narita A blend of Nara and Rita.

Narmada Sanskrit; pleasing.

Nashawna Shawna with the *Na-* prefix.

Nashota Native American; twin.

Nasima Arabic; gentle breeze.

Nasya Hebrew; miracle of God.

Nata Polish; hope.

Natalie Latin; birthday of the Lord, hence Christmas Day. Light use from 1950 peaking in heavy use in 1985. *Other forms*: Nata, Natala, Natalia, Natalya, Natasha,

Stasha, Tasha. *Variants*: Natasa (Czech); Noelle (French); Natalia (German); Natalina (Italian); Natalia, Natka (Polish); Nastasha, Natacha, Natalja, Natalya, Natasha, Talya, Tasha (Russian); Natalija, Tasya, Tusya (Slavonic); Natalia, Talia (Spanish).

Natanya A blend of Natalie and Tanya.

Natasha A Russian form of Natalie. Light use from 1970 peaking in 1990. *Other forms*: Natacha, Tascha, Tasha, Tasya.

Natchka Yurok; from a Native American village name.

Natha Sanskrit; refuge.

Natoma Maidu; upstream, eastern.

Nava, Navene Persian; glad tidings.

Nayana Sanskrit; beautiful eyes.

Nazara Hebrew; the truth.

Nazirah Arabic; an equal.

Neche Ojibwa; friend.

Neda Slavonic; Sunday's child.

Neema Swahili; born during prosperous times.

Negara Balinese; a place-name on the island of Bali.

Neha Sanskrit; rain.

Nehanda Zezuru; hardy.

Nelita A blend of Neda and Lita (Lolita).

Nellie A form of Eleanor. Light use from its peak in 1900 to 1935.

Nema Hebrew; thread, hair.

Nemaha Omaha; muddy.

Nemissa A star maiden in Native American mythology.

Neola Greek; youthful, new.

Neoma Greek; wooded pasture.

Neona Greek; new moon.

Neorah Hebrew; light.

Nerine A sea nymph in Greek mythology. *Other forms*: Nerida, Neridah, Nerina. *Variant*: Nerina (Italian).

Nerissa Greek; daughter of the sea.

Nerita Greek; sea snail.

Neroli Latin; dark. Neroli is an essential oil made from orange blossoms, named after an Italian princess.

Nerys Welsh; lady.

Nessa Cornish; second daughter. *Other forms*: Neisha, Nesha.

Netania Hebrew; gift of God.

Neula Celtic; champion.

Neva Latin; snow.

Nevada From the name of the American State. Spanish; snowy.

Nesya Greek; pure.

Ngaio Maori; from the name of an evergreen tree.

Nia A Welsh name of uncertain meaning.

Niamh Irish Gaelic; radiance, brightness. The name of a goddess in Irish legend.

Nichelle A blend of Nicola and Michelle.

Nichola A form of Nicola. Occasional use from 1955, peaking in 1975.

Nicky A form of Nicola. Occasional use from 1955. *Other forms*: Nicki, Nickie. (See Gender-neutral names.)

Nicola An Italian feminine form of Nicholas. Light use from 1950 peaking in very heavy use in 1975. *Other forms*: Nichelle, Nichola, Nichole, Nicki, Nicky,

Nicolette, Nicoline, Nikola, Nikole, Niki, Nikki. *Variants*: Cosette, Nicole (French); Nikola, Nikoline (German); Niki (Greek); Nicoletta (Italian); Nikita (Russian).

Nicole A French form of Nicola. Light use from 1955 peaking in 1990. *Other forms*: Cole, Nicol.

Nicolette A French diminutive of Nicola. Occasional use from 1950 until it fell out of use in 1990.

Nida Omaha; fairy.

Nigesa Lumasada; born during the harvest season.

Nike Greek; victorious. Nike was the Greek goddess of victory.

Nikita Sanskrit; the earth.

Nikki A form of Nicola. Occasional use from 1970. (See Gender-neutral names.)

Nila, Nyla From the name of the river Nile.

Nima, Nimah Arabic; blessing.

Nina A Russian form of Ann. Occasional use from 1900, peaking in 1950 and 1970. *Other forms*: Nena, Ninette. *Variants*: Ninon (French); Ninotchka (Russian); Nena (Spanish).

Ninita Zuni; little girl.

Nirel, Nirelle Hebrew; light of God.

Nirvana Sanskrit; extinguished. Bliss gained through extinction of desires and entering a state of transpersonal oneness.

Nisa Seneca; moon.

Nisha Sanskrit; night.

Nissa Hebrew; sign, emblem.

Nita Hebrew; planter.

Nitara Hindi; deeply rooted.

Nitha Scandinavian; elf.

Nituna Native American; my daughter.

Nitya Sanskrit; eternal.

Nizana Hebrew; flower bud.

Noami Hebrew; pleasing.

Noelani Hawaiian; beautiful one from heaven.

Noelle French; Christmas. (See Gender-neutral names.)

Nola, Noleen Irish Gaelic; white shoulder.

Nolana Italian; little bell.

Nona, Noni Latin; ninth.

Nora An Irish form of Eleanor. Light use from 1900, peaking in 1925 and declining until it fell out of use in 1960. There was a small revival in 1980 but it was not sustained. *Variants*: Noni, Noreen (Irish).

Norah A form of Nora. Light use from 1900, although this spelling was used more than Nora 1900–35. It then fell out of use. Despite two brief revivals it fell out of use again in 1970.

Nordica French; from the north.

Noreen A diminutive of Nora. Occasional use from 1925 until it fell out of use in 1965. *Other forms*: Norene, Noreyne. *Variant*: Nolina (Hawaiian).

Norelle Scandinavian; from the north.

Norma Latin; pattern, model. Light use from 1900, peaking in 1935 and falling out of use in 1970. *Variants*: Neami, Noma (Hawaiian).

Nova Latin; new. Occasional use in the 1930s. *Other form*: Novia.

Novanda A blend of Nova and Amanda.

Novantha A blend of Nova and Samantha.

Novenda A modern invention linked to the month of November.

Noya Hebrew; beautiful.

Nuala, Nula Irish Gaelic; white shoulder.

Nubira Hebrew; from Nubia.

Nuna Native American; land.

Nuova Italian; new.

Nura Aramaic; light.

Nurita From the flower name.

Nurya Hebrew; fire of the Lord.

Nyala Amharic; Ethiopian mountain goat.

Nydia A character in the novel *The Last Days of Pompeii* by Lord Lytton.

Nyla From the name of the river Nile.

Nylantha A blend of Nyla and Samantha.

Nylara A blend of Nyla and Lara.

Nylora A blend of Nyla and Lora (Laura).

Nyree Maori; family, or wave.

Nyssa Greek; the goal.

O

Ocean Greek; sea, ocean. *Other form*: Oceana. (See Gender-neutral names.)

Octavia Latin; eighth. *Variants*: Octavie (French); Ottavia (Italian).

Odessa From the Russian place-name derived from the Greek; journey or quest.

Odile Old German; riches. *Variants*: Odette (French); Odetta (German).

Odina Algonquian; mountain.

Ofrah Hebrew; lively maiden.

Ohana Hawaiian; spiritual family.

Ojai Chumash; moon.

Okalani Hawaiian; of the heavens, heavenly.

Ola Old Norse; protector.

Olana Arabic; our place on high.

Olathe Native American; beautiful.

Olave, Oleta Old Norse; ancestor.

Oleanda From the plant name oleander.

Olena Russian; cat.

Oleta Latin; truth. *Other form*: Olethea.

Olga Russian/Old Norse; holy. Occasional use from 1900. *Other forms*: Elga, Helga, Olenka, Ollie, Olva. *Variants*: Olina (Czech); Ola, Olenka (Polish); Lelya, Lesya, Olya (Russian).

Olina Hawaiian; filled with happiness.

Olisa Ibo; God.

Olive Latin; olive tree. Light use from 1900, peaking in heavy use in 1925 and then declining until it fell out of use in 1970. *Variant*: Olivia (Italian).

Olivia An Italian form of Olive. Occasional use from 1900 until it fell out of use in 1955. Revived in 1975 and increased to light use by 1990.

Ollie A form of Olivia. (See Gender-neutral names.)

Olwen Welsh; white path. The name of the daughter of a giant in Welsh myth; clover sprang up wherever she walked. Occasional use from 1925 until it fell out of use in 1965. *Other forms*: Alwen, Olwyn.

Olwyn A form of Olwen. Occasional use from 1925 until it fell out of use in 1965. This spelling was used almost twice as much as Olwen until 1955 when Olwen overtook it, and in 1960 both forms were used equally.

Ona Hebrew; graceful.

Onatah Iroquoian; daughter of the earth and the corn spirit.

Onawa Ojibwa; wide awake. *Other forms*: Onaja, Onaway.

Onchiota Iroquoian; rainbow.

Ondine Latin; a wave. Undine was a water sprite in Roman mythology.

Oneida, Onida Iroquoian; looked-for one.

Onella Greek; light.

Oonagh An Irish Gaelic form of Una. Occasional use from 1965.

Ophelia Greek; help. *Variant*: Ophelie (French).

Ophira Hebrew; gold.

Ophrah Hebrew; a fawn. *Other forms*: Ofra, Ophra.

Oprah A form of Orpah, a Hebrew place-name of uncertain meaning.

Ora Maori; life.

Oralia Latin; a border.

Oralee Hebrew; my light. *Other form*: Oralie.

Orana Irish Gaelic; green.

Orane French; rising. *Other forms*: Oraene, Orayne.

Orantha A blend of Orana and Samantha.

Orella Latin; listener. *Other form*: Orela.

Orena Hebrew; pine tree.

Orenda Seneca; the Eternal Flame of Love, which Native Americans believe was placed by the Creator in all of Creation.

Oresa Costanoan; a bear.

Oriana Latin; dawn.

Oriel, Oriella Latin; golden.

Orienne Latin; direction of the sunrise.

Orina A Russian form of Irene.

Orinda Invented by the English seventeenth-century poet, Abraham Cowley.

Orinthia A character in the play *The Apple Cart* by Bernard Shaw.

Oriole Latin; bird with golden plumage.

Orla Irish Gaelic; golden lady.

Orlanda Old German; famous land. A feminine form of Orlando, an Italian version of Roland.

Orlena Latin; gold. *Other forms*: Orlana, Orlaine, Orlane, Orlina.

Orlene A character in the novel *Bearing an Hourglass* by Piers Anthony.

Orly, Orlie Hebrew; my light.

Orna Irish Gaelic; olive-coloured.

Oseye Benin; merry.

Osla Old Norse; consecrated to God.

Osmantha From the name of the osmanthus tree.

Otay Diegueno; thickets, brush.

Ottilie, Ottalie Old German; riches. *Other form*: Ota.

Otuka Chickasaw; chestnut tree.

Ozara Hebrew; treasure, wealth.

Ozora Hebrew; strength.

P

Paige Old English; servant, page. Light use from 1990. Paige is now used only as a girl's name in the UK, but it began as a male name and is still rarely used for boys in the United States. *Other forms*: Page, Payge. (See Gender-neutral names.)

Paka Swahili; kitten.

Pakuna Miwok; deer jumping while running downhill.

Palau Carolinian; the name of one of the Caroline Islands.

Palila Tahitian; bird, hence a free spirit.

Paloma Spanish; dove.

Pamela Probably Greek; all honey. A name invented for a character in the epic poem *Arcadi* by Sir Philip Sidney, and popularized by the novel *Pamela* by Samuel Richardson. Light use from 1900 peaking in heavy use in 1950. *Other forms*: Pam, Pamelina, Pamella, Pammi, Pammie, Pammy. *Variant*: Pamina (German).

Pamelyn A blend of Pamela and Lynda.

Pamira A blend of Pamela and Mira (Myra).

Pandora Greek; very gifted. In Greek mythology, Pandora was the first woman on earth.

Pansy From the flower name. French; thought. Occasional use 1925–35. Unlikely to revive as the word has become a slang term for an effeminate man.

Panya Swahili; tiny one.

Paoha Mono; female water spirits, undines.

Pari Persian; fairy eagle.

Paris In Greek mythology the son of Priam who carried off Helen from Sparta to Troy. (See Gender-neutral names.)

Pat A form of Patricia. (See Gender-neutral names.)

Patoka Kickapoo; a personal name of uncertain meaning.

Patricia Latin; noble person, patrician. A feminine form of Patrick. Light use from 1925, peaking in very heavy use in 1935 and declining into occasional use by 1990. *Other forms*: Pat, Patia, Patrice, Patsy, Patti, Patty, Tricia, Trisha. *Variants*: Patrice (French); Padraigin (Irish Gaelic); Patrizia (Italian).

Paula Greek; small. A feminine form of Paul. Light use from 1935 peaking in 1965. *Other forms*: Paola, Paulette, Pauline, Paulita, Polly. *Variants*: Pavla (Czech); Paule, Paulette, Pauline (French); Paola (Italian); Pola, Polcia (Polish); Pavla (Russian); Paulita (Spanish).

Paulette A French form of Paula. Occasional use from 1955 until it fell out of use in 1975.

Pauline A French diminutive of Paula. Light use from 1900, peaking in heavy use in 1950 and then declining until it fell out of use in 1990. *Other forms*: Paulene, Paulyne. *Variants*: Paulina (Bulgarian); Pavlina (Czech); Paulene, Paulette (French); Poilin (Irish Gaelic); Paolina (Italian); Pawlina (Polish); Pavlina, Pavlinka (Russian); Paulina (Spanish).

Pauma Probably Luiseno; water.

Pavana Spanish; peacock.

Paz Spanish; peace.

Pazi Ponca; yellow bird.

Pearl Middle English; a pearl. Occasional use from 1900. *Other forms*: Pearla, Pearline, Perle. *Variants*: Perla (Italian); Perlita (Spanish); Perl (Welsh).

Peggy A form of Margaret. Light use at its peak in 1900, but then declined and fell out of use by 1955. There were small revivals in 1970 and 1985. *Other forms*: Peg,

Peggie, Peggoty. *Variant*: Peigi (Scottish Gaelic).

Pele The name of the Hawaiian goddess of fire.

Pemba Bambara; the power that controls all life.

Penda Swahili; beloved.

Penelope Greek; weaver. In Greek mythology the wife of Odysseus who when her husband went away to war was besieged by admirers. She said she would select one when her tapestry was finished, but whatever she wove during the day she unpicked secretly at night. At last Odysseus returned from his wanderings and killed the troublesome suitors. Light use from 1900. *Other forms*: Pen, Pennie, Penny. *Variants*: Pipitsa, Popi (Greek); Pela, Pelcia (Polish).

Peni Carrier; mind.

Penna A blend of Penelope and Anna.

Penny A form of Penelope. Occasional use 1950–85, peaking in 1975.

Penta Latin; five.

Penthea Greek; fifth.

Pera, Peri Persian; elf.

Peta Hebrew; bread. Or Blackfoot; golden eagle. Or Sioux; fire. Occasional use from 1980.

Petaluma Probably Miwok; flat-back hill.

Petra Greek; a rock. A feminine form of Peter. Occasional use in the 1960s. *Other form*: Petronella. *Variants*: Pierette, Perrine (French); Petronille (German); Pietra (Italian); Petrina, Petryna (Russian).

Petrina A Russian form of Petra. Occasional use from 1955.

Petronella Greek; small rock. *Variants*: Petronia, Petronilla (Italian).

Petula Possibly Latin; seeker. Occasional use in the 1960s.

Phaedra Greek; bright. *Other forms*: Faydra, Phae. *Variant*: Phedre (French).

Philena Greek; lover of mankind. *Other form*: Philana.

Philippa Greek; lover of horses. A feminine form of Philip. Occasional use from 1900 peaking in 1975. *Other forms*: Filipa, Phillippa, Pip, Pippa. *Variants*: Philippine (French); Filippa, Filippina, Pippa (Italian); Filipa, Ina, Inka (Polish); Felipa (Spanish); Pelipa (Zuni).

Phillippa A form of Philippa. Occasional use from 1955, falling out of use in 1960 but reviving in 1985.

Philomena Greek; beloved. *Variants*: Philomene (French); Filomena (Italian).

Phoebe Greek; pure, bright. Occasional use from 1900. *Other form*: Phebe. *Variant*: Febe (Italian).

Phoenix Greek; purple. In Greek mythology, a bird that arose renewed from the ashes of its funeral pyre. (See Gender-neutral names.)

Phyllida A form of Phyllis. *Variant*: Filide (Italian).

Phyllis Greek; foliage. Light use from 1900, peaking in 1925 and falling out of use in 1965. *Other forms*: Phillida, Phillis, Phyliss, Phylys. *Variant*: Filide (Italian).

Pita Bari; fourth-born daughter.

Polly A form of Margaret. Occasional use from 1900.

Poloma Choctaw; bow.

Poppy Latin; from the flower name. Occasional use from 1925.

Portia From the Roman clan name Porcius. *Other form*: Porsha. *Variants*: Porsche (German); Porzia (Italian).

Prasada Sanskrit; gracious.

Precious Latin; having great value. (See Gender-neutral names.)

Prema Sanskrit; love.

Primrose Latin; first rose. Occasional use from 1900 to 1935. *Other form*: Prymrose.

Priscilla Latin; ancient, traditional. Occasional use from 1900, peaking in 1925. *Other forms*: Cilla, Prisca. *Variants*: Priscille (French); Priska (German); Prisca (Italian).

Priyal Sanskrit; beloved, sweet natured. *Other form*: Priya.

Pualani Hawaiian; heavenly flower.

Puanani Hawaiian; pretty flower.

Pukwana Ojibwa; peace pipe.

Q

Qadira Arabic; powerful.

Qamara Arabic; moon.

Qandi Arabic; sweet.

Qitarah Arabic; fragrant.

Quanda, Quana Old English; companion.

Quaneisha Neisha (Nessa) with the *Qua-* prefix.

Queenie Little queen. Occasional use from 1900 to 1965.

Quenby Scandinavian; womanly. *Other forms*: Quenna, Quinby, Quona.

Querida Spanish; beloved.

Questa, Quetta Latin; song of the nightingale.

Quiana Ana (Ann) with the *Qu-* prefix.

Quillane Irish Gaelic; fair maiden. *Other forms*: Quillaine, Quillayne.

Quinda Latin; fifth. *Other form*: Quinta. *Variant*: Quintana (Italian).

Quinn Irish Gaelic; counsel. *Other forms*: Quin, Quinna, Quinne. (See Gender-neutral names.)

R

Rabia Arabic; fragrant breeze. *Other forms*: Rabea, Rabiah.

Rachael A form of Rachel. Occasional use from 1925 to 1985, peaking in light use in 1980.

Rachel Hebrew; ewe. Light use from 1900 peaking in heavy use in 1985. *Other forms*: Rachael, Rachele, Rachelle, Rae, Rahel, Raquel, Raye, Rochelle, Shelley. *Variants*: Rahil (Bulgarian); Rachelle (French); Rahel (German); Lahela, Rahela (Hawaiian); Raicheal (Irish Gaelic); Rachele (Italian); Rakhila, Rashel (Russian); Rakel (Scandinavian); Raoghnaild (Scottish Gaelic); Raquel (Spanish).

Rachida Arabic; wise.

Radella Old English; elf counsel.

Radha Irish Gaelic; vision. Or Sanskrit; success.

Radinka Slavonic; joyful, full of life.

Radka Bulgarian; joy.

Rae A form of Rachel. Occasional use from 1935 to 1970.

Raeann A blend of Rae and Ann. *Other forms*: Rayanne, Rayona, Reyanne.

Raelaine A blend of Rae and Elaine.

Raelee A blend of Rae and Lee.

Raelene An Australian invented name, probably a diminutive of Rae.

Rafa Arabic; happy, prosperous.

Rafaela, Rafaella, Rafaele Hebrew; God has healed.

Rahima Arabic; compassionate. *Other forms*: Rahaya, Rahi.

Rainbow Old English; rainbow. *Other forms*: Rainbeau, Raynbow.

Raine, Raina Old French; mighty army.

Raiona Maori; lion.

Rajani Sanskrit; night.

Rakanja Muarusha; a Tanzanian name of unknown meaning.

Ramona Old German; wise protection. *Variants*: Raymonde (French); Raimunde (German); Raimonda (Italian).

Rana Arabic; gaze upon, beautiful. *Other form*: Raniyah.

Randall Old English; protected. *Other forms*: Randal, Randel, Randelle. (See Gender-neutral names.)

Rani Hindi; queen. *Other forms*: Ranee, Rania, Ranice.

Ranita Hebrew; joy.

Ranya Arabic; gazing at the beloved.

Raona An anagram of Aaron.

Raphaela Hebrew; God has healed. *Variants*: Rafaella (Italian); Rafaela (Spanish).

Raquel A Spanish form of Rachel.

Rasha Arabic; young gazelle.

Rashawna Shawna with the *Ra-* prefix.

Rashida Arabic; rightly guided.

Rashieka Arabic; descended from royalty. *Other forms*: Rasheka, Rashika.

Rasina Polish; a rose.

Raula Old Norse; wolf counsel. A feminine form of Raoul.

Raven A form of Robin. (See Gender-neutral names.)

Raviana A blend of Raven and Ana.

Rawnie Romany; lady.

Raya Hebrew; friend. Or Javanese; greater.

Rayleen A blend of Rae and Eileen.

Raylyn A blend of Rae and Lyn.

Rayna, Rayne Scandinavian; mighty.

Raza, Razi Aramaic; my secret.

Razina Arabic; contented.

Rebecca Hebrew; to bind, hence loyalty. Light use from 1900, declining in the 1930s but then steadily growing and peaking in very heavy use in 1990. *Other forms*: Beckie, Becky, Bekki, Reba, Rebeca, Rebeka, Rebekah, Reva, Rivka. *Variants*: Reveka (Bulgarian); Rebeque (French); Rebekka (German); Reveka (Greek); Rehana (Hawaiian); Rebekah, Rifka, Rivkah (Hebrew); Rebeka (Hungarian); Renia (Polish); Reveca (Romanian); Revekka (Russian); Rebeca, Reina (Spanish).

Rebekah A Hebrew form of Rebecca. Occasional use from 1965 peaking in 1975.

Reena Greek; peaceful.

Regan A character in the play *King Lear* by Shakespeare. *Other forms*: Reagan, Reegan, Regane, Reganne. (See Gender-neutral names.)

Regina Latin; queen. Occasional use in 1935. *Other forms*: Rega, Regia, Regine. *Variants*: Regine, Reine (French); Rehana (Hawaiian); Rena (Hebrew); Rioghnach (Irish Gaelic); Gina, Raina (Italian); Rane (Norwegian); Renia (Polish); Reina, Raina (Spanish).

Rei Maori; jewel.

Reika Japanese; beautiful flower.

Reinita Spanish; little queen.

Reka A form of Yreka. Shasta; north mountain, meaning Mount Shasta, a Native American sacred site.

Remi, Remy French; from Rheims.

Remira A blend of Remy (Remi) and Mira (Myra).

Rena Hebrew; song, joy. Occasional use from 1935 to 1955.

Renata A form of Irene. *Variants*: Renee (French); Renate (German).

Rene A form of Irene. (See Gender-neutral names.)

Renee French; born again. Occasional use from 1900, peaking in 1935. *Other forms*: Rena, Renie.

Renita A blend of Renee and Anita.

Reshawna Shawna with the *Re-* prefix.

Reuelle Hebrew; friend of God.

Reva Latin; revived.

Rexanne A blend of Rex and Roxanne.

Reyna Greek; peaceful.

Rezi Hungarian; harvester.

Rhanna The name of a Hebridean island in the novels of Christine Marion Fraser.

Rhian Welsh; maiden. Occasional use from 1970.

Rhiannon Welsh; nymph, goddess. Occasional use from 1955 peaking in 1990. *Variant*: Riwanon (Breton).

Rhianwen Welsh; fair maiden.

Rhoda Greek; a rose. Occasional use from its peak in 1900. *Other forms*: Rhody, Roda, Rodina. *Variant*: Wardeh (Arabic).

Rhona Scottish Gaelic; seal, mermaid. Occasional use from 1925, peaking in 1955. *Other form*: Rona.

Rhonda Welsh; gift. Occasional use 1950–75. *Other forms*: Rhondda, Ronda.

Rhonwen Welsh; fair.

Rhyll From the Welsh place-name.

Rhyssa A character in the novel *Pegasus in Flight* by Anne McCaffrey.

Ria Spanish; small river. Occasional use from 1980.

Rialta Italian; deep stream.

Riane, Riana Forms of Rhian.

Richelle A French feminine form of Richard.

Richenda, Richenza Old German; strong ruler. Feminine forms of Richard.

Richmal Old English; name combining ruler with an obscure second element.

Rihana Arabic; sweet basil.

Rika Japanese; village flower.

Rikka Old German; peaceful ruler.

Rikki, Ricki, Rikky Forms of Erica. (See Gender-neutral names.)

Riley Old English; rye meadow. *Other forms*: Rylea, Rylee. (See Gender-neutral names.)

Rilla A character in the *Canopus in Argos: Archives* novel cycle by Doris Lessing.

Rima Arabic; antelope.

Rimona Hebrew; pomegranate.

Rina Hebrew; joy. *Other form*: Rinah.

Rio Spanish; river. (See Gender-neutral names.)

Riona Irish Gaelic; queenly.

Rioni Georgian; the name of a river in Georgia.

Rionna Scottish Gaelic; star.

Ripley Old English; long clearing. (See Gender-neutral names.)

Risa Latin; laughter.

Risha Hindi; born during Taurus.

Rishona Hebrew; first.

Rita A Spanish form of Margaret. Light use from 1925, peaking in 1935 and then declining and falling out of use by 1975. *Other forms*: Reeta, Rheta.

Riva Italian; shore, coast.

Rivamist A blend of river and mist. *Other forms*: RivaMist, Riva-mist, Rivamyst.

Rivana Old French; river. *Other form*: Rivka.

River Latin; river. (See Gender-neutral names.)

Roana A blend of Rose and Ana (Ann). *Other form*: Roanna.

Robbi, Robbie Forms of Roberta. (See Gender-neutral names.)

Roberta Old English; bright fame. A feminine form of Robert. Occasional but steady use from 1900. *Other forms*: Bobette, Bobbie, Bobby, Bobina, Robbi, Robbie, Robinah, Robena, Robin, Robina, Robyn, Ruby, Ruperta. *Variants*: Bobina (Czech); Roberte, Robine (French); Rupetta (German); Berta, Ruperta (Spanish).

Robin A French feminine form of Robert. Occasional use from 1935 peaking in 1950. (See Gender-neutral names.)

Robina Old English; bright fame. A feminine form of Robert. Occasional use from 1900 until it fell out of use in 1970. *Other form*: Robyna.

Robyn Old English; bright fame. A feminine form of Robert. Occasional use from 1950 peaking in 1990.

Rocana A German name of uncertain meaning.

Rochelle French; little rock. Occasional use from 1975 peaking in 1990. *Other forms*: Rochella, Rochette, Shelley.

Roha Maori; a rose.

Rohan Sanskrit; ascending, healing. Also linked to *The Lord of the Rings* by Tolkien. *Other form*: Rohane. (See Gender-neutral names.)

Rohana Hindi; sandalwood.

Rohanda The original name for the planet Shikasta in the *Canopus in Argos: Archives* novel cycle by Doris Lessing.

Rohani Indonesian; spiritual.

Rohina Sanskrit; one who follows the upward path.

Rohita Sanskrit; red like the setting sun.

Rois Latin; a rose.

Roisin An Irish Gaelic form of Rose. Occasional use in 1935, then falling out of use until it revived in 1990. *Other form*: Roisyn.

Rolaine, Rolayne, Rolane Blends of Rois and Elaine.

Rolanda Old German; famous land. *Variants*: Rolande (French); Orlanda (Italian).

Rolantha A blend of Rolanda and Samantha.

Roma Latin; eternal city, hence Rome.

Romaine, Romayne French; from Rome.

Romaire A blend of Roma and Mary.

Romana Latin; Roman woman. *Variants*: Romanette (French); Romantza (German); Romancia (Italian); Romochka (Russian).

Romanda A blend of Roma and Amanda.

Romany Latin; gypsy.

Romi, Romy Hebrew; exalted.

Romola A character in the novel *Romola* by George Eliot.

Rona A form of Rhona. Occasional use from 1925.

Rondelaine, Rondelayne, Rondelane Blends of Rhonda and Elaine.

Roneisha A blend of Rona and Aisha.

Ronelle A blend of Rona and Ella.

Roni Hebrew; my joy.

Ronica A character in the novel *Orion Shall Rise* by Poul Anderson.

Rosa An Italian form of Rose. Occasional use from its peak in 1900 until it fell out of use in 1950. There was a small revival in 1990. *Variants*: Roza, Ruza (Slavonic).

Rosalie Latin; garland of roses. Occasional use from 1900, falling out of use in 1960 and reviving in 1985. *Other forms*: Rosalea, Rosalee, Rosaleen, Rosalia, Rosaline, Rosele, Rozalia. *Variants*: Rosaleen (Irish); Rosalina (Italian).

Rosalind Invented by Edmund Spenser as the name of a character in his poem *The Shepherd's Calendar*, but in the form of Rosalinde it was already in use in Germanic families, with a disputed meaning, probably horse serpent. In Spain it was also in use before Spenser, with the meaning pretty rose. Occasional use from 1900 peaking in 1950. *Other forms*: Ros, Rosaleen, Rosalinda, Rosaline, Rosalyn, Rosalynd, Roseleen, Roselyn, Roslyn, Roz, Rozalin. *Variants*: Rosalinde (German); Rosalinda (Spanish).

Rosalyn A form of Rosalind. Occasional use from 1925 peaking in 1965.

Rosamond A form of Rosamund. Occasional use in 1935.

Rosamund Old German; protector of fame. Occasional use from 1900 to 1955. *Other forms*: Rosamond, Rosamunda, Rosamunde, Rosomon, Roz, Rozamond. *Variants*: Rozamond (Dutch); Rosemonde (French); Rosamunde (German); Rosmunda (Italian); Rosamunda (Spanish).

Rosana A blend of Rose and Ana (Ann).

Rosanda A blend of Rose and Wanda.

Rosanna A blend of Rose and Anna. Occasional use from 1900.

Rosaria Spanish; the rosary.

Rose Latin; a rose. Heavy use at its peak in 1900 but then steadily declining until it fell out of use in 1985. Began a strong revival in 1990. *Other forms*: Rois, Rosa, Rosaleen, Rosalie, Rosella, Rosena, Rosetta, Rosette, Rosie, Rosina, Rosita, Roslyn, Rozina, Rusena, Zita. *Variants*: Rozenn (Breton); Rosen, Rozen (Cornish); Ruzena (Czech); Rosetta (French); Roza, Rozalia (Hungarian); Rois, Roisin, Roisyn (Irish Gaelic); Rosa, Rosena, Rosetta, Rosina, Rozena (Italian); Rozele (Lithuanian); Roza, Rozalia (Polish); Ruza, Ruzha (Russian); Chalina, Chara, Rosalia, Rosita, Zita (Spanish).

Roseanne A blend of Rose and Anne. Occasional use from 1965.

Rosella, Roselle Blends of Rose and Ella.

Roselyn A form of Rosalind. Occasional use from 1965 to 1980.

Rosemarie A form of Rosemary. Occasional use from 1935, peaking in 1950.

Rosemary Latin; dew of the sea. Light use from 1945

peaking in 1950. *Other forms*: Rosemarie, Rozemary. *Variant*: Rosemarie (French).

Rosetta A diminutive of Rose. Occasional use from 1900.

Roshana Persian; light, splendour. *Other forms*: Rashana, Roshan.

Roshawna Shawna with the *Ro-* prefix.

Rosie A form of Rose. Occasional use from 1900 until it fell out of use in 1935. It revived in 1975 and peaked in 1990.

Rosina An Italian form of Rose. Occasional use from 1900.

Rosinda A blend of Rose and Linda.

Roslyn A form of Rosalind. Occasional use from 1925.

Rowan Scottish Gaelic; red-haired. Also a Scandinavian tree name; the mountain ash. Occasional use from 1965. *Other form*: Ro. (See Gender-neutral names.)

Rowanda A blend of Rowena and Wanda.

Rowena Possibly Old German; joyful fame. Occasional use from 1935 peaking in 1955. *Variants*: Rowenta (Italian); Rhonwen (Welsh).

Roxane Probably Persian; dawn. Popularized by Edmond Rostand's play *Cyrano de Bergerac*, and by Daniel Defoe's novel *Roxana*. Occasional use from 1985. *Other forms*: Roxana, Roxann, Roxanna, Roxanne, Roxi, Roxianne, Roxie, Roxine, Roxy. *Variants*: Roushan (Arabic); Roxane (Greek); Rossana (Italian); Roksana (Russian).

Rozelle A blend of Rose and Elle (Ella). *Other form*: Rozella.

Rozene Native American; a rose.

Ruana Hindi; a stringed instrument.

Ruby Latin; from the jewel name meaning red. Occasional use from 1900. *Other forms*: Rubi, Rubia, Rubina.

Rukan Arabic; steady, confident.

Rukiya, Rukiyah Swahili; goddess, angel.

Rumer Romany; a gypsy.

Runa Old Norse; to flow. *Variant*: Rula (Czech).

Rusalka Czech; water nymph.

Ruth Hebrew; companion. Light use from 1900, peaking in 1925 but maintaining a steady level of usage. *Other forms*: Ruthi, Ruthie. *Variant*: Rut (Irish Gaelic).

Ruthann A blend of Ruth and Ann.

Ruthena A blend of Ruth and Athena.

Ruza, Ruzena Czech; a rose.

Ryana Scottish Gaelic; little queen. A feminine form of Ryan. *Other forms*: Riane, Ryenne.

Rylona Lona with the *Ry-* prefix.

Ryo Japanese; dragon.

S

Saada Hebrew; support, help. *Other form*: Saana.

Sabah Arabic; morning, dawn.

Sabbata Abnaki; a Native American form of the French name St Jean Baptiste.

Sabina Latin; woman from the Sabine region of Italy. Occasional use 1935–65. *Variants*: Savine (French); Sabine (German); Saidhbhin (Irish Gaelic); Savina (Italian); Sabinka, Sabka (Polish); Savina (Russian).

Sabira Arabic; patient.

Sabiya Arabic; morning.

Sabrina Celtic; from the name of the mythical character who gave her name to the river Severn. Occasional use from 1980.

Sacha A French form of Alexandra. *Variants*: Sasa, Sasha (Russian). (See Gender-neutral names.)

Sachi, Sachiko Japanese; bliss child.

Sadani Sadani; the name of a tribe in India.

Sadie A form of Sarah. Occasional use from 1960 peaking in 1975. *Other form*: Sade.

Sadira Arabic; ostrich returning from water.

Sadiya Arabic; fortunate. Or Assamese; a place-name in northern Assam.

Safara Swahili; journey, traveller.

Saffron Arabic; crocus. *Other forms*: Saffrane, Safrane.

Safiya Arabic; pure, serene.

Sagara Hindi; ocean.

Sage Latin; healing plant, the herb sage. (See Gender-neutral names.)

Sagina Latin; wise one. *Other form*: Saguna.

Sagirah, Sagira Arabic; little one.

Sahila Sanskrit; guide.

Sai Japanese; intelligence.

Sakara Native American; sweet.

Sakari Todas; sweet one.

Saketa Sanskrit; single-pointed, hence integrity.

Saki Japanese; rice wine, protecting garment, cape.

Sakina Native American; queen.

Sakinah Arabic; tranquillity with God.

Sakura Japanese; cherry blossom, prosperity.

Salama Arabic; peaceful.

Salema Hebrew; peace.

Saliha Arabic; goodness.

Salima Arabic; flawless, whole.

Salina French; dignified.

Sally A form of Sarah. Light use from 1925, peaking in heavy use in 1965. *Other forms*: Sallie, Sallye.

Sally-Ann A blend of Sally and Ann. Occasional use 1950–70.

Sallyanne A blend of Sally and Anne. Occasional use 1950–80. *Other forms*: Salliann, Salli-Anne, Sally-Ann, Sallyann, Sally-Anne.

Salma Arabic; peaceful.

Salome Hebrew; peace. *Other form*: Saloma. *Variants*: Salama (Arabic); Shalom (Hebrew); Salomea (Portuguese); Saloma (Spanish).

Salote Tongan; from the name of a queen of Tonga.

Sam A form of Samantha. (See Gender-neutral names.)

Samadhi Sanskrit; bliss, union with creation.

Samah Arabic; generosity.

Samala Hebrew; prayed for.

Samana A blend of Samantha and Lana.

Samanda A blend of Samantha and Amanda.

Samantha Probably Aramaic; listener. Popularized by the film *High Society* and the television series *Bewitched*. Light use from 1965, peaking in heavy use in 1970 and again in 1985. *Other forms*: Sam, Samanthe, Sammie, Sammy, Symantha. *Variant*: Samanta (Italian).

Samara Hebrew; guarded by God.

Samatha Pali; tranquillity, calm.

Samimah Arabic; true, sincere, generous.

Samina A blend of Samantha and Nina.

Samira Arabic; lively talker, entertainer. *Other forms*: Sameera, Sameerah.

Samora A blend of Samantha and Nora.

Samphire French; from the name of the cliff-growing plant.

Samya Arabic; sublime.

Sanchia Possibly Latin; holy. *Other form*: Sancha.

Sanaya A form of Sanya.

Sandie A form of Sandra or Alexandra. Occasional use from 1965. (See Gender-neutral names.)

Sandina A blend of Sandra and Nina.

Sandra A form of Alessandra, an Italian version of Alexandra. Light use from 1935 peaking in heavy use in 1950. *Other forms*: Sandee, Sandi, Sandie, Sandey.

Sanisa Arikaran; real people.

Santali Santali; the name of a tribe in India.

Santana A shortened form of Santa Anna, the Spanish version of Saint Anne.

Santina Spanish; little saint.

Sanya Sanskrit; born on Saturday. *Other form*: Sanaya.

Sanyu Luganda; happiness.

Sapphire, Sapphyre Hebrew; lapis lazuli. *Other forms*: Safyre, Sapphira.

Saqara Egyptian; place of the falcon. Saqara in Egypt is the site of a number of tombs.

Sara A form of Sarah. Or Sanskrit; essence. Occasional use from 1935 peaking in 1970.

Sarada Sanskrit; goddess of wisdom.

Sarah Hebrew; princess. Heavy use from 1900 peaking in

very heavy use in 1975. *Other forms*: Sada, Sade, Sadella, Sadie, Sahra, Saira, Sallie, Sally, Sara, Sarena, Sarette, Sari, Sarina, Sarita, Sayre, Shari, Sher, Sherrie. *Variants*: Sara (Bulgarian, Czech); Sarotte, Zaidee (French); Xsara (Galician); Sara (German); Zaharia (Greek); Kala (Hawaiian); Sari, Sarika, Sasa, Shari (Hungarian); Saraid, Sorcha (Irish Gaelic); Sara, Serita (Italian); Sala, Sara (Polish); Sala, Salcia (Portuguese); Sarka, Sarochka, Sarra (Russian); Morag, Salaidh (Scottish Gaelic); Sarena, Sarenne, Sarina (Slavonic); Charita, Sara, Sarida, Sarita, Zarita (Spanish); Sara, Sassa (Swedish).

Sarah-Jane A blend of Sarah and Jane. Occasional use from 1970. *Other forms*: Sarahjane, Sarah-Jayne, Sarahjayne.

Sarah-Jayne A blend of Sarah and Jayne. Occasional use from 1980 to 1985.

Sarai Possibly Hebrew; contentious. In the Bible, this was Sarah's name before it was changed by God. *Other forms*: Sarain, Saray, Sarayne.

Saraid Irish Gaelic; the best. *Other forms*: Sarai, Saray, Saraye.

Saraka Crow; a village name of uncertain meaning.

Sarala Sanskrit; honest, sincere.

Sarana Sanskrit; protecting.

Sarantha A blend of Sarah and Samantha.

Sarassa Quapaw; derived from the name of a Native American chief.

Sarella A blend of Sarah and Ella.

Sarika Sanskrit; from the name of a bird, hence a free spirit.

Sarila, Sareela Turkish; waterfall.

Sarinda Sanskrit; a musical instrument.

Sarita Hindi; stream. Or a Spanish form of Sarah.

Sariyah Arabic; clouds at night.

Sarola A blend of Sarah and Lola.

Saruk Arabic; east wind.

Sasha A Russian form of Alexandra. *Other forms*: Sascha, Saschae, Sashah, Sashaye, Sashia. *Variants*: Sacha (French); Sasa (Russian). (See Gender-neutral names.)

Saskia Dutch; a Saxon.

Satara A blend of Sarah and Tara.

Satinka Native American; magic dancer.

Satolah Cherokee; six, sixth-born.

Satori Japanese; sudden enlightenment.

Satya Sanskrit; absolute truth.

Savannah Spanish/Carib; meadow.

Savita Sanskrit; sun.

Sayre Old German; victory. *Other form*: Seah.

Scarlett Old English; bright red. Popularized by the novel *Gone with the Wind* by Margaret Mitchell.

Scirocco, Sirocco Arabic; warm sultry wind in southern Europe.

Seama Keresan; door, gateway.

Sean An Irish Gaelic form of John, used as a feminine name. (See Gender-neutral names.)

Seda Armenian; echo through the woods.

Sedaye Shoshone; lookout place.

Sedona A place-name in Arizona.

Seema Dari; sky, profile.

Seiko Japanese; success.

Seirian Welsh; sparkling.

Sekoma Tswana; a place-name in Botswana.

Selah Native American; still water.

Selanda A blend of Selina and Amanda.

Selara A blend of Selina and Lara

Selena A form of Selina. Occasional use 1955–85.

Selantha A blend of Selina and Samantha.

Selina Greek; moon. The goddess of the moon in Greek mythology. Occasional use from 1900. This spelling has always been at least twice as popular as Selena. *Other forms*: Celena, Celina, Selena, Selene, Silene. *Variant*: Celine (French).

Selinka A blend of Selina and Katinka.

Selma Celtic; beautiful.

Selora A blend of Selina and Lora (Laura).

Semira Hebrew; height of the heavens.

Senara From Zennor, the name of a Cornish saint.

Senga Scottish Gaelic; slender.

Seonaid A Scottish Gaelic form of Janet. *Variant*: Shaynee (Irish Gaelic).

Sequim Probably Clallam; quiet water.

Sequin Arabic; shining costume.

Sequoia Cherokee; giant redwood tree.

Sera Italian; what will be, hence destiny.

Seraiah Hebrew; warrior of God. (See Gender-neutral names.)

Seraphina, Serafina Hebrew; burning, ardent. *Other forms*: Serafia, Seraphia. *Variants*: Serafina (Italian); Sima (Russian); Seraphite (Spanish).

Seren Welsh; starlight.

Serena Latin; peaceful. Occasional use from 1955. *Other forms*: Seraina, Serayna.

Serinda A blend of Serena and Linda.

Seruna Rajasthani; a place-name in Rajasthan.

Severina Latin; from the Roman family name Severinus. *Variants*: Severine (French); Szorenya (Hungarian).

Shae A form of Shea. *Other forms*: Shay, Shaye.

Shaelyn A blend of Shae and Lyn.

Shafaye Faye with the *Sha-* prefix.

Shaheena, Shahina Arabic; falcon.

Shahira Arabic; renowned.

Shahla Dari; beautiful eyes.

Shaina Yiddish; beautiful. *Other form*: Shahna.

Shaira Arabic; thankful.

Shajuana Juana (Juanita) with the *Sha-* prefix.

Shakarah Kara with the *Sha-* prefix.

Shakeena Keena with the *Sha-* prefix. *Other form*: Shakeita.

Shakela Kela (Keela) with the *Sha-* prefix.

Shakila Arabic; pretty.

Shakina Kina with the *Sha-* prefix.

Shakirah, Shakira Arabic; grateful. *Other form*: Shakeera.

Shakti Sanskrit; power. This can mean royal, mantric or creative power. In the Vedic texts it means the active power of a deity symbolized by his wife: the feminine aspect holds the power, while the masculine aspect provides focus and structure.

Shalana Lana with the *Sha-* prefix. *Other form*: Shaleah.

Shalanda Landa with the *Sha-* prefix.

Shalena Lena with the *Sha-* prefix.

Shalisa Lisa with the *Sha-* prefix. *Other form*: Shaleisha.

Shalita Lita (Lolita) with the *Sha-* prefix.

Shalom Hebrew; peace, wholeness.

Shalona Lona with the *Sha-* prefix. *Other form*: Shalonda.

Shalynn Lynn with the *Sha-* prefix. *Other form*: Shalyn.

Shamara Arabic; ready for battle.

Shameka Meka (Michaela) with the *Sha-* prefix.

Shamika Mika (Mikaela) with the *Sha-* prefix.

Shamina Arabic; scent, fragrance.

Shamira Hebrew; precious stone, diamond.

Shan Phonetic form of the Welsh name Sian. *Other forms*: Shana, Shanae, Shanay, Shanaye, Shanda.

Shana Hebrew; God is gracious.

Shanalee A blend of Shan and Lee.

Shanda A blend of Shan and Wanda.

Shandi, Shandie, Shandy Blends of Shan and Wendy.

Shani Swahili; wonderful. *Other form*: Shanida.

Shanice A blend of Shani and Janice.

Shaniqua A blend of Shani and Monique. *Other form*: Shanika.

Shanita Nita with the *Sha-* prefix.

Shanleigh A blend of Shan and Leigh.

Shanna A blend of Shan and Anna.

Shannara A character in the *Shannara* trilogy of novels by Terry Brooks.

Shannon, Shanon Celtic; old wise one. *Other forms*: Shannan, Shanneen, Shannen. Occasional use from 1955.

Shantara A blend of Shan and Tara. *Other form*: Shantana.

Shantha Hindi; peaceful. *Other form*: Shanta.

Shanti, Shantih Sanskrit; peace. *Other forms*: Shantae, Shante.

Shantina A blend of Shan and Tina. *Other forms*: Shanteena, Shantyna.

Shantora A blend of Shan and Tora. *Other form*: Shantori.

Sharada Sanskrit; autumn. *Other form*: Sharadini.

Sharana Sanskrit; take refuge, protection. *Other forms*: Sharan, Sharaine, Sharayne.

Sharanda A blend of Sharana and Ananda.

Shardae, Sharday Punjabi; clarity, compassion.

Sharella A blend of Shara (Sharon) and Ella.

Sharifa Arabic; eminent, honourable.

Sharlene Old English; womanly. A feminine form of Charles. Occasional use in the 1980s.

Sharly A blend of Shara and Carly.

Sharma Old English; inheritance.

Sharon Hebrew; the plain. Light use from 1950 peaking in very heavy use in 1970. *Other forms*: Shaaron, Sharada, Shareen, Shari, Sharia, Sharona, Sharron, Sharyn.

Sharona A blend of Sharon and Rona.

Sharonda A blend of Sharon and Ronda (Rhonda).

Sharron A form of Sharon. Occasional use 1950–80, peaking in 1970.

Sharyn A blend of Shara and Lynda.

Shasta Hokan; forest people. The name of a mountain in California, and of a Native American nation.

Shasti In Hindu mythology, a protective goddess of children.

Shatha Arabic; fragrance.

Shauna A feminine phonetic form of the Irish Gaelic name Sean.

Shavonne, Shavon Phonetic forms of Siobhan. *Other forms*: Chavon, Chevonne, Chivonne, Shevaun, Shivaun.

Shawn An Irish Gaelic form of John used as a feminine name. (See Gender-neutral names.)

Shawna A form of Shauna. *Other forms*: Shawne, Shawnta.

Shawndelle A Canadian form of Shawna.

Shawnee Algonquian; my people, our people. The name of a Native American nation. *Other forms*: Shaunee, Shawni, Shaunie, Shawney, Shawnie.

Shayna Hebrew; beautiful.

Shea Irish Gaelic; hawk-like, fine. *Other forms*: Shae, Shay.

Sheanda A blend of Shea and Amanda.

Sheantha A blend of Shea and Samantha.

Sheba A form of Bathsheba. Hebrew; daughter of an oath.

Sheeana A character in the novel *Dune* by Frank Herbert.

Sheela Sanskrit; character, individualism.

Sheelagh An Irish Gaelic form of Sheila. Occasional use 1935–65.

Sheena Phonetic form of the Scottish Gaelic name Sine, a version of Jean. Occasional use 1950–80. *Other form*: Shena.

Sheila An English version of the Irish Gaelic name Sile, a form of Celia. Light use from 1925 peaking in heavy use in 1935. *Other forms*: Shaela, Shaila, Shayla, Shaylah, Shaylih, Sheelagh, Sheelah, Shelagh, Sheyla, Shiela. *Variants*: Zelizi (Basque); Sheelagh, Shelagh (Irish Gaelic); Sileas, Silis (Scottish Gaelic).

Shelagh An Irish Gaelic form of Sheila. Occasional use from 1925 to 1965.

Shelby Old English; willow village. Popularized by a character in the film *Steel Magnolias*.

Shelley Old English; meadow on a slope. Occasional use from 1950, peaking in 1980. *Other forms*: Shelli, Shellie, Shelly.

Shelly A form of Shelley. Occasional use 1965–85.

Shera Aramaic; light.

Sherah Hebrew; female relative.

Sherala A blend of Sheree and Lala.

Sheralyn A blend of Sheree and Lynda.

Sheree A form of Cherie. Occasional use from 1955. *Other forms*: Sheri, Sherie, Sherrie, Sherry.

Sherelle A blend of Sheree and Ella.

Sherise A blend of Sheree and Cerise. *Other form*: Sherissa.

Sherita A blend of Sheree and Rita.

Sherrie A form of Sheree. Occasional use 1980–5.

Sherril, Sherrill Old English; country hill.

Sheryl A form of Cheryl. Occasional use from 1955.

Sherylynn A blend of Sheryl and Lynn.

Shifra Hebrew; beautiful.

Shika Japanese; gentle deer.

Shikasta The name of a planet in the *Canopus in Argos: Archives* novel cycle by Doris Lessing.

Shiloh Possibly Hebrew; tranquillity. In the Bible, a place near Jerusalem. *Other form*: Shilo. (See Gender-neutral names.)

Shima Japanese; island.

Shimako Japanese; island child.

Shimara A blend of Shima and Mara.

Shimiah Hebrew; to guard.

Shimona Hebrew; little princess. *Other form*: Shimonel.

Shiona A blend of Sheila and Fiona.

Shira, Shiri Hebrew; my song.

Shirley Old English; bright clearing. Popularized by the novel *Shirley* by Charlotte Brontë. Light use from 1925 peaking in very heavy use in 1935. *Other forms*: Shirlee, Shirlie.

Shizu Japanese; quiet, clear. *Variant*: Shizuka (Japanese).

Shona Phonetic form of the Scottish Gaelic name Seonaid, a version of Joan. Occasional use from 1965. *Other forms*: Shonda, Shonta.

Shua A Hebrew name of uncertain meaning.

Shubuta Choctaw; smokey.

Shula Probably Arabic; peace. *Other forms*: Shulie, Shuna. *Variant*: Shola (Polish).

Sian A Welsh form of Jane. Occasional use from 1955, peaking in 1990.

Sibyl, Cybil Greek; prophetess. *Variants*: Sibylle (French); Sibilla (Italian).

Sidonie Old French; a follower of St Denis.

Sienna Italian; a yellow-brown hue that takes its name from the Tuscan city of Siena.

Sierra Spanish; saw. From the Spanish name for a mountain range, whose peaks resemble the teeth of a saw.

Sigourney A form of Sagina. Occasional use from 1990.

Sika Japanese; deer.

Silvana Latin; wood.

Sima Arabic; treasure. Or Comorian; a place-name in the Comoros Islands.

Simone Hebrew; listen attentively. A feminine form of Simon. Occasional use from 1950 peaking in 1980. (See Gender-neutral names.)

Sina The name of the Hawaiian moon goddess.

Sinead An Irish Gaelic form of Janet. Occasional use from 1990. *Variants*: Sineidin (Irish Gaelic); Sine (Scottish Gaelic); Sian (Welsh).

Sinta Choctaw; snake, hence wisdom.

Sintra From the name of a town in Portugal.

Siobhan An Irish Gaelic form of Joan. Occasional use from 1965. *Other forms*: Chavonne, Sioban, Siobhana.

Siri Norman French; conquering impulse. *Other form*: Sirah.

Sisika Native American; thrush, swallow.

Sita Sanskrit; furrow. The goddess of the harvest and wife of Rama in Hindu mythology. *Other form*: Seetha.

Sitala Miwok; display memory.

Sitara Hindi; morning star.

Sitka Tlingit; from the Alaskan place-name of uncertain meaning.

Sivana Assyrian; the ninth month of the Jewish calendar.

Sky Old English; vault of heaven, sky (hence high aspirations). (See Gender-neutral names.)

Skye Dutch; sheltering. Associated with the Hebridean island.

Skyla A character in the novel *Black Lynx* by Elizabeth H. Boyer.

Skylar Dutch; scholar. (See Gender-neutral names.)

Sloane Scottish Gaelic; warrior. (See Gender-neutral names.)

Sofiel, Sofielle The Egyptian or Persian angel of plants.

Sohani, Suhani Arabic; star.

Sol Latin; sun. (See Gender-neutral names.)

Sola Latin; sun.

Solace Latin; to comfort.

Solaire, Solayre Latin/Greek; sunshine and air.

Solana Spanish; sunshine.

Solanda A blend of Sola and Amanda.

Solange Italian; unique, special.

Solantha A blend of Sola and Samantha.

Solara A blend of Sola and Lara.

Soleila French; sun.

Solena, Solina Blends of Sola and Lena.

Solora A blend of Sola and Lora (Laura).

Somer Old English; summer.

Sona Scottish Gaelic; happy, fortunate.

Sonda A blend of Sonya and Wanda.

Sondara A blend of Sonya and Dara.

Sonia A Russian form of Sophia. Occasional use from 1925 peaking in 1965. *Other forms*: Sonja, Sonya, Zonya. *Variants*: Sonja, Sonje (German, Scandinavian); Sonya (Russian).

Sonika Sanskrit; golden. *Other forms*: Sonal, Sonali.

Sonora From the name of the Native American nation.

Sontara A blend of Sonia and Tara.

Sontina A blend of Sonia and Tina.

Sonya A Russian form of Sophia. Occasional use from 1965 to 1980.

Sophia Greek; wisdom. Occasional use 1900–25. It fell out of use in 1930 but revived in 1965, peaking in 1990.

Sophie Greek; wisdom. Occasional use from 1925, rising steadily from 1975 and peaking in heavy use in 1990. *Other forms*: Sofia, Sonia, Sonni, Sophia, Sophy, Sunny, Zophia. *Variants*: Sona (Armenian); Sofia (Bulgarian); Zofie (Czech); Saffi (Danish); Sofie (Dutch); Sofia (German); Sofi, Sofronia, Sophia (Greek); Kopia (Hawaiian); Zsofia (Hungarian); Sofia (Italian); Sofiya (Latvian); Sofiya, Sofja (Lithuanian); Sonja (Norwegian); Zocha, Zofia, Zosha (Polish); Sonia (Portuguese); Sofia (Romanian); Sofia, Sofya, Sonia, Sonya, Sovay (Russian); Sofka, Zofia (Slavonic); Chofa, Sofia, Soficita (Spanish); Sofi, Sonya (Swedish); Sofya (Turkish); Sofiya, Zofia (Ukrainian).

Soraya Persian; princess.

Sorcha Irish Gaelic; bright.

Sorrel French; reddish brown. From the herb name.

Stacey A form of Anastasia. Occasional use from 1960 peaking in heavy use in 1990. *Other forms*: Stacee, Staci, Stacie, Stacy, Staicie, Staicy, Staycee, Stayci. *Variants*: Stasa, Staska (Czech); Steise (Irish Gaelic); Stasya, Tasenka, Tasya (Russian); Tasia (Spanish).

Stacy A form of Stacey. Occasional use from 1970 peaking in 1985.

Starla Old Norse; star. *Other form*: Starlyte. *Variant*: Rionna (Scottish Gaelic).

Stefanie A form of Stephanie. Occasional use from 1980. *Other forms*: Steffie, Steffy. *Variant*: Steffi (German).

Stella Latin; star. Occasional use from 1900 peaking in 1925. *Variants*: Estelle (French); Estella (Spanish).

Stephanie A French feminine form of Stephen. Light use from 1925 peaking in heavy use in 1990. *Other forms*: Stefa, Stefania, Stefanie, Steffie, Stephenie, Stevana, Stevie. *Variants*: Stefania, Stefka (Czech); Etiennette, Stefanie, Trinnette (French); Stefani, Stefanie, Steffi (German); Stamatios, Stefania (Greek); Kekepania (Hawaiian); Stefna (Hungarian); Stefania (Italian); Stefanija (Lithuanian); Stefa, Stefania, Stefcia, Stefka (Polish); Estefana, Estefania (Portuguese); Panya, Stefanie, Stepanida, Steshka, Stepa (Russian); Estefania, Stefania (Spanish); Stefkha, Stepanyda (Ukrainian).

Stevie A form of Stephanie. *Other form*: Stevi. (See Gender-neutral names.)

Storm Old Norse; storm. (See Gender-neutral names.)

Subira Swahili; our patience has been rewarded.

Sue A form of Susan. Occasional use in 1980.

Suha Arabic; star.

Sukalena Choctaw; camps on the bank of the river.

Sukha Sanskrit; happiness, bliss.

Suki Japanese; beloved.

Sukina A blend of Suki and Kina.

Sukuma Sukuma; the name of a tribe in Tanzania.

Suky A form of Susan. *Other forms*: Suki, Sukey, Suki, Sukie.

Sula Icelandic; sun.

Suma Serbo-Croatian; forest. Or Nyakyusa; ask.

Sumalee Thai; beautiful flower.

Sumay Chamoro; a place-name on the island of Guam.

Sumaya A Muslim name of uncertain meaning. *Other forms*: Sumayah, Sumayyah.

Sumi Japanese; elegant, refined.

Summer Old English; summer.

Sunda Sunda; the name of a tribe on the island of Java.

Sundarah A blend of Suna (Sunita) and Darah (Dara).

Sunila Sanskrit; dark blue.

Sunita, Suneetha Sanskrit; good guidance. *Other forms*: Suna, Sunya.

Sunny Old German; from the word linked to happy, fortunate. (See Gender-neutral names.)

Suraiya Sanskrit; beautiful.

Surata Gujarati; blessed joy.

Surya Hindi; sunshine. The Hindu equivalent of the sign Leo.

Susan Hebrew; lily. Light use from 1900, rising rapidly into very heavy use in 1950, peaking in 1955 and then declining into occasional use by 1990. *Other forms*: Shoshana, Shushanah, Siusan, Sosanna, Sue, Suki, Susanna, Susannah, Susanne, Susie, Suzanna, Suzanne, Suzette, Suzie, Zsa Zsa. *Variants*: Suzan, Zuza, Zuzana (Czech); Susette, Suzanne, Suzette (French); Susanne, Susette (German); Suse (Hawaiian); Shoshana, Shoshonna, Sonel (Hebrew); Shuka, Zsa Zsa, Szuzsanna (Hungarian); Sosanna (Irish); Susanna, Suzanna (Italian); Zuzanna, Zuzia (Polish); Suzana (Romanian); Susanka (Russian); Siusan (Scottish); Siusaidh (Scottish Gaelic); Chana, Susana (Spanish).

Susanna An Italian form of Susan. Occasional use from 1965. *Other form*: Xuxa (Brazilian).

Susannah A form of Susanna. Occasional use from its peak in 1900.

Susanne A form of Susanna. Occasional use 1950–85, peaking in 1970.

Susantha A blend of Susan and Samantha.

Suselle, Suzella Blends of Susan and Ella.

Susie A form of Susan. Occasional use from 1900.

Suzanna An Italian form of Susan. Occasional use 1965–85.

Suzanne A form of Suzanna. Occasional use from 1925 peaking in light use in 1965.

Sybil Greek; prophetess. *Other forms*: Cybil, Sibyl. *Variants*: Sibylla (Dutch); Cybele, Sibylle (French); Sibeal (Irish Gaelic); Sibilla (Italian).

Sycana Klamath; grassy plain.

Sydnie, Sydnee, Sydney Norman French; from the French place-name Saint-Denis. *Variants*: Sidonie (French); Sidonia (Italian). (See Gender-neutral names.)

Sylvaine, Sylvayne, Sylvane Latin; dweller in a wood.

Sylvia Latin; wood. Light use from 1900, peaking in heavy use in 1935 and then declining into occasional use. *Other forms*: Silvana, Silvia, Silvie, Sylva, Zilvia. *Variants*: Silvie, Silviane, Sylvie (French); Xylia (Greek); Silvana, Silvestra, Silvia (Italian); Zilvia (Polish).

Syna Greek; together.

Syra From the name of the star system Sirius.

Sysha Old German; sweet.

T

Tabia Swahili; talented.

Tabina Arabic; follower of Muhammad.

Tabitha Aramaic; gazelle. *Other forms*: Tabatha, Tabetha, Tabotha. Popularized by the television series *Bewitched*. *Variants*: Tabea (German); Dorcas (Greek).

Tachia Formosan; the name of a river in Taiwan.

Tacoma Algonquian; mountain; or the sacred places of the gods.

Tacy, Taci, Tacey Latin; peace.

Tahani Arabic; congratulations.

Tahira Arabic; pure.

Tahoe Washo; lake.

Tahuata Marquesan; the name of one of the Marquesas Islands.

Tahuna Maori; beach.

Taimana Maori; diamond.

Taisha Chinese; peace.

Taja Persian; crown.

Takala Hopi; corn tassel.

Takara Japanese; treasure.

Takira Kira with the *Ta-* prefix.

Takiyah African; righteous.

Takoha Maori; free from fear or suspicion.

Tala Native American; stalking wolf. *Other form*: Talana.

Talanda A blend of Talia and Amanda.

Talantha A blend of Talia and Samantha.

Talara A blend of Talia and Lara.

Talas Kirghiz; a place-name in Kirghizstan.

Talasha Choctaw; palmettos are there.

Taleisha Leisha with the *Ta-* prefix.

Talena Lena with the *Ta-* prefix.

Talia Aramaic; young lamb. *Other forms*: Talie, Tally.

Talinda A blend of Talia and Linda.

Talita A blend of Talia and Lita (Lolita).

Talitha Aramaic; little girl.

Tallis A character in the novel *Lavondyss* by Robert Holdstock.

Tallulah Native American; running water.

Tally A form of Talia. (See Gender-neutral names.)

Talma Hebrew; hill.

Talona A blend of Talia and Lona.

Talora Hebrew; dew of the morning.

Talula Choctaw; leaping water.

Talwa Creek; town.

Talwyn Cornish; fair brow.

Talya A Russian form of Natalya. *Other forms*: Tali, Tally.

Tamaha Choctaw; town.

Tamaahine Maori; girl.

Tamaka Japanese; bracelet.

Tamantha A blend of Tasmin and Samantha.

Tamaqua Delaware; little beaver stream.

Tamar Hebrew; palm tree. Or Celtic; water spirit, undine. Occasional use from 1935. *Other forms*: Tama, Tamah, Tammie, Tammy. *Variant*: Tamara (Russian).

Tamara A Russian form of Tamar. Occasional use from 1970. *Other forms*: Tamarah, Temira. *Variants*: Mara (Czech); Tomochka (Russian).

Tamarisk Latin; from the name of the flowering tree.

Tamatha Arabic; to walk around.

Tambra Phonetic form of the word timbre. Greek; drum, the quality of sound.

Tameka Aramaic; twin. *Other form*: Tamesha.

Tamika Japanese; people.

Tamila Possibly Sanskrit; southern.

Tamla From Tamla Motown, the name of an American record label.

Tamlyn A blend of Tamsin and Lynda.

Tammy A form of Tamsin, Tamara, etc. Occasional use from 1965 peaking in 1975. *Other forms*: Tami, Tamme, Tammie.

Tamsin Aramaic; twin. Occasional use from 1960. *Other forms*: Tam, Tamasin, Tamasine, Tammie, Tammy, Tamsen, Tamsyn, Tamzyn. *Variant*: Tamsyn (Cornish).

Tanada Aleutian; small island.

Tanala Malagasy; people of the forest.

Tanana Athapascan; people of the mountain and the river.

Tandy Old English; team.

Taneisha A blend of Tanya and Aisha. *Other form*: Tanesha.

Tanga From the names of the dances tango and rumba.

Tangerine From the name of the orange fruit linked with Tangier. *Other forms*: Tangeryne, Tangina.

Tangina A character in the film *Poltergeist*. *Other form*: Tangie.

Tangye Possibly Breton; fire dog. A useful name for a child born under this sign in Chinese astrology. (See Gender-neutral names.)

Tani, Tanie Japanese; valley.

Tania A form of Tanya. Occasional use from 1960 peaking in 1965.

Tanira A blend of Tania and Mira (Myra).

Tanis Egyptian; an ancient temple site in Egypt.

Tanisha Hausa; born on Monday.

Tanith Phoenician; the name of the Phoenician goddess

of love. *Other forms*: Tanita, Tanitha, Tanytha.

Tanmaya A blend of Tanya and Maya.

Tansy From the name of the wild flower.

Tanya Greek; great one. Occasional use from 1955 peaking in 1990. *Other forms*: Tania, Tanis, Tanna, Titania. *Variants*: Tanja (German); Taneya (Russian); Tanja (Scandinavian).

Tanza Old German; dance, dancer.

Taoa, Tayoa Futuna; the name of a village in the Futuna Islands.

Taos Tewa; a New Mexico place-name of uncertain meaning.

Tara Irish Gaelic; hill. Or Sanskrit; star. In Irish mythology the name of a site linked with the early Irish kings. Popularized by the television series *The Avengers*. Occasional use from 1970. *Other forms*: Tarah, Taraya, Tari, Taryn.

Taralynda, Taralyn Blends of Tara and Lynda.

Taraneh Persian; melody.

Tarasa Nicobarese; the name of one of the Nicobar Islands.

Tarawa Gilbertese; big island. The name of one of the Gilbert Islands.

Tarika Possibly Arabic; conqueror. A feminine form of Tarik.

Tarita A Polynesian form of Dorothy.

Taroka Bengali; star.

Tarova Corsican; the name of a river on the island of Corsica.

Taryn A blend of Tara and Lynda. *Other forms*: Tarryn, Taryne.

Tasarla Romany; dawn.

Tasha A form of Natasha. *Other forms*: Tacha, Tascha, Tashia, Tasia. *Variants*: Tazia (Italian); Taska (Latvian); Tashi, Tasia (Slavonic).

Tashana Shana with the *Ta-* prefix.

Tashawna Shawna with the *Ta-* prefix.

Tasheena Sheena with the *Ta-* prefix.

Tasida Sarcee; horse rider.

Tasya A form of Tasha.

Tatum Old English; cheerful. Or Algonquian; great talker.

Tavia A form of Octavia. *Variant*: Tawia (Polish).

Tawana Wana (Wanda) with the *Ta-* prefix.

Tawiah Ga; first child after twins.

Tawny Romany; little one. *Other forms*: Tawnee, Tawnie, Tawney.

Tawnya A blend of Tawny and Tanya.

Tayanita Cherokee; young beaver.

Taylor Old English; worker with cloth. *Other forms*: Tay, Taye, Teylor. (See Gender-neutral names.)

Tayna A blend of Taylor and Ina. *Other forms*: Tena, Teyna.

Taytay Tagalog; a place-name in the Philippines.

Tazara Zara with the *Ta-* prefix.

Tazlina Athapascan; swift river.

Tazmin, Tazmyne Forms of Tamsin

Teanna Anna with the *Te-* prefix.

Tecca Cornish; fairer.

Tecla Greek; God's glory. *Other form*: Thecla. *Variant*: Tekla (Swedish).

Tecoma Shoshone; small mountain standing alone.

Tegan Welsh; beautiful. *Other forms*: Teagan, Tiegan, Tigi.

Tegwen, Tegwyn Welsh; beautiful and blessed.

Tehya Native American; precious.

Temba Zulu; hope.

Temira Hebrew; tall.

Tempest, Tempestt Latin; storm.

Tenesha Nesha (Nessa) with the *Te-* prefix.

Tenshi Japanese; angel.

Teocali Aztec; temple.

Teoma Scottish Gaelic; active.

Terah Hebrew; cycle, duration. *Other forms*: Tera, Terra. (See Gender-neutral names.)

Teralyn A blend of Terah and Lyn.

Terantha A blend of Terah and Samantha.

Terella A blend of Teresa and Ella.

Teresa An Italian form of Theresa. Light use from 1925 peaking in 1965. *Variant*: Teresita (Spanish).

Terina A blend of Teresa and Rina.

Terri A form of Teresa. Occasional use from 1955. *Other forms*: Terree, Terriah, Terrie. (See Gender-neutral names.)

Terrie A form of Teresa. Occasional use 1955–80.

Terri-Lynn A blend of Terri and Lynn.

Tessa A form of Teresa. Occasional use from 1935. *Other forms*: Teisha, Tess, Tessie.

Tessara Latin; fourth.

Teya Native American; precious. *Other forms*: Tayah, Taye, Tayna, Tayra, Taysha, Tayva, Tiyah.

Thabana Sotho; mountain.

Thalia Greek; blossom, plenty, joy. The name of the Greek Muse of comedy. *Other form*: Thalea.

Thana Arabic; praise. *Other forms*: Thani, Thania, Thanie.

Thandie A form of Thandiwe. Zulu; loved one.

Thara Arabic; wealth.

Theana Greek; divine name.

Thelma Probably Greek; will. A character in the novel *Thelma, a Norwegian Princess* by Marie Corelli. Light use from 1900 until it fell out of use in 1960. There was a small revival in 1990.

Thema Akan; queen.

Theodora Greek; God's gift. Occasional use until 1930 when it fell out of use. Two small revivals in 1980 and 1990. *Other forms*: Dora, Fedora, Tedda, Teodora, Thaddea, Theda, Thekla, Theodosia. *Variants*: Teodora (Italian); Fedora, Feodora (Russian); Theadora (Spanish).

Theola Greek; divine.

Theolyn A blend of Theola and Lynda.

Theona, Theone, Theonie Greek; godly.

Theora Greek; watcher for God.

Thera Greek; untamed.

Theresa Greek; summer, harvest. Light use from 1900, peaking in 1965 and then declining. *Other forms*: Teresa, Teresina, Teressa, Teri, Terrie, Tess, Tessa, Thera, Therese, Tressa, Zita. *Variants*: Tereza (Bulgarian); Terezia, Reza, Rezka (Czech); Therese (French); Resi, Theresia, Tresa, Trescha (German); Tassos (Greek); Rezi, Teca, Terez, Treska (Hungarian); Toireasa, Treasa (Irish Gaelic); Teresa, Teresina (Italian); Terese (Norwegian); Tesia, Tereska (Polish); Terezilya, Zilya (Russian); Tesilya (Slavonic); Terez, Tereza, Theresita (Spanish).

Thetis In Greek mythology Thetis was the mother of Achilles.

Thirza Hebrew; pleasantness.

Tia Egyptian; princess. Or Spanish; aunt. *Other forms*: Tea, Teah.

Tiana Greek; princess.

Tiara Czech; coronet. *Other form*: Tiarra.

Tierra Spanish; land.

Tiffany Greek; manifestation of God. Occasional use 1970–80. *Other forms*: Teffany, Tifaine, Tifanie, Tiffanie, Tyffany.

Tigra Italian; tiger.

Tika Maori; truth, justice.

Timandra Greek; honour.

Timora Hebrew; tall.

Timpa Ute, Gosiute; rock.

Tina A form of Christina. Light use from 1935 peaking in 1960.

Tinesha Nesha (Nessa) with the *Ti-* prefix.

Tirana Gheg; a place-name in Albania.

Tirza Spanish; cypress tree.

Tista Sikkimese; the name of a river in Sikkim.

Titania Greek; great one. *Other form*: Tatanya.

Tivka Hebrew; hope.

Tivona Hebrew; lover of nature.

Tizana, Tizane, Tyzayne Hungarian; gypsy.

Tohona Native American; river.

Tokaina Athapascan; trees by the river.

Toketee Chinook; pretty.

Tokopah Shoshone; high spring.

Tomah Coahuila; a Native American village name.

Tonala Zapotec; a place-name in Mexico.

Toni A form of Antonia. Occasional use from 1955 peaking in 1990. *Other forms*: Tonia, Tonie. *Variant*: Tola (Polish). (See Gender-neutral names.)

Tonia A form of Antonia. Occasional use 1960–85.

Tonya Slavonic; fairy queen.

Topanga Indonesian; support, hence caring, supportive. Also a Native American place-name in California. Popularized by the television series *Boy Meets World*.

Topaz Greek; yellow gem-stone. *Other forms*: Topaza, Topaze, Topayze. (See Gender-neutral names.)

Topeka Kansa; good place for wild potatoes.

Tora Japanese; tiger. *Other form*: Toora.

Toranda A blend of Tora and Amanda.

Tori Maori; cat. Or a form of Victoria. (See Gender-neutral names.)

Toria Old English; hill.

Torina From Torino (Turin) in Italy. *Other forms*: Torene, Toryna.

Torrance Irish Gaelic; tall tower. (See Gender-neutral names.)

Tory A form of Victoria. (See Gender-neutral names.)

Tova, Tovah Hebrew; good. *Other form*: Tove.

Toya Sioux; green.

Toyah Middle English; amorous dalliance.

Tracey From the Norman place-name linked to Thracius. Light use from 1960 peaking in very heavy use in 1965. This has been the more popular spelling since 1985 although it has vied almost equally with Tracy since 1960, sometimes one having a slight edge and sometimes the other. *Other forms*: Tracee, Traci, Tracie, Tracina, Traeci, Traice.

Tracie A form of Tracey. Occasional use 1965–85.

Tracilee A blend of Tracie and Lee.

Tracilyn A blend of Tracie and Lyn.

Tracy From the Norman place-name linked to Thracius. Popularized by the film *High Society*. Light use from 1955 peaking in heavy use in 1965. This was the original form of the name.

Trella A form of Estrella, the Spanish version of Esther.

Treska A Hungarian form of Theresa. Or Macedonian; the name of a river in Macedonia.

Tressa Cornish; third daughter.

Treya French; third.

Tricia, Trycia Forms of Patricia.

Trillow Old English; from the Devon place-name.

Trina A form of Katrina. Occasional use from 1965.

Triona A form of Catriona.

Tristan Probably Celtic; noise, din. *Other forms*: Tristana, Trystana, Trystine. (See Gender-neutral names.)

Troyla Irish Gaelic; foot soldier. *Other forms*: Troi, Troia, Troiana, Troya.

Trudi A form of Trudy. Occasional use from 1955 peaking in 1970.

Trudy A form of Gertrude. Occasional use from 1950. *Other forms*: Truda, Trudi, Trudie, Trula. *Variants*: Trude (Danish); Trudel (Dutch); Druda, Traude (German).

Tuella, Tula Hindi; born during Capricorn.

Tukwila Native American; land of hazelnuts.

Tumaca Pima; curved peak.

Turaya Arabic; star.

Turquoise French; jewel from Turkey. *Other forms*: Turkoise, Turquoyse.

Twila, Twyla Middle English; two threads woven together, hence harmony.

Tyanna Anna with the *Ty-* prefix.

Tyna Scottish Gaelic; dark grey.

Tyne Welsh; river name meaning to flow.

Tynesha Nesha (Nessa) with the *Ty-* prefix.

Tyra Scandinavian; warrior. Tyr was the god of battle in Scandinavian mythology. *Other form*: Tyrina.

Tyrona From County Tyrone in Ireland.

U

Ualani Hawaiian; heavenly rain.

Udelle Old English; small valley with yew trees.

Uhane Hawaiian; soul or spirit of a person, holy spirit.

Uhura Swahili; freedom. Popularized by the original television series of *Star Trek*, in which Nichelle Nichols played the communications officer, a major breakthrough for an African-American actress at that time. When she considered leaving the series Martin Luther King persuaded her to stay, saying that she would become a role model for a whole generation.

Ula, Ulla Celtic; sea jewel.

Ulani Hawaiian; cheerful, merry.

Ulema, Ulima Arabic; learned, wise.

Ululani Hawaiian; heavenly inspiration.

Uma Sanskrit; flax, hence flaxen-haired.

Una Latin; one, unity. Occasional use from 1900 until 1960 when it fell out of use. *Other forms*: Ona, Oona. *Variant*: Oonagh (Irish Gaelic); Euna (Scottish Gaelic).

Unaka Cherokee; white.

Unity Latin; one, oneness.

Ursula Latin; she-bear. Occasional use from 1900. *Other forms*: Orsola, Ursa, Ursala, Ursola, Ursulina. *Variants*: Vorsila (Czech); Sula (Estonian); Ursule (French); Ulla, Ursel (German); Orsola, Ursina (Italian); Urzula (Latvian); Ursule (Romanian); Ursola, Ursulina (Spanish).

Usha Sanskrit; dawn.

Uta German; riches.

Utara Sumatran; north, northerner.

Utina Native American; woman of my country.

V

Vachelle French; keeper of cattle.

Vada Latin; to go, travel. Popularized by the film *My Girl*. *Other forms*: Vayda, Vaydra.

Vala Old German; chosen one.

Valda Old German; battle heroine. Occasional use 1935–55. *Other forms*: Vaelda, Velda.

Valeda Old German; wholesome.

Valentina Latin; vigorous. *Other form*: Valene. *Variants*: Walentyna (Polish); Tyna, Valentyna (Russian).

Valerie A French form of the Latin name Valeria. Light use from 1900, peaking in heavy use in 1950 and then declining and falling out of use by 1980. *Other forms*: Val, Valari, Valarie, Valery, Valerye, Valora. *Variants*: Valeria (Italian); Waleria (Polish); Lera, Valya (Russian); Valeska (Slavonic); Valeriana (Spanish).

Valeska Russian; glory.

Valetta From the Maltese place-name.

Valma Welsh; May-flower. *Other forms*: Valmai, Valmay.

Valona Tosk; a place-name in Albania.

Valora Latin; to be strong.

Vanda Slavonic; traveller. Occasional use 1935–75.

Vandella A blend of Vanda and Ella.

Vanessa The invention of Jonathan Swift from the elements of the surname Von Homrigh and the first name Esther of a woman friend. Occasional use from 1950 peaking in the 1970s. *Other forms*: Nessa, Nessie, Vania, Vannie, Vanny, Vanya. *Variant*: Vanika (Russian).

Vania A feminine version of Vanya, the Russian form of John. *Other form*: Vanya. (See Gender-neutral names.)

Vanina A blend of Vanessa and Nina.

Vanna Cambodian; golden.

Vanora Celtic; white wave.

Vanua Bislama; our land.

Varda Hebrew; a rose.

Varella A blend of Varda and Ella.

Varina, Varene Blends of Varda and Irene. *Other form*: Varuna.

Varsha Sanskrit; rain.

Vasara Sanskrit; morning.

Vashti Persian; beautiful.

Veda Sanskrit; knowledge, wisdom.

Veena Sanskrit; a sitar, a stringed instrument.

Vela Greek; sails.

Velanda A blend of Vela and Amanda.

Velantha A blend of Vela and Samantha.

Velda Old German; field.

Velika Russian; great.

Velinda A blend of Vela and Linda.

Velintha A blend of Vela and Cynthia.

Venda Bantu; the name of a tribe in Zimbabwe.

Veneta, Venitia Latin; woman of Venice.

Ventura Spanish; good fortune.

Vera Russian; faith, hence faithful. Light use from 1900, peaking in heavy use in 1925 and then declining and falling out of use by 1990. *Other forms*: Vere, Verada. *Variants*: Viera (Czech); Wiera (Polish); Verinka, Verushka, Verusya (Russian); Virenda (Slavonic); Wera (Swedish).

Verada Latin; truthful, forthright.

Verana Spanish; summer.

Verbena From the herb name.

Verella A blend of Vera and Ella.

Verena, Verina Latin; truth. *Variant*: Veran (French).

Verity Latin; truth. Occasional use from 1935.

Verna, Verla Latin; truth.

Veronica Latin; true image. Occasional use from 1900, peaking in 1950 and falling out of use in 1985. *Other forms*: Veronika, Veronique, Vonnie. *Variants*: Veronika (Czech); Veronique (French); Veronike (German); Berenike (Greek); Veronika (Scandinavian).

Vespera Greek; evening star (usually a reference to Venus when seen in the west after sunset).

Vesta, Vestoria Vesta was the Roman goddess of the hearth.

Vevina, Vevin, Vevan Irish Gaelic; fair lady.

Vianna Anna with the *Vi-* prefix.

Vicki A form of Victoria. Occasional use from 1955.

Vickie A form of Victoria. Occasional use 1965–75.

Vicky A form of Victoria. Occasional use from 1950 peaking in 1985. *Other forms*: Vicki, Vickie, Vikki.

Victoria Latin; victory. Light use from 1900, peaking in heavy use in 1980. *Other forms*: Vicki, Vickie, Vicky, Victorine, Viki, Vikie, Vikki, Vita, Vitoria, Viqui. *Variants*: Bittore, Bixenta (Basque); Boudicca (Celtic); Viktorie, Viktorka (Czech); Viktorija (Dutch); Victoire, Victorine (French); Viktoria (German); Nike (Greek); Wikolia (Hawaiian); Vittoria, Vittorina (Italian); Viktorija (Latvian, Lithuanian); Viktoria (Norwegian); Wikitoria, Wisia (Polish); Vitoria (Portuguese); Tora, Vika, Viktoria, Viktoriushka (Russian); Bhictoria (Scottish Gaelic); Viki (Serbo-Croatian); Toya, Victorina, Viqui, Vita, Vittoria (Spanish); Viktoria (Swedish).

Vida Spanish; life. Occasional use 1935–55.

Vikki A form of Victoria. Occasional use from 1970 peaking in 1980.

Vimala Sanskrit; pure.

Vinaya Sanskrit; behaving properly.

Vinca Latin; periwinkle. From the name of the flowering plant.

Viola Latin; violet.

Violet Middle English; from the flower name. Heavy use in 1900, but then declining and falling out of use by 1985. *Other forms*: Vi, Viola, Violeta, Violetta, Violette, Voleta, Yolanda. *Variants*: Viola, Viole, Violette (French); Violetta (Italian); Violante (Spanish).

Virginia Latin; maidenly. Occasional use from 1950 peaking in 1965. *Other forms*: Ginnie, Ginny, Virgie.

Variants: Virginie (French); Vegenia (Hawaiian); Gina (Italian); Ginata, Ginetta (Spanish).

Vita Latin; life.

Vitara A blend of Vita and Tara.

Vitesse French; swiftness.

Viveka Sanskrit; discrimination.

Vivian A form of Vivien. Occasional use 1900–60. *Variant*: Beibhinn (Irish Gaelic). (See Gender-neutral names.)

Vivien Latin; alive, lively. Occasional use from 1925 peaking in 1950. *Other forms*: Bibiana, Fithian, Vevay, Viv, Viveca, Vivi, Vivian, Vivie, Vivienne, Vyvyan. *Variants*: Vivienne (French); Viviane (German); Viviana (Italian). (See Gender-neutral names.)

Vivienne A form of Vivien. Occasional use from 1900, peaking in 1950 and falling out of use in 1980.

Voda Czech; water.

Volanta, Volante Italian; flying.

Voleta French; flowing veil.

Vondra Czech; loving woman.

Vonora A blend of Vona (Wanda) and Nora.

W

Wadena Ojibwa; little round hill.

Wahida Arabic; unique.

Wairua Maori; soul.

Wakana Sioux; holy woman.

Wakanda Sioux; power of the spirit.

Walida Arabic; new-born girl.

Wanda Slavonic; traveller. Occasional use from 1955. *Other forms*: Vanda, Vona, Wandy, Wenda, Wendeline.

Variants: Wanaka, Wanika (Hawaiian); Vanda (Italian); Wandzia (Polish); Vanda (Russian); Wanja (Swedish).

Waneta Native American; one who charges about.

Wanetta Old English; young pale one.

Waratah Tasmanian; a place-name on the island of Tasmania.

Wasima Arabic; pretty.

Wauna Miwok; snow geese calling as they fly overhead.

Wayah Cherokee; wolf.

Wenda Welsh; fair and good.

Wendelin, Wendelene Old English; wanderer. *Other forms*: Wendaline, Wendelle.

Wendy Probably invented by J. M. Barrie for the heroine of his play *Peter Pan*. He based the name upon the nickname Fwendy-Wendy (a pet form of friend) given to him by a child he met. There was also a German name Wendelgard, and this may have had Wendy as a short form. But even if the name was not originated by Barrie, it was certainly popularized by the success of his play. Light use from 1925, peaking in heavy use in 1960 and then declining into occasional use. *Other forms*: Wendi, Wendie, Wendye.

Wenona Old English; joy.

Wesla Old English; west meadow.

Whitley Middle English; white glade.

Whitney Old English; white island. *Other forms*: Whitne, Whitnee, Whitneigh, Whitnie, Whytne, Whytny, Witney. (See Gender-neutral names.)

Wilhelmina A German feminine form of William. *Other forms*: Billie, Mina, Minnie, Williamina. *Variants*: Vilhelmine (Danish); Valma (Finnish); Guillemette,

Guillelmine, Vilette (French); Helmine, Minna, Wilhelmine, Wilma (German); Guglielma (Italian); Vilma (Russian); Vilhelmina, Minka (Slavonic); Guillelmina (Spanish); Vilhelmina (Swedish).

Willa Old English; desirable.

Willow Old English; from the tree name, hence slender and graceful. Occasional use from 1980. *Other forms*: Willoe, Wyllow, Wyloe, Wylow. (See Gender-neutral names.)

Wilona Old English; desired.

Winema Native American; woman chief.

Winifred Welsh; blessed reconciliation. Heavy use in 1900 but then declined and fell out of use in 1965. There were small revivals in 1980 and 1990. *Other forms*: Freda, Fredi, Vinette, Wenefreda, Win, Winefred, Winnie, Winny, Wyn, Wynelle, Wynette, Wynne. *Variants*: Jenifry (Cornish); Venefrida (Italian).

Winnie A form of Winifred. Occasional use 1900–35. (See Gender-neutral names.)

Winola Old German; gracious friend.

Winona, Winonah Sioux; first-born daughter. *Other form*: Wynona. Popularized by H. L. Gordon's poem *Winona*.

Wira Celtic; lady of the castle.

Wynema, Winema Moquelumnan; woman chief.

Wynn Welsh; white, pure. *Other forms*: Wynette, Wynne.

Wyshe Old German; desire, aspiration.

X

Xandra A Spanish form of Alexandra.

Xanthe, Xan Greek; golden yellow. *Other forms*: Xantia, Xanthia, Zan.

Xela Mayan; my mountain home.

Xena, Xenia Greek; hospitable.

Xia Chinese; the name of the first dynasty in Chinese history.

Ximena Greek; heroine. *Variant*: Chimene (French).

Xylla A form of Sylvia.

Y

Yael, Yaelle Hebrew; mountain deer.

Yahala Seminole; an orange.

Yakima A Native American tribal name.

Yakira Hebrew; precious, beloved.

Yama Sanskrit; path, way. *Variant*: Yana (Pali).

Yamina Arabic; right, proper.

Yana A Russian form of Joanna. *Other form*: Yanni.

Yancey, Yancie Dutch; daughter of John. (See Gender-neutral names.)

Yaren Nauruan; from Yaren, the capital of Nauru.

Yarrow From the name of the plant.

Yasmeen Farsi; flower.

Yasmin Persian; from the flower name. Occasional use from 1965. *Other forms*: Jasmin, Jasmine, Yasmine, Yasmyne. *Variant*: Jessamine (French).

Yasna Arabic; flower. *Other forms*: Yaz, Yesenia, Yesna.

Yasu Japanese; tranquil.

Yazata Avesta; worthy of praise.

Yeda Hebrew; heart's ease.

Yedda Old English; singer.

Yelena Latin; lily blossom.

Yetta Old German; mistress of the house.

Yocona Probably Choctaw; reach.

Yoko Japanese; positive child, girl.

Yola A Spanish form of Yolanda.

Yolanda Greek; violet flower. Occasional use from 1980. *Other forms*: Eolande, Iolanthe, Jolanda, Jolenta, Olinda, Yola, Yolande, Yolana, Yolanta, Yolanthe. *Variants*: Yolande (French); Iolanthe (German); Iolana, Iolani (Hawaiian); Jolanka (Hungarian); Iolande, Jolanda (Italian); Jola, Jolanta (Polish); Yola (Spanish).

Yolandra A blend of Yolanda and Sandra.

Yolantha A blend of Yolanda and Samantha.

Yolara A blend of Yolanda and Lara.

Yona Hebrew; dove.

Yootha A form of Ute, an old German name meaning prosperity.

Yovela, Yovella Hebrew; rejoicing.

Ysanne A blend of Ysabel (Isabel) and Anne.

Yula Celtic; altar. *Other form*: Ula.

Yulan Chinese; jade orchid.

Yva A character in the novel *2061: Odyssey Three* by Arthur C. Clarke.

Yvelda A blend of Yvette and Velda.

Yvette Old French; archer. Occasional use 1960–75. *Variants*: Iveta (Czech); Evette, Ivette (French); Yvetta (Italian); Ivona (Russian).

Yvonne Scandinavian; archer. Light use from 1925, peaking in 1955 and falling out of use in 1990. *Other forms*: Evona, Evonne. *Variants*: Evonne (French); Iwona (Polish); Ivone (Portuguese); Ivona (Russian).

Z

Zabrina Old English; noble maiden. *Other forms*: Zabrena, Zabryna.

Zada Arabic; lucky.

Zadah Arabic; prosperous.

Zadina A blend of Zadah and Dina (Dinah).

Zadora A form of Isadora.

Zafirah Arabic; successful.

Zahara Swahili; flower.

Zaheera Hebrew; golden.

Zahira, Zahirah Arabic; luminous, shining.

Zahra Arabic; blossom.

Zaida Spanish; heron. *Other form*: Zaiga.

Zaka Hebrew; bright, clear.

Zakira, Zakina Arabic; remembrance.

Zakiya Arabic; intelligent.

Zala Spanish; greeting.

Zalika Swahili; born to royalty.

Zalina A blend of Zala and Lina.

Zamarra Spanish; shepherd's coat.

Zamia The Jamaica sago tree.

Zamira, Zamyra Hebrew; song.

Zamora A form of Samora.

Zana A character in the novel *Unbalanced Earth* by Jonathan Wylie.

Zande Zande; the name of a tribe in West Central Africa.

Zandina A form of Sandina.

Zandora A Slavonic form of Alexandra.

Zandra A form of Xandra. *Other form*: Zondra.

Zanina A blend of Zanna and Nina.

Zanna A Latvian form of Jane. *Other forms*: Zanetta, Zhane.

Zante From the name of the Greek island.

Zara Arabic; splendour, brightness of the dawn. Occasional use from 1970. *Other forms*: Zarah, Zaretta, Zayra.

Zaranda A blend of Zara and Amanda. *Other form*: Zarantra.

Zareba Arabic; in the (sheep)fold, hence protected.

Zareena, Zarina Persian; golden.

Zarella, Zarala Blends of Zara and Ella.

Zaria Slavonic; dawn.

Zarifa Arabic; graceful.

Zarina, Zahrina Spanish; empress.

Zarisa, Zariza, Zarissa Hebrew; industrious.

Zarita A blend of Zara and Rita.

Zarona A blend of Zara and Rona.

Zathara Invented for an American radio soap opera in the 1930s.

Zayante A Native American personal name of uncertain meaning.

Zayna, Zaynah Arabic; beautiful. *Other form*: Zaina.

Zaza Hebrew; movement. *Other forms*: Zazie, Zazy.

Zea Latin; the herb rosemary.

Zebrina From the name of the flowering herb.

Zefira Italian; breeze, zephyr. *Other forms*: Zefyra, Zephyra.

Zehara Hebrew; light.

Zehira Hebrew; protected.

Zeira Aramaic; small.

Zelda A form of Griselda. Old German; grey battle.

Zelene Old English; sunshine.

Zelenka Czech; innocent.

Zelia Latin; zealous. *Other forms*: Zeyla, Zillah.

Zelinda Hebrew/Latin; beautiful dawn.

Zelinka A Slavonic form of Zelia.

Zelma A form of Selma.

Zemela Phrygian; honey-laden. The name of the
  Phrygian earth goddess.

Zemira Hebrew; song of joy. *Other forms*: Zemirah,
  Zemora.

Zemirah Hebrew; song of joy. *Other form*: Zemora.

Zena Persian; woman. Occasional use from 1925.
  Other forms: Azena, Zenia.

Zenda Persian; sacred. (See Gender-neutral names.)

Zenka Slavonic; ice glade.

Zenna Persian; woman.

Zephira Hebrew; morning.

Zephyra Greek; soft gentle breeze. In Greek mythology
  Zephuros was the god of the west wind.

Zera Hebrew; seeds.

Zerdali Swahili; wild apricot.

Zerelda A blend of Zera and Imelda.

Zerlina Old German; serene beauty.

Zerlinda Hebrew/Spanish; beautiful dawn.

Zeta Hebrew; an olive.

Zetsi Nepalese; first daughter.

Zetta Greek; sixth born.

Zeva Greek; sword.

Zeyla A form of Zelia.

Zhenya A form of the Russian name Yevgenia, a feminine version of Eugene.

Zia Arabic; light.

Ziana Hebrew; abundance. *Other form*: Zindzi.

Ziazan Armenian; rainbow.

Zigena, Zigana Hungarian; gypsy girl.

Zimra Hebrew; song.

Zina Nsenga; spirit name.

Zinevra Celtic; white wave.

Zingara Italian; gypsy.

Ziona, Zeona Hebrew; excellent. *Other forms*: Zina, Zinnia.

Zira Hebrew; arena.

Zita Spanish; a rose.

Ziva Greek; to seek. Or Hebrew; shine brightly. *Other forms*: Zivara, Zivarah.

Zivana Slavonic; lively.

Zoanna A character in the novel *Orc's Opal* by Piers Anthony and Robert E. Margroff.

Zoe Greek; life. Occasional use from 1900, peaking in light use in 1975, then declining but rising again in 1990. *Other forms*: Zoey, Zowie. *Variants*: Zoa (French); Zoia, Zoya (Russian).

Zohara Hebrew; radiant light.

Zohreh Persian; happiness.

Zola Greek; duty.

Zona Latin; sound.

Zonta, Zontah Sioux; trustworthy.

Zora Arabic; dawn. *Other forms*: Zorah, Zorana.

Zorana A blend of Zora and Ana (Ann).

Zorella, Zorelle Blends of Zora and Ella.

Zorina, Zorene Slavonic; golden sunrise.

Zorita Spanish; wood pigeon.

Zowie A form of Zoe. Occasional use 1980–5.

Zoya A Russian form of Zoe.

Zuleika Arabic; beautiful. *Variant*: Suleika (German).

Zulema, Zulima Arabic; peace. *Variant*: Zulemita (Spanish).

Zumaya Spanish; barn owl. *Other form*: Zuma.

Zylpha Hebrew; sprinkling. *Other form*: Zyla.

A-Z names for boys

A

Aaron Hebrew; high mountain. Occasional use from 1925 peaking in light use in 1990. *Other forms*: Ahron, Ari, Arnie, Aron, Ronnie. *Variants*: Haroun (Arabic); Aronne (German); Aharon (Hebrew); Aron (Irish); Aronne (Italian); Aronek (Polish); Aarao (Portuguese); Aronos (Russian).

Abdul Arabic; servant of God. *Variant*: Abdala (Swahili).

Abiel Hebrew; God is my father.

Abraham Hebrew; father of a multitude. Occasional use from 1900 until 1970. *Other forms*: Abe, Abram, Avram, Bram. *Variants*: Ibrahim (Arabic); Bram (Dutch); Avram (Greek); Avraham (Hebrew); Abrahamo, Abramo (Italian); Abrao (Portuguese); Abrahan, Abran (Spanish); Arram (Swedish).

Adair Scottish Gaelic; oak tree ford.

Adam Hebrew; red earth. Occasional use from 1900 falling out of use in 1935. Revived in 1955 and then rose steadily into heavy use by 1990. *Other forms*: Adan, Addison, Adom, Edom. *Variants*: Adamek, Damek (Czech); Aatami (Finnish); Adi (Hebrew); Adrien (Hungarian); Adhamh (Irish Gaelic); Adamo (Italian); Adomas (Lithuanian); Adas, Adok (Polish); Adao (Portuguese); Adamka, Adas (Russian); Edom, Keady, Keddy (Scottish); Adhamh (Scottish Gaelic); Adan

(Spanish); Adem (Turkish); Adda (Welsh).

Adar Arabic; ruler, prince.

Adiel Hebrew; ornament of God.

Adrian Latin; man from Hadria in northern Italy. Light use from 1900 peaking in heavy use in 1965. *Other forms*: Ade, Adrien, Arne, Arnie. *Variants*: Adrien (French); Adorjan (Hungarian); Adriano (Italian); Adriao (Portuguese); Andreyan, Andri (Russian); Adriano (Spanish); Hadrian (Swedish).

Adriel Hebrew; God is my majesty.

Aerion Welsh; heir.

Aeron Welsh; battle. (See Gender-neutral names.)

Aidan Scottish Gaelic; fire. Occasional use from 1955 peaking in 1990. *Other forms*: Aiden, Eden. *Variants*: Aodren (Breton); Edan (Irish Gaelic); Aodh (Scottish Gaelic); Addan (Welsh).

Aiden A form of Aidan. Occasional use 1965–85.

Ainsley Scottish Gaelic; one's own meadow. *Other form*: Ainslie.

Akbar Arabic; praised.

Akeem Nigerian; most wise.

Akron Greek; summit.

Alan Possibly Scottish Gaelic; bright, handsome. Light use from 1900, peaking in very heavy use in 1950 and then declining into occasional use by 1990. *Other forms*: Al, Alain, Alein, Aleyn, Allan, Allen, Allyn, Alun. *Variants*: Alain (French); Ailin (Irish Gaelic); Alano (Italian, Spanish); Alao (Portuguese); Ailean (Scottish Gaelic); Alun (Welsh).

Alaric Old German; noble ruler.

Alastair A Scottish Gaelic form of Alexander. Occasional use from 1935, peaking in 1985. *Other forms*: Alistair, Alister. *Variant*: Alasdair (Scottish Gaelic).

Alben Latin; fair-haired. *Other forms*: Alban, Alby. *Variants*: Albin (Breton); Aubin (French); Binek (Polish); Alva (Spanish).

Albert Old German; noble-bright, illustrious. Very heavy use at its peak in 1900 but then steadily declined into occasional use by 1990. *Other forms*: Albie, Bert, Bertie, Del, Elbet, Elvert, Halbert, Hobbie, Imbert. *Variants*: Albertik (Czech); Aubert (French); Adalbert, Albrecht (German); Alvertos (Greek); Alberto (Italian, Spanish); Albek, Bertek (Polish); Ailbert (Scandinavian); Ailbeart (Scottish Gaelic).

Alden, Aldon Old English; elf hill down. *Variant*: Aldous (German).

Alder From the tree name.

Alec A form of Alexander. Occasional use from 1900.

Aled Probably Welsh; to pour forth.

Alex A form of Alexander. Occasional use from 1935 peaking in 1990.

Alexander Greek; protector of men. Light use from 1900 peaking in heavy use in 1990. *Other forms*: Alastair, Alec, Alek, Alex, Alexis, Alick, Alix, Eckie, Sander, Sandy, Zander. *Variants*: Alexan (Armenian); Alekka, Aleksandur, Sander (Bulgarian); Santo (Cornish); Alexandr, Lekso, Olexa (Czech); Iskander (Dari); Aleksander (Estonian); Alexandre, Sacha (French); Alik, Axel (German); Alexandros, Alekos, Zander (Greek); Alika (Hawaiian); Elek, Sandor (Hungarian); Alastar (Irish); Alsandair (Irish Gaelic); Alessandro, Lissandro, Sandro (Italian); Aleksandrs (Latvian); Alexandras (Lithuanian); Aleksander, Olek (Polish); Alexio (Portuguese); Alexandru (Romanian);

Aleksandr, Aleksei, Alexandr, Alexei, Olesko, Sasha, Sashenka, Shura (Russian); Alastair, Alistair (Scottish); Alasdair (Scottish Gaelic); Alejandro, Jandino, Jando (Spanish); Aleksander, Oleksander (Ukrainian).

Alfie A form of Alfred. Occasional use from 1965.

Alford Old English; elf ford.

Alfred Old English; elf, hence wise, counsel. Heavy use at its peak in 1900 but then declined steadily into occasional use by 1990. *Other forms*: Alf, Alfie, Avery, Fred, Freddie, Freddy. *Variants*: Ailfrid (Irish); Alfredo (Italian, Spanish).

Ali Arabic; greatest. (See Gender-neutral names.)

Alick A form of Alec. Occasional use 1935–65.

Alistair A form of Alastair. Occasional use from 1950 peaking in 1975.

Alister A form of Alastair. Occasional use 1935–85.

Allan A form of Alan. Occasional use 1900–85, peaking in light use in 1950.

Allen A form of Alan. Occasional use 1900–85.

Alon Hebrew; oak tree.

Alroy Scottish Gaelic; red-haired.

Alston Old English; elf stone.

Alton Old English; elf stream source.

Alun A Welsh form of Alan. Occasional use 1950–70.

Alvar Old German; elf army. *Variant*: Alvaro (Portuguese).

Alvin Old German; old friend. *Other forms*: Alvan, Alvyn, Alwyn. *Variants*: Aluin (French); Alwin (German); Alvino (Italian); Aluino (Spanish).

Alvis Old Norse; all knowing. *Other form*: Alvey.

Alwyn A form of Alvin. Occasional use from 1925. *Other forms*: Alwin, Aylwin, Elwyn.

Amal Arabic; hope.

Ambak Ndali; from Ambakisye, a name meaning God has been merciful.

Ambrose Greek; immortal. Occasional use 1900–70. *Other forms*: Ambie, Ambros, Amby, Brose, Emrys. *Variants*: Ambroz, Broz (Czech); Ambroise (French); Ambrosius (German); Ambros (Irish Gaelic); Ambrogio (Italian); Ambrozy, Mroz (Polish); Ambrosio (Spanish); Emrys (Welsh).

Amos Hebrew; troubled. Occasional use 1900–70.

Anan Hebrew; cloud.

Anand Sanskrit; happiness, bliss. (See Gender-neutral names.)

Anchali Taos; painter.

Anders Greek; manly.

Andre A French form of Andrew. Occasional use from 1965.

Andrew Greek; brave. Light use from 1900 peaking in very heavy use in 1965. *Other forms*: Anders, Anderson, Andie, Andre, Andrey, Andy, Dandie, Dando, Dandy, Drew, Tandy. *Variants*: Ander (Basque); Andrev (Breton); Andrei, Andrej (Bulgarian); Andrej, Ondro (Czech); Anker (Danish); Andries (Dutch); Antero (Finnish); Andre (French); Andreas (German); Andreas, Evagelos (Greek); Analu (Hawaiian); Andor, Andras (Hungarian); Aindreas, Aindriu (Irish Gaelic); Andrea (Italian); Andrejs (Latvian); Andrius (Lithuanian); Anders (Norwegian); Andrzej, Jedrek (Polish); Andres (Portuguese); Andrei (Romanian); Andrei, Andrik (Russian); Aindrea, Anndra (Scottish Gaelic); Andres, Necho (Spanish);

Anders (Swedish); Andriuy (Ukrainian); Andras (Welsh).

Angelo An Italian form of Angel. Greek; being of light, angel.

Ango Cornish; blacksmith.

Angus Scottish Gaelic; unique choice. Occasional use from 1965. *Other forms*: Ennis, Gus. *Variants*: Aengus (Irish Gaelic); Aonghas (Scottish Gaelic).

Annan Scottish Gaelic; one who lives by the river.

Ansel Old German; divine helmet, hence protected by God. *Other form*: Anselm. *Variants*: Anselme (French); Anselmo, Elmo (Italian, Spanish); Anzelm (Polish).

Anson Old English; son of Ann.

Anthony From the Roman family name Antonius. Light use from 1900, rising steadily and peaking in very heavy use in 1965. *Other forms*: Antone, Antony, Nanty, Tony. *Variants*: Andoni (Basque); Antonin (Czech); Antoine (French); Anton (German); Andonis, Tonis (Greek); Akoni (Hawaiian); Antal (Hungarian); Antain (Irish Gaelic); Antonio (Italian); Antavas (Lithuanian); Antoni, Tonek (Polish); Antin, Tusya (Russian); Antjuan (Spanish).

Antony A form of Anthony. Occasional use from 1925 peaking in light use in 1960.

Anyon Celtic; anvil. *Variants*: Enyon (Cornish); Einion (Welsh).

Ara Old German; eagle. Or Maori; path, awake. (See Gender-neutral names.)

Aramis A character in the novel *The Three Musketeers* by Alexandre Dumas.

Aran Thai; forest.

Archer Old English; bowman.

Ardal Irish Gaelic; high valour.

Ardan Irish Gaelic; tall fellow.

Arden Latin; enthusiastic.

Ardley Old English; the home meadow.

Argyle Scottish Gaelic; place of the Gaels.

Arial Welsh; vigour, courage.

Ariel Hebrew; lion of God. (See Gender-neutral names.)

Arley, Arleigh Hebrew; pledge. *Variants*: Arlen (Irish); Arles (Scandinavian).

Arlin Old German; eagle wood. *Other form*: Arlen.

Arlo Old English; fortified hill.

Armand, Armin Old German; warrior. *Variants*: Hermann (German); Armando (Italian); Mandek (Polish); Arman (Russian); Armondo (Spanish).

Armon Hebrew; castle.

Arno Old German; eagle wolf.

Arnold Old German; strong as an eagle. Occasional use 1900–70. *Other forms*: Arnald, Arnell, Arne, Arness, Arnet, Arney, Arnie, Arno, Arnot, Arny, Ernald. *Variants*: Arnaud (French); Arndt (German); Arno, Arnoldo (Italian); Arnaldo (Spanish); Arnallt (Welsh).

Arnon Hebrew; roaring waters.

Arran From the name of the Scottish island. Occasional use from 1955. *Other forms*: Arron, Aryn.

Arthur Possibly Celtic; bear. Or Irish Gaelic; stone. Very heavy use at its peak in 1900, but then declined and fell out of use by 1970. There was a small revival in 1990. *Other forms*: Art, Artie, Artur, Azor, MacArthur. *Variants*: Artis (Czech); Arto (Finnish); Artus (French); Athanasios, Thanos (Greek); Artur (Irish Gaelic);

Arturo, Turi (Italian, Spanish); Artek (Polish); Atur (Scandinavian); Artair (Scottish Gaelic).

Arun Hindi; sun.

Arvin Old German; man of the people.

Arwel Welsh; prominent.

Aryn Possibly a form of Arran.

Asa Hebrew; healer. (See Gender-neutral names.)

Asgard Old Norse; hall of the gods. Asgard was the abode of the gods in Scandinavian mythology.

Ashby Old English; farm by the ash trees.

Asher Hebrew; happy, blessed. (See Gender-neutral names.)

Ashford Old English; river crossing by the ash trees.

Ashley Old English; ash wood. Occasional use from 1900 rising into light use by 1990. *Other form*: Ash. (See Gender-neutral names.)

Ashton Old English; ash tree village. Occasional use in 1900 and then fell out of use until there was a small revival in 1980.

Aspen Old German; from the name of the tree in the poplar family. (See Gender-neutral names.)

Aston Old English; eastern village.

Astor Irish Gaelic; loved one.

Athol Scottish Gaelic; juniper tree.

Auberon Old German; little elf ruler. *Other form*: Oberon.

Aubin Latin; fair.

Aubrey Old German; elf ruler. Occasional use 1900–70. *Other forms*: Aelfric, Alberic, Auberon, Avery, Oberon. *Variants*: Auberi (French); Alberich (German); Alberik (Swedish). (See Gender-neutral names.)

Aulay A Scottish Gaelic form of Olaf. *Variants*: Amhlaibh (Scottish Gaelic).

Aurek Polish; golden-haired.

Austen A form of Austin. Occasional use in 1925 and again 1980–5.

Austin Latin; majestic. Occasional use from 1900. *Other forms*: August, Augustine, Austen, Gus. *Variants*: Tauno (Finnish); Auguste (French); August (German); Aguistin, Oistin (Irish Gaelic); Agostino (Italian); Augustyn (Polish); Avgust (Russian); Augusto (Spanish); Awstin (Welsh).

Avery A form of Alfred. (See Gender-neutral names.)

Axton Old English; stone for sharpening axes.

Ayrton Old English; village on the river Aire.

B

Bailey Old French; outer courtyard of a castle.

Baird Scottish Gaelic; minstrel. *Variants*: Barde (French); Bard (Irish Gaelic).

Balfour Scottish Gaelic; from the Gaelic greeting meaning the blessings of God on the harvest.

Balin Old English; valiant.

Bamber Old English; from the place-name meaning Bimme's bridge.

Barclay Old English; birch meadow.

Barden Old English; valley where barley is grown.

Barnaby Hebrew; son of consolation. Occasional use from 1970. *Other forms*: Barnabas, Barney, Barnie, Barny, Burnaby. *Variants*: Barnaba (Czech); Barnabe (French); Barna (Hungarian); Barnaib (Irish Gaelic); Barnaba, Barna (Italian); Bernabe (Spanish); Barinthus (Welsh).

Barnum Old English; barley storehouse.

Barrie A form of Barry. Occasional use from 1925, peaking in 1950. (See Gender-neutral names.)

Barrington Old English; village of Beorn's (or Bara's) people. Occasional use 1925–80.

Barry Irish Gaelic; like a spear. Light use from 1925 peaking in heavy use in 1950 and then declining. *Other forms*: Barri, Barrie, Barrington, Barris. *Variants*: Baz, Bazza (Australian); Barri (Welsh).

Bartholomew Aramaic; son of Tolmai. Occasional use from 1925. *Other forms*: Bardo, Bart, Bartel, Barth, Bartle, Bartlett, Bartold, Barton, Bertel, Meo, Tolly, Tolomey. *Variants*: Bartek (Czech); Bardo (Danish); Bartholomeus (Dutch); Barthelemy (French); Bartel, Bertel (German); Bartal, Bartos (Hungarian); Bairtlimead (Irish Gaelic); Bartolo, Bartolomeo (Italian); Bartek, Barthel (Polish); Varfolomei (Russian); Parlan (Scottish Gaelic); Jerney (Slovenian); Bartoli, Bartolome, Toli (Spanish); Barthelemy (Swedish).

Barton Old English; village near the barley field.

Basil Greek; kingly. Occasional use 1900–50. *Other forms*: Basile, Baz. *Variants*: Bazil, Vasil (Czech); Basile (French); Basle (German); Vasilis (Greek); Bazel (Hungarian); Breasal (Irish Gaelic); Basilio (Italian); Bazek (Polish); Vassily, Vasya (Russian); Basilius (Swedish).

Beavis Old English; strong as an ox. *Other forms*: Bevis, Beavys.

Bede Old English; prayer.

Bellamy French; fair friend.

Bello Fultani; helper or promoter of Islam.

Ben A form of Benjamin. Occasional use from 1950

peaking in light use in 1990. *Other forms*: Bennie, Benny, Benson.

Benedict Latin; to bless. Occasional use from 1965. *Other forms*: Bendix, Benet, Beniton, Bennett, Benny, Dix. *Variants*: Benoit (French); Benedikt (German); Benedek (Hungarian); Benedetto (Italian); Benek (Polish); Venedikt, Venya (Russian); Bengt (Scandinavian); Benneit (Scottish Gaelic); Benito (Spanish).

Benjamin Hebrew; son of my right hand. Occasional use from 1900 until it fell out of use in 1955. Revived in 1965 and rose steadily into heavy use by 1990. *Other forms*: Ben, Benji, Bennie, Benny, Yemin. *Variants*: Benkamin (Basque); Veniamin (Bulgarian); Beni (Finnish); Verniamin (Greek); Peni, Peniamina (Hawaiian); Beinish, Binyamin (Hebrew); Beno (Hungarian); Beircheart (Irish Gaelic); Beniamino (Italian); Benjamins (Latvian); Beniamin (Polish, Romanian); Venyamin (Russian); Beatham (Scottish Gaelic); Benja, Mincho (Spanish).

Benson Son of Benjamin.

Beren Old German; bear spear.

Bernard Old German; bold as a bear. Light use from 1900 peaking in 1925. *Other forms*: Barn (Australian), Barnard, Barnet, Barney, Barret, Bern, Berni, Bernie, Bernis, Levar. *Variants*: Bernez (Breton); Bernek (Czech); Barnard, Bernadin (French); Berend, Bernhard (German); Vernados (Greek); Bernat (Hungarian); Bernardo, Bernardino (Italian); Bernardyn (Polish); Bergards (Russian); Bernt, Bjorn (Scandinavian); Bearnard (Scottish and Irish Gaelic); Barnardo, Nardo (Spanish).

Bert A form of Robert, Hubert or Albert. Occasional use 1900–50 peaking in 1925. *Other forms*: Bertie, Berty, Burt.

Bertie A form of Robert, Hubert or Albert. Occasional use from its peak in 1900 to 1950.

Bertram Old German; bright raven. Occasional use 1900–60. *Other forms*: Bertie, Bertran, Bertrand, Bertrem. *Variants*: Bertrand (French); Bertrando (Italian); Beltran (Spanish).

Bevan Welsh; son of Evan.

Bill A form of William. Occasional use 1965–85.

Billy A form of William. Occasional use from 1950 peaking in 1990. *Other form*: Bill.

Birch From the tree name. Old English; white.

Blade Celtic; glory.

Blaine Scottish Gaelic; yellow-haired. Occasional use from 1965. *Other form*: Blayne.

Blair Scottish Gaelic; clearing. Occasional use from 1965.

Blake Old English; pale, shining. (See Gender-neutral names.)

Bo Chinese; precious. (See Gender-neutral names.)

Bobby A form of Robert. Occasional use from 1980. *Other form*: Bob.

Boden French; herald.

Bogart Celtic; marshlands.

Bojan Czech; battle.

Bonar Old French; courteous, gentle.

Booker Old English; scholar, bookman.

Boone Old French; good.

Borden Old English; from the boar's den.

Boris Russian; warrior.

Bowen Celtic; son of Owen.

Bowie Celtic; yellow-haired.

Boyd Scottish Gaelic; yellow hair. Occasional use 1955–65.

Bracken Old Norse; fern, bracken.

Braden Irish Gaelic; salmon.

Bradley Old English; broad meadow. Occasional use from 1960 peaking in light use in 1990. *Other forms*: Brad, Braden.

Brady Old English; broad island.

Bramble Old English; blackberry.

Bramley Old English; clearing where broom grows.

Bran Welsh; raven.

Brandon Old English; hill covered with broom.

Brannan Irish Gaelic; sad raven.

Brannock Irish Gaelic; young raven. *Variants*: Brannoc (Cornish); Brynach (Welsh).

Branson From the place-name Branston. Old English; Bran's farm.

Brant Old German; fiery.

Branton Old English; Bran's village.

Branwell Cornish; raven's well.

Braxton Old English; Brock's village.

Brecon Welsh; king.

Brendan Possibly Irish Gaelic; raven. Occasional use from 1950. *Other forms*: Bramwell, Bran, Brand, Brandon, Brant, Brendon, Brennan.

Brendon A form of Brendan. Occasional use 1955–85.

Brent Old English; high place. Occasional use from 1960.

Brenton Old English; high town.

Brett Latin; a Briton. (See Gender-neutral names.)

Brewster Middle English; brewer.

Brian Possibly Irish Gaelic; strong. Light use from 1925, peaking in very heavy use in 1935 and then declining into occasional use by 1990. *Other forms*: Briant, Briar, Brien, Brion, Bryan, Byron. *Variants*: Brien (French); Briano (Italian); Palaina (Hawaiian).

Briar Greek; strong.

Brioc From the Romano-British name Brigacos and in the form Bryok the name of a Welsh saint. *Variants*: Brieuc (Breton); Breock (Cornish); Breok, Bryock (Welsh).

Brion A character in the novel *Deryni Rising* by Katherine Kurtz.

Brishan Romany; born in the rain.

Britt A form of Brett. (See Gender-neutral names.)

Brock, Broc Old English; a badger.

Brody From the barony of Brodie.

Bromley Old English; brown clearing. *Other form*: Brom.

Bron Afrikaans; source.

Bronson Old English; son of the brown-haired man.

Brook, Brooks Old English; dweller by the stream. (See Gender-neutral names.)

Bruce French; woods. Occasional use from 1900 peaking in 1960. *Other forms*: Brucey, Brucie.

Bruno Italian; brown-haired.

Bryan A form of Brian. Occasional use 1925–85 peaking in 1935.

Bryce Welsh; alert. *Other form*: Brice.

Bryden Old English; bird valley.

Brymer Old English; bright.

Bryn Irish Gaelic; strength with virtue. Or Welsh; hill.

Brynmor Welsh; great hill.

Buck Old English; stag.

Buckley Old English; beech meadow.

Burgess Old English; town dweller.

Burke Old German; castle.

Burl Latin; coarse hair.

Burley Old English; clearing belonging to a fort or manor.

Burrell, Burr Middle English; prickly plant.

Burton Old English; bright fame.

Burwood Old English; wood on the hillside.

Busby, Buzz Old Norse; village in a thicket.

Byron Old English; barn. Occasional use from 1950 peaking in 1985. *Other form*: Biron.

C

Cabot Old English; barn where jackdaws gather.

Caddock Welsh; keen in battle.

Cadell, Cade Welsh; warrior. *Other forms*: Cadoc, Caddock.

Cadern Welsh; strong in battle.

Cador Cornish; warrior.

Cael A form of Caelan, a Scottish version of Nicholas.

Cai A Welsh form of Caius, a Roman name meaning to rejoice. *Variants*: Ke, Kaie (Breton).

Caird Scottish Gaelic; blacksmith.

Calayan Ilocano; the name of an island in the Philippines.

Caleb Hebrew; dog, hence loyal, faithful.

Callum A Scottish Gaelic form of Columba, a Latin name

meaning dove. Light use from 1985. *Other form*: Calum.

Calum A form of Callum. Occasional use from 1965 peaking in 1990.

Calvin Latin; bald. Occasional use 1955–85. *Other forms*: Cal, Calvyn, Vinnie. *Variant*: Calvino (Italian).

Cameron Celtic; bent nose. Occasional use from 1965 peaking in 1990. *Other form*: Camron. (See Gender-neutral names.)

Camlo Romany; handsome, lovable. *Other form*: Camlan.

Candan Turkish; sincere.

Caradoc Celtic; beloved. *Variant*: Caradawg (Welsh).

Caramon A character in the novel *Time of the Twins* by Margaret Weis and Tracy Hickman.

Carl A German form of Charles. Light use from 1925 peaking in 1980. *Variants*: Kale (Hawaiian); Carlo (Italian); Kalle (Scandinavian); Carlos (Spanish).

Carlin Scottish Gaelic; little champion.

Carlton Old English; Carl's village. Occasional use 1955–70. *Other form*: Carleton.

Carmody Manx Gaelic; god of arms.

Carney Irish Gaelic; victorious warrior. *Other form*: Kearney.

Carollan Irish Gaelic; little champion.

Carrick Irish Gaelic; a rock.

Carroll An Irish form of Charles. *Other form*: Carol. *Variants*: Karel (Czech); Karol (Polish). (See Gender-neutral names.)

Carson Old English; son of the marsh dweller. (See Gender-neutral names.)

Carter Old English; maker of carts. (See Gender-neutral names.)

Cary, Carey Old English; pleasant stream. (See Gender-neutral names.)

Casey Irish Gaelic; watchful. (See Gender-neutral names.)

Casimir Slavonic; he announces peace. *Other form*: Caz. *Variants*: Kazimir (Czech, German); Kazmer (Hungarian); Casimiro (Italian); Kazek, Kazimierz (Polish); Casimiro (Spanish).

Caspar Persian; treasurer. *Variants*: Gaspard (French); Kaspar (German); Gaspar (Hungarian); Gasparo (Italian); Kasper (Polish).

Cassidy Celtic; ingenious. (See Gender-neutral names.)

Cavan, Cavin Irish Gaelic; gentleness.

Cecil Latin; dim-sighted. Light use from its peak in 1900 to 1970. A name with so negative a meaning that it is unlikely to revive. *Variant*: Cecilio (Italian).

Cedar Greek; from the name of the coniferous tree with fragrant wood, once considered a sign of wealth in those who possessed things made from it. (See Gender-neutral names.)

Cedric A character in *Ivanhoe* by Sir Walter Scott. Occasional use 1900–50. *Other form*: Cedrick.

Ceejay A combination of the initials C and J.

Celestin Latin; heavenly.

Chad Celtic; warrior.

Chakotay Native American; a character in the television series *Star Trek: Voyager*.

Chan Sanskrit; shining.

Chandan Sanskrit; sandalwood paste.

Chandler Old English; candle maker.

Channing Old English; knowing.

Charles Old English; manly. Very heavy use at its peak in 1900 but then steadily declined into occasional use by 1970. In 1975 began to rise into light use again. *Other forms*: Carl, Carling, Carlisle, Carlton, Carroll, Cary, Cathal, Chad, Charlie, Chas, Chay, Chuck, Karl. *Variants*: Xarles (Basque); Karel, Karol (Czech); Karel (Dutch); Kaarle (Finnish); Charlot (French); Carl, Karl (German); Karoly (Hungarian); Searlas (Irish Gaelic); Carlo (Italian); Karlis (Latvian); Karol (Polish); Karlin (Russian); Tearlach (Scottish Gaelic); Carlos (Spanish); Kalle (Swedish); Siarl (Welsh).

Charlie A form of Charles. Occasional use 1900–25, and then from 1980 on. (See Gender-neutral names.)

Chase Old French; hunter.

Chauncey Latin; chance, luck.

Chayton Sioux; falcon.

Che A Spanish form of Joseph.

Chem, Chen Chinese; great, magnificent.

Chenac Karok; stream mouth.

Chesney French; oak grove.

Chester Latin; fort. *Other form*: Chet.

Chet Thai; brother.

Chetlo Chinook; oyster.

Chetwin Old English; going home along a winding path.

Chevy Welsh; ridge.

Cheyni French; oak tree.

Chico Nahuatl; poppy.

Chris A form of Christopher or Christian. (See Gender-neutral names.)

Christian Latin; a Christian. Occasional use from 1900 peaking in 1975. *Other forms*: Chris, Christie, Christy, Kerstan, Kit, Kreston, Kris, Krispin, Zan. *Variants*: Kristen (Danish); Chretien (Finnish); Christophe (French); Carsten, Krischan (German); Christianos, Kristos (Greek); Kerestel (Hungarian); Christiano (Italian); Krist (Norwegian); Crystek, Krystek, Krystian (Polish); Cristiano (Portuguese); Christie (Scottish); Kristian (Swedish). (See Gender-neutral names.)

Christopher Greek; one who carries Christ in his heart. Occasional use from 1900, rising steadily and peaking in very heavy use in 1990. *Other forms*: Chris, Christal, Christie, Christo, Christy, Chrystal, Cris, Gilchrist, Kester, Kit, Kris. *Variants*: Kristapor (Armenian); Kristofor (Bulgarian); Kitto (Cornish); Kristof, Krystof (Czech); Christoffer (Danish); Christofel (Dutch); Risto (Finnish); Christophe, Kristophe (French); Christoph, Kriss, Kristoph (German); Christophoros, Khristos (Greek); Kilikikopa (Hawaiian); Kristof (Hungarian); Criostal, Criostoir (Irish Gaelic); Cristoforo, Kristoforo (Italian); Kriss, Kristaps (Latvian); Krystupas (Lithuanian); Kristoffer (Norwegian); Krysztof (Polish); Cristovao (Portuguese); Cristofor (Romanian); Christofer, Khristofor (Russian); Christie, Kester (Scottish); Gille Criosd (Scottish Gaelic); Cristobal, Cristoval, Tobal, Tobalito (Spanish); Kristofer, Kristofor, Kristoff (Swedish); Khrystofor (Ukrainian).

Chumani Sioux; dewdrops.

Churstan Old English; church stone.

Cian Scottish Gaelic; long-lived.

Ciaran Irish Gaelic; dark-haired.

Clancy Irish Gaelic; tribe, clan.

Clarence Old English; from the place-name Clare in

Suffolk, probably named after a Celtic river. Occasional use 1900–35 then falling out of use. A small revival in 1965 was not sustained.

Clark Old English; secretary, scholar. Occasional use from 1970.

Claude Latin; from the Roman name Claudius, meaning lame. Occasional use from 1900 until it fell out of use in 1955 probably due to the unfortunate meaning. *Other form*: Claud. *Variants*: Claudius (Dutch); Claudian (German); Claudio (Italian, Spanish).

Clayton Old English; village built in clay land. Occasional use 1960–80. *Other forms*: Clay, Clayland.

Cleary Scottish Gaelic; scholar.

Clem A form of Clement. Latin; merciful. *Variants*: Clementius (Dutch); Klemens (German); Kelemen (Hungarian); Clemente (Italian, Spanish); Kliment (Russian); Cliamain (Scottish Gaelic). (See Gender-neutral names.)

Cleon Greek; famous.

Clifford Old English; a crossing near the cliff. Light use from 1900 peaking in 1925. *Other form*: Cliff.

Clifton Old English; village near the cliff.

Clint Old English; village on a hill. Occasional use 1960–80. *Other forms*: Clinton, Clynt.

Clive Old English; steep bank. Occasional use from 1925 peaking in light use in 1955. *Other forms*: Cleavon, Cleave, Cleveland, Clifford, Clifton.

Clovis Old German; famous warrior.

Clyde Welsh; heard from afar.

Coburn Middle English; small stream.

Cody Irish Gaelic; riches. (See Gender-neutral names.)

Colby Old English; dark-haired. (See Gender-neutral names.)

Colin A form of Nicholas. Light use from 1900 peaking in heavy use in 1960. *Other forms*: Colan, Collin. *Variants*: Coilean, Coilin, Colan (Irish Gaelic); Caelan, Cailean (Scottish Gaelic).

Colman Irish Gaelic; dove. *Other form*: Colm. *Variants*: Kolman (Czech); Colombain (French); Kalman (Hungarian); Columbano (Italian).

Colum Scottish Gaelic; dove.

Conal, Conlan Irish Gaelic; mighty.

Conan Irish Gaelic; wolf. *Variants*: Konan (Breton); Kenan (Cornish); Kynon (Welsh).

Conn Irish Gaelic; sense, intelligence.

Connor Irish Gaelic; high desire. Occasional use from 1955 peaking in 1990. *Other form*: Conor. *Variant*: Connaire (Irish Gaelic).

Conor A form of Connor. Occasional use from 1995.

Conrad Old German; brave counsel. Occasional use from 1900. *Other forms*: Konrad, Kurt. *Variants*: Cort (Danish); Curt, Koenraad (Dutch); Conrade (French); Konrad, Kort, Kurt (German); Corradino, Corrado (Italian); Conrado (Spanish).

Conroy Irish Gaelic; hound of the plain.

Conway Welsh; holy river.

Coran, Corran Irish Gaelic; boat.

Corbin, Corby, Corbet Old French; raven.

Cord, Corden Old French; craftsman in leather.

Corey, Cory Scottish Gaelic; ravine. (See Gender-neutral names.)

Coriander Greek; from the name of the herb.

Corin Probably Latin; spear. Occasional use 1965–75. *Other form*: Coryn.

Cormac Irish Gaelic; charioteer. *Variant*: Cormag (Scottish Gaelic).

Cornelius Latin; horn-coloured (hair). Occasional use from 1900. *Other forms*: Cornell, Cory. *Variants*: Cornell (French); Conchobhar (Irish Gaelic); Cornelio (Italian, Spanish); Kornel, Nelek (Polish).

Corwin Old English; heart's companion.

Cory, Corry Scottish Gaelic; ravine. *Other form*: Corey. (See Gender-neutral names.)

Courtney Latin; courtyard. (See Gender-neutral names.)

Craddock Welsh; amiable. *Variant*: Caradoc (Welsh).

Craig Celtic; rocky crag. Light use from 1950 peaking in heavy use in 1975. *Variants*: Creag, Creagh (Scottish Gaelic).

Cranford Old English; crane ford.

Cranston Old English; village where cranes gather.

Crary Welsh; pleasant stream.

Crawford Old English; crow ford.

Crispin Latin; curly-haired. *Other form*: Crispian. *Variants*: Krispijn (Dutch); Krispin (German); Crispino (Italian).

Crofton Irish Gaelic; village with cottages.

Cronan Greek; companion.

Curran Irish Gaelic; hero. *Other form*: Corran.

Curtis Latin; courtyard. Occasional use from 1960. *Other forms*: Courtland, Courtney, Curt. *Variant*: Curcio (Spanish). (See Gender-neutral names.)

Cymry Welsh; of Wales. (See Gender-neutral names.)

Cynan Welsh; great.

Cyprian Latin; from Cyprus. *Other form*: Zyprian. *Variants*: Cyprianus (German); Cipriano (Italian, Spanish).

Cyril Greek; lord, ruler. Light use from 1900, peaking in 1925 and falling out of use in 1965. *Other forms*: Ciro, Cy, Cyrill, Kyril. *Variants*: Kiril (Bulgarian); Cyrillus (Dutch); Cyrille (French); Kyrill (German); Kyriako (Greek); Ciorial, Coireall (Irish Gaelic); Cirillo (Italian); Kirill, Kiryl (Russian); Cyrillus (Scandinavian); Kiril (Slavonic); Cirilo, Ciro (Spanish). (See Gender-neutral names.)

Cyrus Persian; sun. *Other forms*: Cy, Cyris. *Variants*: Kir (Bulgarian); Ciro (Italian, Spanish).

D

Dacey Irish Gaelic; southerner. (See Gender-neutral names.)

Dagan Scandinavian; sunrise.

Dain Old English; hardy Dane.

Dakarai Shona; happiness.

Dakota Dakota; alliance of friends. From the name of the Dakota Native American nation, one of the three branches of the Sioux. (See Gender-neutral names.)

Dale Old English; from the valley. Occasional use from 1935 peaking in 1980. *Other forms*: Dael, Dallan, Dalton. *Variant*: Dalibor (Czech).

Daley Irish Gaelic; assembly. Occasional use from 1950.

Dallas Irish Gaelic; wise. (See Gender-neutral names.)

Dalton Old English; village in the valley.

Damian Greek; to tame. Occasional use from 1950 peaking in 1975. *Other form*: Damien. *Variants*: Damien

(French); Damjan (Hungarian); Damiano (Italian); Damiao (Portuguese); Damyan, Dema (Russian).

Damien A French form of Damian. Occasional use from 1970.

Damon Greek; to tame. Occasional use from 1980. *Other forms*: Darmon, Daymon, Daymond.

Danby Old Norse; from the Danish settlement.

Dando A form of Andrew.

Dane Old English; a Danish settler. Occasional use from 1975. *Variant*: Dayne (Scandinavian).

Danek A Polish form of Daniel.

Daniel Hebrew; God is my judge. Light use from 1900, rising rapidly from 1970 into very heavy use and peaking in 1990. *Other forms*: Dan, Dannie, Dannson, Danny, Dennel. *Variants*: Danel (Basque); Danil (Bulgarian); Danek, Dano (Czech); Dane (Dutch); Taneli (Finnish); Donois (French); Kana, Kanaiela (Hawaiian); Daneil, Dasco (Hungarian); Daniele (Italian); Daniels (Latvian); Danielus (Lithuanian); Danek (Polish); Danila (Romanian); Danil, Danila, Danilo, Danya (Russian); Dusan (Serbo-Croatian); Dani (Slovenian); Danilo, Nelo (Spanish); Danylko (Ukrainian); Deinol (Welsh).

Danny A form of Daniel. Occasional use from 1950. (See Gender-neutral names.)

Dante Latin; enduring. *Other form*: Donte.

Darcy Irish Gaelic; dark-haired. (See Gender-neutral names.)

Daren A form of Darren. Occasional use 1960–80 peaking in 1965.

Darin A form of Darren. Occasional use 1965–70.

Darius, Darian Persian; kingly. *Variant*: Dario (Italian).

Darnell Middle English; hidden nook.

Darran A form of Darren. Occasional use 1965–85.

Darrel A form of Darrell. Occasional use 1960–85.

Darrell Old English; grove of oak trees. Occasional use from 1925. *Other forms*: Darel, Darol, Darrel, Darrill, Darroll, Darry, Derrel, Derry.

Darren Old English; small rocky hill. Light use from 1960 peaking in very heavy use in 1970. *Other forms*: Daran, Daren, Darin, Darnell, Daron, Darran, Darrin, Darron, Darry. *Variant*: Dario (Italian).

Darrin A form of Darren. Occasional use in 1965.

Darron A form of Darren. Occasional use 1960–75.

Darryl A form of Daryl. Occasional use from 1955.

Darshan Sanskrit; seeing, grace. In the Hindu tradition, darshan is being in the presence of a holy or revered person.

Darvin A blend of Darren and Marvin.

Darwin, Darwyn Old English; river where oaks grow.

Daryl Old English; loved one. Occasional use from 1950. *Other forms*: Darryl, Daryll. (See Gender-neutral names.)

Daryll A form of Daryl. Occasional use from 1965.

Dasan Pomo; bird clan leader.

Dashell, Dashiell Possibly Old French; ash tree of the elves.

Daud Arabic; beloved. *Variants*: Daudi (East African); Dodi (Egyptian).

Daven Scandinavian; two rivers.

David Hebrew; beloved by God. Light use from 1900, peaking in very heavy use in 1950 and then declining into heavy use by 1990. *Other forms*: Dabney, Dave,

Davey, Davis, Davy, Dawes, Dawson, Dewey, Tab.
Variants: Daoud (Arabic); Tavid, Tavit (Armenian); Dabi
(Basque); Daveth, Davy (Cornish); Davidek (Czech);
Taaveti, Taavi (Finnish); Havika, Kavika, Kawika
(Hawaiian); Tevel (Hebrew); Daibhead, Daibhi (Irish
Gaelic); Davide, Davidde (Italian); Davids (Latvian);
Dovidas (Lithuanian); Davy (Manx Gaelic); Davi,
Dawid (Polish); Davi (Portuguese); Danya, Daveed,
Dodya (Russian); Dabhaidh (Scottish Gaelic); Dafydd,
Dai, Deio, Dewi (Welsh).

Davin Irish Gaelic; dear. *Variant*: Davon (American).

Davon An American form of Davin. *Other form*: Davell.

Dax French; water.

Dayton Old English; bright village.

Dean Old French; leader. Occasional use from 1925
peaking in light use in 1980. *Other forms*: Deane, Dene,
Denton. *Variant*: Dino (Italian).

Declan From the Irish saint's name of uncertain
meaning. Occasional use from 1990.

Dee Welsh; black. (See Gender-neutral names.)

Delaney Irish Gaelic; skilful warrior.

Delroy A form of Leroy, a French name meaning son of
the king. Occasional use from 1960.

Delshay Shay with the *Del-* prefix.

Delvin Greek; dolphin.

Demarco Marco with the *De-* prefix. *Other form*:
Demarcus.

Demario Mario with the *De-* prefix.

Dempsey Irish Gaelic; the proud one. *Other form*:
Dempster.

Denby Old Norse; Danish settlement.

Denholm Old English; home of the Dane.

Denis A form of Dennis. Occasional use 1900–85 peaking in light use in 1925.

Dennis A French form of Dionysus, the Greek god of wine. Light use from 1900 peaking in heavy use in 1925. On average this spelling has been about five times as popular as Denis. *Other forms*: Denis, Denison, Denny, Denzil, Dion, Dwight, Ennis. *Variants*: Denis, Deon, Dion (French); Dionys (German); Dionysus (Greek); Denes (Hungarian); Dionisio (Italian); Dionizy (Polish); Denka, Denya (Russian); Dionis, Nicho (Spanish).

Denton Old English; happy home.

Denver Old English; green valley.

Denzil From the Cornish place-name Denzell meaning high. Occasional use 1900–65. *Other form*: Denzel.

Derby Old English; deer park village. *Other form*: Darby. (See Gender-neutral names.)

Derek Old German; famous ruler. Light use from 1925 peaking in heavy use in 1935. *Other forms*: Darrick, Derick, Derrek, Derrick, Deryk, Dirk, Ricky. *Variants*: Diederick, Dirk (Dutch); Dietrich (German).

Deri Welsh; oak tree.

Derick A form of Derek. Occasional use 1925–80.

Dermot Scottish Gaelic; free of envy. Occasional use in the 1950s. *Variants*: Diarmaid (Irish Gaelic); Diarmid, Diarmuid (Scottish Gaelic).

Deron Hebrew; bird, hence a free spirit.

Derrick A form of Derek. Occasional use from its peak in 1925 to 1985.

Derry Irish Gaelic; red-haired. (See Gender-neutral names.)

Derwin, Derwyn Old German; animal lover.

Deshawn Shawn with the *De-* prefix.

Desmond Latin; the world. Occasional use from 1900 peaking in 1925. *Other forms*: Des, Desi, Dezi. *Variant*: Dezi (Spanish).

Deveren Celtic; dweller on the Ebura river.

Devin Celtic; poet. *Other form*: Devan.

Devlin Irish Gaelic; brave.

Devon Old English; dweller in the deep valley. Occasional use 1965–70.

Dewayne Wayne with the *De-* prefix.

Dewi A Welsh form of David. Occasional use 1955–80.

Dexter Latin; right-handed, hence skilful. Occasional use 1955–75.

Dharman Sanskrit; duty, destiny.

Diarmid Scottish Gaelic; free of envy.

Dickon, Dickson, Dixon, Dikken Son of Richard.

Digby Dutch; dyke. Occasional use 1935–50.

Diggory From Sir Degarre, the hero of a medieval romance.

Dillon Irish Gaelic; faithful.

Dinos Greek; firm, constant.

Dinsdale Old English; the enclosure belonging to Deighton.

Dion A French form of Dennis. Occasional use 1955–75.

Dirk A Dutch form of Derek. Occasional use 1965–70. *Variant*: Dierk (German).

Dominic Latin; belonging to God. Occasional use from 1900 peaking in 1975. *Other forms*: Dominick, Nicky. *Variants*: Dominik, Domek (Czech); Dominique

(French); Domonkos (Hungarian); Damhlaic, Damhnaic (Irish Gaelic); Domenico (Italian); Donek, Niki (Polish); Chuma, Domingo, Mingo (Spanish).

Don A form of Donald. Occasional use 1955–65.

Donald Irish; world ruler. Light use from 1900, peaking in heavy use in 1935 and declining into occasional use by 1950. *Other forms*: Don, Donal, Donnie, Donny, Donovan, MacDonald. *Variants*: Tauno (Finnish); Donovan (Irish Gaelic); Donaldo (Italian); Donalt (Norwegian); Dolly (Scottish); Domhnall (Scottish Gaelic); Pascual (Spanish).

Donat French; gift. *Variant*: Donato (Italian).

Donny A form of Donald. *Variant*: Donnaidh (Scottish Gaelic). (See Gender-neutral names.)

Donovan An Irish Gaelic form of Donald.

Doran Irish Gaelic; descendant.

Dorian Greek; gift. Occasional use from 1935. *Other forms*: Doran, Dorran, Dory.

Dormin Potawatomi; maize, corn.

Dougal Irish Gaelic; black stranger. *Other forms*: Dugal, Dugald. *Variant*: Dughall (Scottish Gaelic).

Douglas Scottish Gaelic; dark blue water. Occasional use from 1900 peaking in light use in 1925. *Other forms*: Doug, Dugal, Dougie, Dugald. *Variants*: Koukalaka (Hawaiian); Dougal (Irish); Dugald, Dughall (Scottish); Dubhghlas (Scottish Gaelic).

Doyle Irish Gaelic; assembly.

Drake Old English; dragon. *Variant*: Drago (Italian).

Drew A Scottish form of Andrew. Occasional use 1965–75.

Drogo Middle English; thirsty.

Druce Celtic; capable.

Dryden Old English; dry valley.

Duane Irish; black. Occasional use from 1970. *Other forms*: Dwain, Dwayne.

Dudley Old English; Dudda's meadow. Occasional use 1900–65.

Dugan Scottish Gaelic; dark-skinned.

Duke French; leader.

Duncan Celtic; warrior with dark skin. Occasional use from 1900 peaking in 1965. *Variant*: Donnchad (Scottish Gaelic).

Dunstan Old English; brownstone fortress.

Durril Romany; berry.

Dustin Old English; brownstone quarry.

Dusty A form of Dustin. (See Gender-neutral names.)

Dwayne A form of Duane. Occasional use in 1985.

Dylan Welsh; sea. In Welsh mythology, a god of the waves and waters of the sea. Occasional use from 1970 peaking in 1975. *Other forms*: Dill, Dillon.

Dyson From the surname linked to Denis.

E

Eaglen Old English; valley of the eagles.

Eamonn An Irish Gaelic form of Edmund. Occasional use in the 1960s. *Other form*: Eamon. *Variant*: Eumann (Scottish Gaelic).

Earl Old English; nobleman, prince. Occasional use 1900–70.

Earthan Irish Gaelic; strong of faith.

Eason Scottish Gaelic; son of Adam.

Ebon Marshallese; the name of one of the Marshall Islands.

Edan Irish Gaelic; flame, hence fiery one. Or Hebrew; delight.

Eddie A form of Edward. Occasional use 1900–75.

Eden Hebrew; delightful, pleasant. Or Babylonian; a plain. Occasional use from 1935. (See Gender-neutral names.)

Edgar Old English; prosperous spearsman. Light use at its peak in 1900, then declining and falling out of use in 1975. *Other forms*: Ed, Eddie, Eddy, Edgard, Teddie. *Variants*: Edko (Czech); Edgard (French); Edgardo (Italian, Spanish); Garek (Polish); Edgard (Russian); Adair (Scottish Gaelic).

Edlan Old English; prosperous village.

Edmond A form of Edmund. Occasional use 1935–50.

Edmund Old English; prosperous protector. Occasional use from a peak in 1900. Fell out of use in 1970 but revived in 1985. *Other forms*: Eamon, Ed, Edmon, Edmond. *Variants*: Edmond (Dutch); Esmond (French); Odo (Hungarian); Eamon (Irish Gaelic); Edmondo (Italian); Mundek (Polish); Edmon (Russian); Eumann (Scottish Gaelic); Edmundo, Mundo (Spanish); Iemwnt (Welsh).

Edson Son of Edward.

Edur Basque; snow.

Edward Old English; prosperous guardian. Heavy use from 1900, peaking in 1925 and then declining into light use. *Other forms*: Ed, Eddie, Eddy, Edison, Edson, Eduard, Ewart, Ned, Neddy, Ted, Teddie, Teddy. *Variants*: Eduard (Dutch, German); Edouard (French); Ekewaka (Hawaiian); Eadbhard (Irish Gaelic); Edoardo (Italian); Ewart (Norman French); Edek (Polish);

Eduardo, Duarte (Portuguese); Edgard (Romanian); Edvard (Scandinavian); Eideard (Scottish Gaelic); Eduardo (Spanish); Edwart, Iorwerth (Welsh).

Edwin Old English; prosperous friend. Light use from 1900, peaking in 1925 and then declining into occasional use. *Other forms*: Ed, Eduin, Edwyn. *Variants*: Eadaoin (Irish Gaelic); Eduino (Italian, Spanish).

Effro Welsh; awake.

Egan Scottish Gaelic; fire. *Variants*: Eginer, Fingar (Breton); Aodhgan, Hagan (Irish Gaelic); Iagan (Scottish Gaelic).

Egon Old German; formidable.

Einar Old Norse; warrior chief. *Variant*: Ejnar (Danish).

Eiran Irish; peace.

Ejau Ateso; we have received.

Elan Hebrew; tree. Or Native American; friendly. (See Gender-neutral names.)

Elber Old English; elf grove.

Eldon Old English; elf down.

Elgan Welsh; bright circle.

Elgin Old English; noble.

Eli Hebrew; God is high. *Variants*: Elie (French); Elia (Italian); Elias (Spanish).

Elijah Hebrew; the Lord is my God. Occasional use 1935–80. *Other forms*: Elias, Eliott, Ellis, Ellison, Elson, Ilija. *Variants*: Elya (Czech); Elie (French); Ilias (Greek); Ilya (Russian); Ilya, Ilija (Slavonic); Elia (Zuni).

Elisha Hebrew; God is my salvation. Occasional use from 1965 peaking in 1990. *Other forms*: Elias, Elison, Ellas, Ellis, Elson. *Variants*: Elya (Czech); Elias (Dutch, German); Elisee (French); Elihu (Greek); Eliseo (Italian,

Spanish); Elek (Polish); Elis (Welsh). (See Gender-neutral names.)

Elliot A form of Elijah. Occasional use from 1970 peaking in 1990. *Other forms*: Eliot, Elliott, Ellott.

Elliott A form of Elliot. Occasional use from 1970 peaking in 1990.

Ellis A form of Elisha. Occasional use from 1900. *Other forms*: Elis, Ellice. *Variant*: Elis (Welsh).

Elmer Old English; noble fame.

Elmore Old English; elm tree moor.

Elroy A form of Delroy.

Elton Old English; old village.

Elvis Old German; old friend. Occasional use from 1990. *Other forms*: Alvan, Alvis, Elvert, Elvin, Elvys.

Elwood Old English; elf woods.

Elwyn, Elwin Welsh; kind and fair.

Emer Old English; uncle. (See Gender-neutral names.)

Emery Old German; industrious leader. *Other forms*: Emerson, Emmery, Emory. *Variants*: Emeri (French); Emmerich (German); Imre (Hungarian); Amerigo (Italian, Spanish).

Emlyn A form of Emil. Latin; from the Roman clan name Aemilius. *Variants*: Emile (French); Emilio (Italian, Spanish).

Emmanuel Hebrew; God with us. *Other forms*: Emanuel, Immanuel. *Variants*: Imanol (Basque); Eman (Czech); Immanuel (German); Maco (Hungarian); Emanuele (Italian); Manoel (Portuguese); Emanuel (Scandinavian); Manuel (Spanish). (See Gender-neutral names.)

Emrys A Welsh form of Ambrose. Occasional use 1935–55.

Enli Dene; dog, hence loyal, faithful.

Ennis Greek; mine.

Enoch Possibly Hebrew; experienced, dedicated. Occasional use 1900–35. *Variant*: Enos (Greek).

Enyon Cornish; anvil.

Eric Old Norse; eternal ruler. Light use from 1900, peaking in heavy use in 1925 and then declining into occasional use. *Other forms*: Erich, Erik, Eryk, Rick. *Variants*: Jerik (Danish); Eriq (French); Erich (German); Elika (Hawaiian); Erico (Italian); Eriks (Russian); Eirik, Erik, Erkki (Scandinavian).

Erin Irish Gaelic; western island, hence Ireland. (See Gender-neutral names.)

Ernest Old German; resolute, sincere. Very heavy use at its peak in 1900, but then declined steadily and fell out of use in 1970. *Other forms*: Earnest, Ern, Ernie, Erno, Erny. *Variants*: Arno (Czech); Ernestus (Dutch); Ernestin (French); Ernst (German); Erno (Hungarian); Ernesto (Italian, Spanish).

Ernie A form of Ernest. Occasional use 1955–80.

Erol Turkish; strong, courageous.

Errando Basque; bold.

Errol Latin; to wander. Occasional use 1925–75. *Other forms*: Erroll, Rollo.

Erskine Scottish Gaelic; green ascent.

Erwin, Ervin Old German; honourable friend. *Other forms*: Irvin, Irwin. *Variants*: Erwan (Breton); Ervins (Latvian); Erwinek, Inek (Polish).

Eryl Welsh; watcher. (See Gender-neutral names.)

Esme French; to esteem. Occasional use from 1900.

Esmond Old English; protective grace.

Essien Ochi; sixth-born son.

Ethan Hebrew; strong, firm. *Variants*: Eitan, Etan (Hebrew).

Euan A phonetic form of the Scottish Gaelic name Eoghann, which may be a form of Eugene but may also be from a Celtic source meaning born of the yew tree. Occasional use 1955–80. *Other forms*: Ewan, Ewen, Owen.

Eugene Greek; well-born. Occasional use 1925–70. *Other forms*: Eugen, Gene, Owen. *Variants*: Evzen, Zenda (Czech); Eugenius (Dutch); Eugen (German); Iukini (Hawaiian); Jano, Jeno (Hungarian); Eoghan (Irish Gaelic); Eugenio (Italian); Genek (Polish); Eugenio (Portuguese); Eugeni, Genya, Yevgeni, Zhenka (Russian); Egen (Scandinavian); Euan, Ewan (Scottish); Eoghann (Scottish Gaelic); Eugenio, Gencho (Spanish); Owain, Owen (Welsh).

Eustace Greek; fruitful. *Variants*: Eustatius (Dutch); Eustache (French); Eustasius (German); Iustas (Irish Gaelic); Eustazio (Italian); Eustaquio (Spanish).

Evander Greek; good man.

Ewan A form of Euan. Occasional use 1950–85.

Everard Old German; tough as a boar. *Other form*: Everett. *Variants*: Everhart (Dutch); Evraud (French); Eberhard (German).

Ewart Possibly a Norman French form of Edward. Occasional use 1900–35.

Ezra Hebrew; help. *Other forms*: Azur, Ezri. *Variants*: Esdras (French, Spanish); Esra (German); Ezera (Hawaiian). (See Gender-neutral names.)

F

Fabian Latin; bean farmer. *Variants*: Fabien (French); Faber (German); Fabiano (Italian); Fabek (Polish); Fabiao (Portuguese); Fabiyan (Russian).

Faraday Old English; day traveller.

Faramond Old English; protected journey.

Farand Old German; pleasant.

Faris Arabic; knight.

Farley Old English; wayside place.

Farquhar Scottish Gaelic; very dear one. *Variant*: Fearchar (Scottish Gaelic).

Farrar Latin; blacksmith.

Farrel Celtic; courageous.

Felix Latin; happy, fortunate. Occasional use from 1935. *Other forms*: Feliks, Phelim. *Variants*: Felice (Italian); Feliks (Russian); Felo (Spanish).

Fenton Old English; village by the marsh.

Ferdinand Old German; courageous peacemaker. *Other forms*: Ferdie, Fernand, Nando. *Variants*: Fernand (French); Nandor (Hungarian); Ferdinando (Italian); Fernando, Hernando (Spanish).

Fergal Irish Gaelic; strong man.

Fergus Scottish Gaelic; supreme choice. Occasional use from 1965. *Variant*: Fearghas (Scottish Gaelic).

Fernley Old English; clearing with ferns. (See Gender-neutral names.)

Ferris Latin; strong as iron.

Fidel Latin; faithful. *Variants*: Fidele (French); Fidelio (Italian).

Finbar Irish Gaelic; fair-haired. *Variant*: Fymber (Cornish).

Fingal Scottish Gaelic; a Norwegian.

Finian Scottish Gaelic; fair-haired.

Finlay Scottish Gaelic; fair hero. *Other forms*: Findley, Finley. *Variant*: Fionnlagh (Scottish Gaelic).

Finn Irish Gaelic; fair.

Fintan Irish Gaelic; little fair one.

Fitz Norman French; son.

Flann Old English; arrow.

Flint Old English; a rock.

Florian Latin; from the Roman name Florianus. *Variant*: Floriano (Italian).

Floyd Welsh; grey-haired.

Flynn Irish Gaelic; bright red.

Forbes Irish Gaelic; prosperous. *Variant*: Foirbeis (Scottish Gaelic).

Fordel Romany; forgive.

Forrest Latin; woods.

Foster Possibly Middle English; forester.

Francis Latin; free. Light use at its peak in 1900 steadily declining into occasional use. *Other forms*: Chico, Fran, Franchot, Franco, Frank, Frankie, Franklyn, Franz, Pancho. *Variants*: Patxi (Basque); Francois, Franchot (French); Franciskus, Franz (German); Palani (Hawaiian); Proinsias (Irish Gaelic); Francesco, Franco (Italian); Frans (Scandinavian); Frang (Scottish Gaelic); Chico, Francisco, Paco, Pancho, Paquito, Quico (Spanish); Ffransis (Welsh).

Frank A form of Francis. Heavy use at its peak in 1900 steadily declining into occasional use. *Variants*: Franc

(French); Franck, Franz (German); Franco (Italian, Spanish); Frang (Scottish Gaelic).

Frankie A form of Francis. Occasional use 1965. (See Gender-neutral names.)

Franklin Latin; freeholder. Occasional use 1900–80. *Other form*: Franklyn.

Fraser French; charcoal maker. Occasional use from 1955. *Other forms*: Frasier, Frazier. *Variant*: Friseal (Scottish Gaelic).

Fred A form of Frederick. Occasional use from 1955. *Other forms*: Freddie, Freddy.

Frederick Old German; peaceful ruler. Very heavy use at its peak in 1900 but then steadily declining into occasional use. *Other forms*: Fred, Freddie, Freddy, Freeman, Fritz, Rickie, Ricky. *Variants*: Fridrich (Czech); Frederik (Danish, Dutch, Swedish); Frederic (French); Friedrich, Fritz (German); Peleke (Hawaiian); Frederico (Italian); Fredek (Polish); Fridrich (Russian); Frederigo, Fico (Spanish).

Fremont Old German; noble protector.

Frey Old English; lord. The god of prosperity in Scandinavian mythology.

Fulton Old English; field near the village.

Fyfe Scottish Gaelic; man from the kingdom of Fife.
Fynn Irish Gaelic; fair.

G

Gabriel Hebrew; God is my strength. *Other forms*: Gabe, Gabin, Gabby, Gable. *Variants*: Gabris (Czech); Gabe (Hebrew); Gabor (Hungarian); Gabriele (Italian); Gavril (Russian); Riel (Spanish).

Galen Greek; healer, calm. *Other form*: Gaelen. *Variant*: Galeno (Spanish).

Gallin Celtic; little stranger.

Galton Old Norse; high village.

Galvin, Galvyn Irish Gaelic; fair.

Ganesh, Ganesha Sanskrit; lord of the hosts. The name of the elephant-headed elder son of Shiva, revered in India as the god of wisdom. Ganesh is also linked with the overcoming of obstacles and auspicious beginnings. (See Gender-neutral names.)

Gannon Irish Gaelic; little loved one.

Gardiner Latin; keeper of the garden.

Garek A Polish form of Edgar. *Other form*: Gerik.

Gareth Old Norse; from the garden. Light use from 1955, peaking in 1980. *Other forms*: Garet, Garret, Garth, Gary. *Variant*: Gairiad (Irish Gaelic).

Garfield Old English; spear field. *Other form*: Gary.

Garin, Garen Old English; small rocky hill.

Garmon, Garman Old English; spearman.

Garnett Probably Old English; protection. (See Gender-neutral names.)

Garrett An Irish form of Gerard. *Other forms*: Garett, Jarrett.

Garridan Romany; you hid.

Garry A form of Gary. Occasional use 1950–85 peaking in 1960.

Garth Old Norse; enclosure.

Garton Old English; village shaped like a triangular spearhead.

Garvey Old English; spear bearer.

Garvin Irish Gaelic; rugged, tough.

Gary Possibly Old German; spear bearer. Light use from 1935, peaking in very heavy use in 1965 and then declining into light use again. Gary has always exceeded the popularity of the other form Garry by about five to one. *Other forms*: Garrie, Garry.

Gavin Welsh; little hawk. Occasional use from 1925 peaking in 1985. *Other forms*: Gavan, Gaven, Gawain, Walwyn.

Gawain, Gawaine Welsh; courteous. *Variant*: Gawen (Cornish).

Gene A form of Eugene. (See Gender-neutral names.)

Geoffrey Old English; gift of peace. Light use from 1900, peaking in 1950 and declining into occasional use. *Other forms*: Geoff, Godfrey, Jeff, Jeffrey, Jeffry. *Variants*: Jeffra (Cornish); Geoffroi (French); Gottfried (German); Siothrun (Irish Gaelic); Giotto, Goffredo (Italian); Geofri (Romanian); Sieffre (Welsh).

George Greek; farmer. Very heavy use at its peak in 1900 but then steadily declined down into occasional use by 1970. Some signs of revival into light use by 1990. *Other forms*: Geordie, Georgie, Georgy, Jorge, Sior, Yorick. *Variants*: Semer (Amharic); Gevorak (Arabic); Georg (Bulgarian); Jordi (Catalan); Jory (Cornish); Jurik (Czech); Joris (Dutch); Georges (French); Georg, Jorg, Jurgen (German); Giorgis (Greek); Keoki (Hawaiian); Seoirse (Irish Gaelic); Giorgio (Italian); Joji (Japanese); Jurgis (Lithuanian); Jurek (Polish); Egor, Yuri, Zhorka (Russian); Jorgen (Scandinavian); Geordie (Scottish); Seoras, Seorsa (Scottish Gaelic); Jorge (Spanish); Joran, Jorgen (Swedish); Sior (Welsh).

Georgie A form of George. (See Gender-neutral names.)

Geraint Welsh; old, hence wise. *Variant*: Gerens (Cornish).

Gerald Old German; spear-ruler. Light use from 1900, peaking in 1935 and then declining into occasional use. *Other forms*: Ged, Gerold, Gerrie, Gerry, Jerald, Jerall, Jerrell, Jerrold, Jerry. *Variants*: Geralde, Geraud, Giraud (French); Gerolt (Dutch); Gerhold, Gerold (German); Gellert (Hungarian); Gearalt, Gearoid (Irish Gaelic); Geraldo, Giraldo (Italian); Gerek (Polish); Garold, Kharald (Russian); Jarell (Scandinavian); Geraldo (Spanish); Gerallt (Welsh).

Gerard Old German; spear-brave. Occasional use from 1900 peaking in 1955. *Other forms*: Erhard, Gardell, Garey, Garrard, Garrick, Garry, Garvey, Gary, Gerbert, Gerrard, Gerrie, Gerry, Gervase, Girard, Jarrett, Jerrie, Jerry. *Variants*: Geraud (French), Gerhard, Gerhardt (German); Garrett (Irish); Gearard, Giorard (Irish Gaelic); Gerardo, Gherardo (Italian); Gerek (Polish); Gerardo (Spanish); Gerhard (Swedish, Danish).

Gerrard A form of Gerard. Occasional use 1935–55.

Gervaise Old German; a compound of spear and a second element of unknown meaning. *Other forms*: Garvais; Gervais, Gervase. *Variants*: Gervaas (Dutch); Gervais (French); Gervas (German); Gervasio (Italian, Spanish); Gerwazy (Polish); Gervasi (Russian). (See Gender-neutral names.)

Gethin Welsh; dusky.

Gideon Hebrew; warrior, destroyer.

Gifford Old German; bold giver.

Gilbert Old German; will to be bright or famous. Occasional use from a peak in 1900 to 1970. *Other forms*: Bert, Bertie, Gibb, Gibson, Gil, Gilburt, Gill, Wilbert, Wilbur, Will. *Variants*: Guilbert (French); Gilbrecht, Giselbert (German); Kiribati (Gilbertese); Gilibeirt (Irish Gaelic); Gilberto (Italian, Spanish); Gilleabart (Scottish Gaelic).

Gilby Old Norse; estate near the ravine. *Other form*: Gil.

Giles Greek; young goat, hence a goatskin shield. Occasional use from 1900 peaking in 1975. *Other forms*: Gil, Gelean, Gyles. *Variants*: Egide, Gilles (French); Egidius, Gill (German); Egidio (Italian); Sileas (Scottish Gaelic); Gil (Spanish).

Ginger A reference to ginger-coloured hair. (See Gender-neutral names.)

Glen Celtic; secluded wooded valley. Occasional use from 1900 peaking in 1970. *Other forms*: Glennon, Glyn. *Variants*: Glyn, Glynn (Welsh).

Glendon Celtic; valley fortress.

Glenn Celtic; secluded wooded valley. Occasional use from 1950 peaking in 1955.

Glyn A Welsh form of Glen. Occasional use from 1925 peaking in 1965. *Other form*: Glynn.

Godfrey Old German; God's peace. Occasional use 1900–60. *Variants*: Godefroi (French); Gottfried (German); Gofrai, Gothfraidh (Irish Gaelic); Goffredo (Italian); Gofraidh, Goraidh (Scottish Gaelic); Godofredo (Spanish); Gottfrid (Swedish).

Gomer Hebrew; to complete.

Gondar From the name of the ancient royal town in Ethiopia.

Gordon Possibly Greek; bold. Occasional use 1900–85 peaking in light use in 1925. *Other forms*: Gorden, Gordie, Gorton. *Variants*: Gordan (Irish); Geordan (Scottish).

Gowan Tiv; rainmaker.

Grady Scottish Gaelic; illustrious and noble.

Graeme A form of Graham. Occasional use from 1950 peaking in 1965.

Graham Old English; homestead in a gravelly place. Light use from 1900, peaking in heavy use in 1950 and declining into occasional use by 1990. *Other forms*: Graeme, Grahame. *Variants*: Greachan (Irish Gaelic); Graeme (Scottish).

Grahame A form of Graham. Occasional use from 1935.

Grainger Old French; farm steward.

Grant Middle English; giver. Occasional use from 1950 peaking in 1990.

Granville Old French; from the big town. Occasional use 1900–60. *Other form*: Grenville.

Graydon Old English; grey hill.

Grayson Old English; son of the steward.

Greendale Old English; green valley.

Gregory Greek; vigilant. Occasional use from 1950 peaking in 1975. *Other forms*: Greg, Gregor, Gregus. *Variants*: Grigor (Bulgarian); Greggor (Dutch); Gregoire (French); Gregor, Gregorius (German); Grigorios (Greek); Greagoir, Grioghar (Irish Gaelic); Gregorio (Italian); Grigori, Grisha (Russian); Gregor (Scottish); Griogair (Scottish Gaelic); Gregorio (Spanish); Gries (Swedish); Grigor (Welsh).

Grenville A form of Granville. Occasional use 1935–60.

Griffin, Griffith Forms of the Welsh name Gruffudd, which combines chief with an unknown second element.

Grover Old English; one who grows trees.

Gus A form of Gustave. Old German; staff of the Goths. *Variants*: Gustaff (Dutch); Kosti (Finnish); Gustav (German); Gustavo (Italian); Tavo (Slavonic); Gustaf (Swedish).

Guy Old French; a guide. Occasional use from 1900

peaking in 1990. *Variants*: Veit (Dutch); Gui (French); Wido (German); Guido (Italian); Wyatt (Norman French); Vito (Spanish).

Gwilym A Welsh form of William. *Variant*: Guin (Scottish Gaelic).

Gwyn Welsh; fair.

Gwynfor Welsh; fair lord.

H

Habib Syriac; beloved.

Hadar Hebrew; glory.

Haddon Scottish Gaelic; heathland.

Hadley Old English; meadow near the heath.

Hadrian Greek; rich. Occasional use 1965–70.

Hagan Old German; strong defence.

Hagen Irish Gaelic; little one.

Hakan Native American; fiery.

Halcyon Greek; kingfisher, a bird thought by the ancients to calm the sea beneath its floating nest hence calm, peaceful, happy.

Halford Old English; valley ford.

Hallam Old English; dweller on the hill slope.

Halsey Old English; neck-like spur of land.

Halton Old English; village on the slope of a hill.

Hamilton Old English; crooked hill.

Hamish A phonetic form of the Scottish Gaelic name Seumas, a version of James. Occasional use from 1965. *Variant*: Seamus (Irish Gaelic).

Hamlin, Hamlyn Old English; home by the brook.

Hammond Old English; village dweller.

Hanford Old German; hill ford.

Hanif Kiswahili; believer.

Hanson Son of Hans, a German form of John.

Harford Old English; ford of the hares.

Harith Arabic; able to make money.

Harker Old English; listener.

Harlan Middle English; strand of hemp.

Harley Old English; from the hare meadow.

Harold Old English; leader of the army. Heavy use at its peak in 1900, then steadily declining and falling out of use by 1975. *Other forms*: Arold, Hal, Haldon, Halford, Harald, Harlow, Harry, Parry. *Variants*: Jindra (Czech); Herold (Dutch); Arold, Arry (French); Henrik (Hungarian); Aralt (Irish Gaelic); Araldo, Arrigo (Italian); Haralds (Latvian); Heronim (Polish); Enric (Romanian); Garald (Russian); Harald (Scandinavian); Arailt, Haral (Scottish Gaelic); Haraldo (Spanish).

Harper Old English; harp player. (See Gender-neutral names.)

Harrison Son of Harry.

Harry A form of Henry. Heavy use at its peak in 1900 then declining and falling out of use in 1975. Revived in 1980 and rose into light use again by 1990. *Variants*: Hale (Hawaiian); Arrigo (Italian).

Hart Old English; stag.

Hartley Old English; stag wood.

Hartman Old German; strong man.

Haru Japanese; born in spring.

Harvey Old German; worthy of battle. Occasional use from 1925 peaking in 1970. *Other forms*: Erve, Harv, Harvie, Hervey. *Variants*: Herve (French); Herwig (German).

Hasan Arabic; handsome, good. *Variant*: Husani (East African).

Haslam Old English; place of hazel trees.

Haven, Havin Middle English; harbour.

Hayden Old English; hay pasture. Occasional use from 1965. *Other forms*: Haydn, Haydon, Hayes.

Haydn A form of Hayden. Occasional use from 1955 peaking in 1965.

Haydon A form of Hayden. Occasional use 1955–65.

Haynes A form of Hans, a German version of John.

Heaton Old English; high village.

Hector Greek; steadfast. Occasional use 1900–35. *Variants*: Hectoire (French); Ettore (Italian); Eachann, Eachdhonn (Scottish Gaelic).

Hedley Old English; clearing with heather. *Other form*: Heddle.

Hefin Welsh; summery.

Henry Old German; home ruler. Heavy use at its peak in 1900 then declining into occasional use, almost disappearing in the 1970s. A revival in 1985 took it into light use again by 1990. *Other forms*: Hal, Hank, Harrison, Harry, Heine, Heinz, Hendrik, Henty, Herriot, Herry, Rik. *Variants*: Henna (Cornish); Hinrich (Czech); Hendrik (Dutch, Danish); Henrik (Finnish, Swedish); Henri (French); Heine, Heinrich, Heinz (German); Enrikos (Greek); Hanale (Hawaiian); Anrai, Annraoi, Einri, Hanraoi (Irish Gaelic); Arrigo, Enrico, Enzio (Italian); Henryk (Polish); Henrique (Portuguese); Enric (Romanian); Eanruig (Scottish Gaelic); Enrique, Kiki, Quico (Spanish); Harri (Welsh).

Herbert Old German; shining army. Heavy use at its peak in 1900 but then declined and fell out of use in

1965. A small revival in 1975 was not sustained, probably because the name had by then become a slang term for a pompous and foolish person. *Other forms*: Bert, Bertie, Harbert, Herb, Herbie. *Variants*: Harbert (Dutch); Aribert (French); Heribert (German); Hoireabard (Irish Gaelic); Erberto (Italian); Heriberto (Spanish).

Herman Old German; soldier. *Variants*: Armand (French); Hermann (German); Ermanno (Italian); Mandek (Polish); Armando (Spanish); Hermann (Swedish).

Herrick Old German; army leader.

Hesketh Old Norse; horse track.

Heywood Old English; high wood.

Hickory Native American; from the name of the broad-leaved tree.

Hinto Dakota; blue.

Hiram Hebrew; noble born.

Hobart Old German; famous spear.

Hogan Irish Gaelic; youthful. Or Navajo; dwelling, home. Or Native American; morning star. *Other form*: Hoagy.

Hogon Dogon; spiritual leader.

Holden Old English; deep valley.

Hollis Old Norse; hero.

Honovi Hopi; strong deer.

Horace Greek; to see. Light use in 1900 then declining and falling out of use by 1980. *Other forms*: Horatio, Horatius. *Variants*: Horatz (Dutch); Horatius, Horaz (German); Orazio (Italian); Horacio (Spanish).

Horton Latin; garden.

Hoshi Japanese; star.

Houston Old English; Hugh's village.

Howard Old English; guardian of the home. Occasional use from 1900 peaking in 1960. *Other forms*: Howey, Howie, Ward. *Variant*: Haoa (Hawaiian).

Hoyt Middle English; ship.

Hubert Old German; bright in mind. Occasional use from 1900 to 1935. *Other forms*: Hobart, Hubie. *Variants*: Hubertek (Czech); Hubertus (Dutch); Hugbert (German); Hoibeard (Irish Gaelic); Oberto, Uberto (Italian); Beredei (Russian); Huberto (Spanish).

Hudson Son of Hudd, a form of Hugh.

Hugh A form of Hubert. Occasional use from 1900 peaking in 1935. *Other forms*: Hew, Hobart, Hub, Huey, Hughie, Hugo, Huw. *Variants*: Hugo (Dutch, German, Spanish); Hugues (French); Aodh (Irish Gaelic); Ugo (Italian); Aoidh (Scottish Gaelic); Hugon (Spanish); Huw (Welsh).

Hugo A Dutch, German and Spanish form of Hugh. Occasional use from 1980.

Humphrey Old German; strength in peace. *Variants*: Omffra (Cornish); Onfroi (French); Humfried, Hunfrid (German); Onofredo, Onofrio (Italian); Onufry (Polish); Hunfredo, Onofre (Spanish); Humfrid (Swedish).

Hunt Old English; to search.

Hunter Old English; huntsman.

Huntley Old English; hunting meadow.

Hurley Celtic; sea tides.

Hute Native American; star in the Big Dipper.

Huw A Welsh form of Hugh. Occasional use from 1965.

Hyak Chinook; hurry.

Hylton Old English; village on the hill. Occasional use 1935–80. *Other form*: Hilton.

Hyman Old English; dweller in a high place.

Hywel Welsh; eminent. *Variants*: Hoel (Breton); Howell (Cornish).

I

Iain A form of Ian. Occasional use from 1950 peaking in 1980.

Ian A Scottish form of John. Occasional use from 1900, peaking in very heavy use in 1965 and then declining into light use by 1990. *Other form*: Iain. *Variant*: Eion (Irish Gaelic).

Ianto A Welsh form of John. *Other form*: Yanto.

Idris Welsh; ardent lord.

Ingemar Old Norse; fame of Ing, the god of peace in Norse mythology.

Iniko Ibibio; born during difficult times.

Innis Scottish Gaelic; island.

Iolo Welsh; worthy lord.

Ira Hebrew; watcher. (See Gender-neutral names.)

Irving Scottish Gaelic; handsome. *Other forms*: Irvin, Irvine.

Isaac Hebrew; he will laugh. Occasional use from 1900, falling out of use from 1935 until it revived in 1975. *Other forms*: Ike, Isaak, Isak, Izaak. *Variants*: Ishaq (Arabic); Izak (Czech); Izaak (Dutch); Isaak (German); Yitzhak (Hebrew); Iosac (Irish Gaelic); Isacco (Italian); Aizik (Russian); Isak (Swedish).

Isador Greek; gift of Isis. *Other form*: Isadore. *Variants*: Isidor (German); Isidoro (Italian); Izydor (Polish); Isadore, Isidro (Spanish).

Isaiah Hebrew; God is my salvation. Occasional use from 1900.

Ishmael Hebrew; God has heard. Occasional use from 1980.

Ivan A Russian form of John. Occasional use from 1900 peaking in 1935.

Ives Old English; young archer. *Variant*: Yves (French).

Ivor Old Norse; warrior bowman. Occasional use from 1900 peaking in 1925. *Other forms*: Ivar, Iver. *Variants*: Ibon (Basque); Yves (French); Ivo (German); Iomhar (Irish Gaelic); Iwo (Polish); Iomhair (Scottish Gaelic); Ifor (Welsh).

J

Jace A character in the novel *Death Dream* by Ben Bova.

Jacinto A Spanish form of Hyacinth. Greek; the flower name meaning blue gem or sapphire. *Variants*: Hyacinthus (Dutch); Hyacinthe (French); Hyazinth (German); Giacinto (Italian). (See Gender-neutral names.)

Jack A form of John. Light use from 1900, peaking in 1925 and declining into occasional use in 1950. Revived in 1980 and rose into heavy use by 1990. *Variant*: Jacca (Cornish).

Jackie A form of John. (See Gender-neutral names.)

Jackson Son of Jack.

Jaco A Portuguese form of Jacob. *Other forms*: Jayco, Jayko.

Jacob Hebrew; a supplanter. Occasional use from 1900 rising into light use by 1990. *Other forms*: Cob, Cobb, Jack, Jackie, Jackson, Jacky, Jaco, Jacobson, Jago, Jake, Jock, Kivi, Yago. *Variants*: Jokubas, Kuba, Kubik

(Czech); Jaako (Finnish); Jacques (French); Jakob (German); Iakobos (Greek); Jakab, Kobi (Hungarian); Giacobo, Giacomo, Jacopo (Italian); Jekebs, Jeska (Lithuanian); Jakub, Koby (Polish); Jaco (Portuguese); Jakov, Yakov, Yasha (Russian); Diego, Iago, Jacobo (Spanish); Iago (Welsh).

Jacy Kiowa; the powers of the moon.

Jaden Hebrew; God has heard. *Other form*: Jadon (See Gender-neutral names.)

Jago A Cornish form of James.

Jahan Swahili; dignity.

Jaime A Spanish form of James. *Other form*: Jamie. (See Gender-neutral names.)

Jak Serbo-Croatian; strong.

Jake A form of Jack. Occasional use from 1970 peaking in light use in 1990.

Jako Timori; the name of an island off the eastern coast of Timor.

Jamal Arabic; handsome.

James An English form of Jacob. Very heavy use in 1900 but then declined into light use by 1960. Revived in 1965, and then rose steadily into very heavy use again by 1990. *Other forms*: Hamish, Iago, Jaime, Jaimie, Jamey, Jamie, Jan, Jaomi, Jayme, Jas, Jem, Jim, Jimbo, Jimmie, Jimmy, Seamus, Shamus. *Variants*: Jacobe (Basque); Jagu (Breton); Jaume (Catalan); Jago, Jamma (Cornish); Jakob (Danish); Jaap (Dutch); Jaakko, Jaakoppi (Finnish); Coco, Jacques (French); Xaime (Galician); Jakob (German); Iokovos (Greek); Kimo (Hawaiian); Yaakov (Hebrew); Dzimi, Zsaki (Hungarian); Shamus (Irish); Seamus, Seumus (Irish Gaelic); Giacomo (Italian); Diogo, Jaco, Jaime (Portuguese); Iocob (Romanian); Jasha, Yacob, Yasha

(Russian); Hamish, Jamie (Scottish); Seumas (Scottish Gaelic); Chago, Diego, Jaime, Jayme, Santiago, Tiago (Spanish); Jakob (Swedish); Dymtro (Ukrainian); Iago (Welsh).

Jamie A Scottish form of James. (See Gender-neutral names.)

Jan A Dutch form of John. *Variants*: Janek (Polish); Janne (Swedish). (See Gender-neutral names.)

Jando A Spanish form of Alexander.

Janek A Polish form of John.

Jansen Scandinavian; son of Jan. *Other form*: Janson.

Jaomi A form of Jamie. (See Gender-neutral names.)

Jared, Jarrod Hebrew; descendant.

Jarek Slavonic; born in January.

Jaron Hebrew; cry out. Or Czech; firm peace.

Jarrad Hebrew; descendant.

Jarvis Old German; war leader.

Jason Greek; healer. Occasional use from 1955, peaking in very heavy use in 1970 and declining into light use by 1990. *Other forms*: Jaeson, Jayson.

Jasper Greek; from the name of the translucent green gemstone. *Variants*: Gaspard (French); Geaspar (Irish Gaelic); Gaspare (Italian); Jesper (Scandinavian); Gaspar (Spanish).

Javin Hebrew; understanding. *Other forms*: Javan, Javon, Jevan.

Jay Latin; from the name of the bird. Occasional use from 1970. (See Gender-neutral names.)

Jayce A combination of the initials J and C. *Other forms*: Jaycey, JC. (See Gender-neutral names.)

Jayden A blend of Jay and Brayden.

Jed Hebrew; a form of Jedidiah, meaning friend of the Lord.

Jedrek Polish; strong, manly.

Jeffery A form of Jeffrey. Occasional use 1925–70.

Jeffrey Old English; gift of peace. Light use from 1900 peaking in 1960. *Other forms*: Geoffrey, Jeff, Jefferey, Jeffery, Jeffry, Jeffy. *Variants*: Jeffra (Cornish); Geoffroi, Jeoffroi (French); Gottfried (German); Geoffredo, Giotto (Italian); Geofri (Romanian); Gotfrid (Russian); Boromir (Serbo-Croatian); Fredo, Gofredo (Spanish).

Jenkin Flemish; little John.

Jenson A form of Jensen (Jansen).

Jeremy Hebrew; God will uplift. Light use from 1935 peaking in 1965. *Other forms*: Gerrie, Gerry, Jere, Jeremiah, Jerrie, Jerry. *Variants*: Jeremie (French); Jeremias (German, Dutch); Kele (Hawaiian); Jeremiah, Nemet (Hungarian); Geremia (Italian); Jeremija (Russian); Jeremias (Spanish); Jeremia (Swedish).

Jermyn Hebrew; may God exalt.

Jerome Greek; of holy name. Occasional use from 1950. *Other forms*: Gerome, Gerry, Jeronim, Jerram, Jerry. *Variants*: Jeroen (Dutch); Hieronymus (German); Hieronymos (Greek); Geronimo (Italian); Jeronimo (Spanish).

Jerrell A blend of Jerald (Gerald) and Darryl.

Jeshua Hebrew; Jehovah saves.

Jesse Hebrew; wealthy. Occasional use from 1900. *Other form*: Jess. (See Gender-neutral names.)

Jethro Hebrew; abundance, excellence.

Jim A form of James. Occasional use from 1900. *Other forms*: Jimmie, Jimmy.

Jimiyu Abaluhya; born in the dry season.

315

Jirar, Jirair Armenian; strong, industrious.

Jocelyn Old German; descendant of the Goths. *Other form*: Joss. (See Gender-neutral names.)

Jodan A blend of Joe and Daniel.

Jodi A form of Joseph. (See Gender-neutral names.)

Joe A form of Joseph. Occasional use from 1900. (See Gender-neutral names.)

Joel Hebrew; God is willing. Occasional use from 1960. *Other form*: Yoel. (See Gender-neutral names.)

John Hebrew; God is gracious. Very heavy use from 1900, peaking in 1935 and declining gradually into light use by 1990. *Other forms*: Evan, Ewan, Haines, Hanan, Haynes, Iain, Ian, Ivan, Jack, Jackie, Jan, Jehan, Jenkin, Jennings, Jock, Johnnie, Johnny, Jon, Jovan, Owen, St John, Sean, Shaun, Shawn, Yan, Yancy, Zan, Zane. *Variants*: Hovan, Ohari (Armenian); Iban, Yon (Basque); Yann (Breton); Ioan (Bulgarian); Joan (Catalan); Jowan (Cornish); Jan, Janco (Czech); Jan, Jens (Danish); Jan, Jantje, Yan (Dutch); Johan (Estonian); Hannes, Jani, Janne, Jukka (Finnish); Jean (French); Xoan (Galician); Hans, Hansel, Jan, Johann (German); Ioannes, Ioannikios, Ioannis (Greek); Yohance (Hausa); Keaka, Keoni (Hawaiian); Yochanan (Hebrew); Jancsi, Janos (Hungarian); Keon, Shane, Shaun, Shawn, Shay (Irish); Eoin, Seaghan, Sean, Seon (Irish Gaelic); Gian, Giovanni (Italian); Janis (Latvian); Jonas, Jonelis (Lithuanian); Jan, Jens (Norwegian); Jehan (Persian); Jan, Janek (Polish); Joao (Portuguese); Iancu, Ioan, Ion (Romanian); Ivan, Vanya (Russian); Euan, Ian, Jonty (Scottish); Eoin, Seathan (Scottish Gaelic); Juan, Juanito (Spanish); Hansel, Jan, Jens (Scandinavian); Ohannes (Turkish); Evan, Ewen, Ianto, Ieuan, Iwan, Jevan, Owen, Sion, Yanto (Welsh).

Johnathan A form of Jonathan. Occasional use from 1950.

Johnny A form of John. Occasional use 1965–85. *Other form*: Johnnie.

Jolyon A form of Julian. Occasional use from 1950.

Jon A form of John. Occasional use from 1935.

Jonas Hebrew; dove. Occasional use 1900–60. *Other form*: Johah. *Variants*: Giona (Italian); Iona (Russian); Yunus (Turkish).

Jonathan Hebrew; God has given. Occasional use from 1900, rising rapidly into heavy use in 1965 and peaking in 1990. *Other forms*: Johnathan, Jon, Jonathon, Jonny. *Variants*: Yanton (Cornish); Ionakana (Hawaiian); Ionatan (Irish); Seonac (Irish Gaelic); Gionata (Italian); Yonathan (Spanish).

Jonathon A form of Jonathan. Occasional use from 1955 peaking in 1990.

Jonty A Scottish form of John. *Other forms*: Jontay, Jonte. *Variant*: Seantaigh (Scottish Gaelic).

Jorah Hebrew; autumn rain. *Other form*: Jora.

Joram Hebrew; God is exalted.

Jordan Hebrew; to flow down. Occasional use 1925–85, suddenly rising into heavy use in 1990. *Other forms*: Jared, Jordain, Jordon, Jory, Judd, Yarden. *Variants*: Jourdan (French); Giordano (Italian); Jordao (Portuguese). (See Gender-neutral names.)

Jorel A name inspired by Jor-el, the father of the comic-strip hero Superman, who first appeared in *Action Comics* in 1938. Superman was written by Jerry Siegel, drawn by Joseph Shuster and later featured in a radio show, a novel, films and a television series.

Joren Scandinavian; love of the chief.

Joseph Hebrew; Jehovah will increase. Heavy use at its peak in 1900 then declining into light use by 1950. This was sustained until 1990 when it rose into heavy use again. *Other forms*: Beppo, Che, Jo, Jody, Joe, Joey, Pepe. *Variants*: Yousef, Yusuf (Arabic); Hovsep, Yousef (Armenian); Joseba (Basque); Iosif, Yosif (Bulgarian); Iosif, Joza, Jozka (Czech); Josephus (Dutch); Joosef, Jooseppi (Finnish); Josephe (French); Xose (Galician); Josef (German); Iosif (Greek); Iokepa, Keo (Hawaiian); Joska, Jozsef, Jozsi (Hungarian); Seosamh (Irish Gaelic); Beppo, Giuseppe (Italian); Jo (Japanese); Jazeps (Latvian); Juozapas, Juozas (Lithuanian); Josep, Juzef (Polish); Jose (Portuguese); Iosif, Yousef (Romanian); Iosif, Iossip, Osip, Yeska, Yusif (Russian); Seosaidh (Scottish Gaelic); Josep (Serbo-Croatian); Che, Jose, Pepe, Pepito (Spanish); Josef (Swedish, Norwegian); Osip, Yosyf (Ukrainian); Ioseff (Welsh).

Josh A form of Joshua. Occasional use from 1985.

Joshua Hebrew; God is my salvation. Occasional use in 1900, then falling out of use until it revived in 1975. Then a rapid rise into very heavy use in 1990. *Other forms*: Josh, Mosha. *Variants*: Josue (French); Josua (German); Yehosha (Hebrew); Jozsua (Hungarian); Giosia (Italian); Joaquim (Portuguese); Iosua (Romanian); Joaquin, Josue (Spanish); Josua (Swedish).

Joss Breton; champion. Or a form of Jocelin or Jocelyn.

Jotham Hebrew; God is perfect.

Jovan Latin; majestic, like Jove. Jupiter (or Jove) was the supreme god in Roman mythology.

Jude Hebrew; praised. (See Gender-neutral names.)

Julian Probably Greek; soft-haired. Occasional use from 1925 peaking in 1965. *Other forms*: Jolin, Jolyon, Jules, Julien, Julius, Julyan. *Variants*: Julen (Basque); Jule,

Jules (French); Giuliano, Giulio (Italian); Juliusz (Polish); Julio (Spanish).

Juniper Latin; from the plant name. (See Gender-neutral names.)

Justin Latin; fair, just. Occasional use from 1960 peaking in light use in 1970. *Other forms*: Jeston, Justus, Justyn. *Variants*: Yesten, Yestin (Cornish); Justyn (Czech); Joost (Dutch); Justine (French); Just (German); Giustino (Italian); Justek (Polish); Iustin, Yustyn (Russian); Justinus (Scandinavian); Justino, Justo (Spanish); Iestyn, Jestin (Welsh).

K

Kacy A form of Casey. *Other form*: Kacey. (See Gender-neutral names.)

Kadar Arabic; powerful.

Kado Japanese; gateway.

Kaemon Japanese; joyful.

Kahale Hawaiian; home.

Kai Hawaiian; sea. Or Hopi; willow tree. (See Gender-neutral names.)

Kalil Arabic; good or beloved friend.

Kamau Kikuyu; quiet warrior.

Kamuzu Ngoni; medicine.

Kane Welsh; handsome.

Kanoa Polynesian; free. Or Hawaiian; key, hidden meaning. (See Gender-neutral names.)

Kaori Japanese; strong.

Karim Arabic; noble, generous. *Other forms*: Kareem, Kario.

Karl A German and Scandinavian form of Charles. Occasional use from 1935, peaking in 1965 and then continuing in steady light use. *Variants*: Karel, Karol (Czech); Karlen (Russian).

Kasey A form of Casey. (See Gender-neutral names.)

Kasiya Ngoni; separate, able to stand alone.

Kato Runyankore; second-born of twins.

Kayin Nigerian; celebrated.

Kayle Hebrew; faithful. (See Gender-neutral names.)

Kealan Irish Gaelic; slender.

Keaton Old English; where hawks fly.

Keefe Irish Gaelic; wellbeing.

Keenan Irish Gaelic; enduring.

Kegan Celtic; son of Egan.

Keir Scottish Gaelic; swarthy.

Keith Probably Scottish Gaelic; wood. Light use from 1925, peaking in heavy use in 1950 and then declining into occasional use by 1985.

Kelby Old German; farm by the spring.

Kelly Irish Gaelic; brave warrior. (See Gender-neutral names.)

Kelsey Old English; victory at sea. (See Gender-neutral names.)

Kelson A character in the novel *Deryni Rising* by Katherine Kurtz.

Kelvin Old English; friend of ships. Occasional use from 1950 peaking in 1965. *Other forms*: Kelvyn, Kelwin.

Kemen Basque; strength.

Kendall Celtic; ruler of the valley (See Gender-neutral names.)

Kendrick Scottish Gaelic; son of Henry.

Kennedy Irish Gaelic; helmeted chief. *Variant*:

Ceannaideach (Scottish Gaelic).

Kenneth Scottish Gaelic; handsome. Light use from 1900, peaking in very heavy use in 1925 and then declining into occasional use by 1970. *Other forms*: Ken, Kenn, Kennie, Kenny, Kent, Kenton, Kenward, Kenyon. *Variants*: Kennet, Kent (Scandinavian); Coinneach (Scottish Gaelic); Chencho, Inocente (Spanish); Cennydd (Welsh).

Kenny A form of Kenneth. Occasional use from 1980.

Kent Celtic; high peace.

Kerel Afrikaans; young.

Kerey Romany; homeward bound.

Kern Celtic; little dark one.

Kerry, Kerrin Irish Gaelic; the place of Ciar's people. (See Gender-neutral names.)

Kerwin, Kerwyn Irish Gaelic; dark-haired.

Keshawn Shawn with the *Ke-* prefix.

Ketan Sanskrit; home.

Kevan A form of Kevin. Occasional use 1950–65.

Kevin Irish Gaelic; handsome at birth. Light use from 1925 peaking in very heavy use in 1960. *Other forms*: Cavan, Kev, Kevan, Keven. *Variants*: Coemgen (Breton); Keverne (Cornish); Caoimhin (Irish Gaelic).

Khyan Possibly Arabic; tent maker.

Kiaran From the Irish saint's name of uncertain meaning.

Kibbe Nayas; night bird.

Kibo Uset; capable, wise.

Kieran Irish Gaelic; black, dark-haired. Light use from 1980. *Other forms*: Ciaran, Kiaran, Kieron, Kyran. *Variant*: Ciaran (Irish Gaelic).

Kieron A form of Kieran. Occasional use from 1965.

Kifeda Luo; only boy in a family of girls.

Kiko Dutooro; born on a misty day.

Kim A form of Kimball. Welsh; war leader. (See Gender-neutral names.)

Kincaid Scottish Gaelic; battle chief.

Kingsley Old English; king's wood or clearing. Occasional use from 1935 until it fell out of use in 1965. There was a small revival in 1990. *Other forms*: Kingsleigh, Kinsley.

Kingston Old English; the king's town.

Kinton Hindi; crowned.

Kiran Sanskrit; ray of sunshine.

Kirby Old English; church farm. (See Gender-neutral names.)

Kirk Old Norse; church. Occasional use from 1955 peaking in 1985.

Kirkwood Scottish/Old English; wood by the church.

Kito Swahili; jewel.

Kofi Twi; born on Friday.

Kogon Uzbek; a place-name in Uzbekistan.

Kohana Sioux; swift. (See Gender-neutral names.)

Kono Moquelumnan; squirrel eating a pine nut.

Koriander, Coriander Greek; from the name of the herb.

Kory, Korey Forms of Corey. (See Gender-neutral names.)

Kris A form of Kristian. (See Gender-neutral names.)

Krishna Sanskrit; black, dark. The name of one of the most important deities in the Hindu system.

Kristian A Danish form of Christian. Occasional use

from 1960 peaking in 1990. *Other form*: Kris. *Variants*: Krischan (German); Krystek (Polish). (See Gender-neutral names.)

Kumar Sanskrit; boy, prince.

Kurt A German form of Conrad. Occasional use from 1970.

Kurtwood Old German; enclosed wood.

Kuruk Pawnee; a bear.

Kuzih Carrier; good speaker.

Kwan Korean; strong.

Kyle Scottish Gaelic; hill where cattle graze. Occasional use from 1980 peaking in light use in 1990. *Other forms*: Kiel, Kile, Ky, Kyler.

Kynan Irish Gaelic; chief.

L

Lachlan Scottish Gaelic; a Viking, man from the land of lochs (Norway). *Variants*: Lachunn (Scottish Gaelic).

Lado Fante; second-born son.

Laird Scottish; wealthy landowner, lord.

Lakotah Sioux; friend to us. The name given to the Teton branch of the Sioux. (See Gender-neutral names.)

Lamar French; the lake. (See Gender-neutral names.)

Lamont Old Norse; lawyer.

Lance A form of Lancelot. Old German; land. Occasional use 1950–75. *Variant*: Lando (German).

Lando A Spanish form of Roland.

Landon, Langdon Old English; from the long hill.

Larry A form of Laurence. Occasional use 1950–80.

Larson, Larsen Son of Lars, a Swedish form of Laurence.

Latham Old English; land that is owned.

Laurence Latin; man from Laurentium. Occasional use from 1900 peaking in 1950. *Other forms*: Laurent, Laurie, Lauriston.

Laurie A form of Laurence. (See Gender-neutral names.)

Lawford Old English; ford in the hills.

Lawrence Latin; man from Laurentium. Occasional use from 1900 peaking in 1950. This has been the most widely used spelling of the name in the majority of decades since 1900, although it was overtaken by Laurence 1955–80. *Other forms*: Lanty, Larken, Larkin, Larry, Larson, Laurence, Laurie, Lawry, Lon, Lonnie, Lorence, Lorin, Lorn, Rance. *Variants*: Laurentz (Basque); Lauritz (Danish); Laurens (Dutch); Laurent (French); Laurenz, Lorenz (German); Lorant, Lorenca (Hungarian); Lanty (Irish); Labhras (Irish Gaelic); Lauro, Loren, Lorenzo, Loretto, Renzo (Italian); Laurenco (Portuguese); Lavrenti, Larya, Lavro (Russian); Lars (Scandinavian); Labhruinn (Scottish Gaelic); Chencho, Laurencio, Lorenzo (Spanish); Lauris (Swedish).

Lawson Son of Lawrence. Occasional use 1925–70.

Lawton Old English; village on the hill.

Leaf Old English; the plant term used as a name. (See Gender-neutral names.)

Lee Old English; wood, clearing. Light use from 1900 peaking in heavy use in 1980. (See Gender-neutral names.)

Leighton Old English; place on a waterway. Occasional use 1965–80. *Other forms*: Layton, Leyton.

Lenno Native American; man.

Lennon Irish Gaelic; meadow.

Lennor Romany; spring and summer.

Lennox Irish Gaelic; grove of elms.

Leo Latin; lion. Occasional use from 1900. *Variants*: Leosko (Czech); Leon (German, Irish); Lio (Hawaiian); Leos (Polish); Leao (Portuguese); Lev (Russian).

Leon A German and Irish form of Leo. Occasional use from 1925 peaking in 1975. *Other forms*: Leighon, Leondris. *Variants*: Leosko (Czech); Leonidas (Greek); Leone (Italian); Leonas (Lithuanian); Leonek, Leos (Polish); Leao (Portuguese); Levka (Russian); Leonardo (Spanish).

Leonard Old German; strong as a lion. Light use from 1900 peaking in heavy use in 1925. *Other forms*: Len, Lennard, Lennie, Lenny, Lonnard, Lonnie, Lony. *Variants*: Lienard (French); Leonhard (German); Leander (Greek); Leonardo (Italian, Spanish); Leonek, Nardek (Polish); Leonid, Lonya (Russian); Lennart, Leontes (Scandinavian); Leinhard (Swiss).

Leopold Old German; brave people. *Variant*: Leopoldo (Italian).

Leroy French; the king. Occasional use from 1960. *Other forms*: Elroy, Lee Roy, Leroi.

Leshawn Shawn with the *Le-* prefix.

Leslie Old French; meadowlands. Light use from 1900, peaking in heavy use in 1925 and then declining into occasional use. *Other form*: Les. (See Gender-neutral names.)

Lester Old English; a camp.

Levar Hebrew; attached.

Lewis An English form of Louis. Occasional use from 1900, falling out of use in 1975 but reviving in 1980 and rising sharply into light use in 1990. *Variants*: Luthais (Scottish Gaelic); Lewys (Welsh).

Liam French; to bind, hence loyalty. Occasional use from 1955 peaking in heavy use in 1990. *Other form*: Lyam.

Lincoln Latin/Old English; settlement by the lake.

Lindell Old English; valley of the linden (lime) trees.

Linden Old German; lime tree. (See Gender-neutral names.)

Lindley Old English; linden (lime tree) field.

Lindo Old German; gentle man.

Linford, Lynford Old English; ford near the linden (lime) trees.

Lionel Latin; little lion. Occasional use from 1900, peaking in 1935 and falling out of use in 1975. *Other forms*: Leonel, Lynel. *Variant*: Lionello (Italian).

Lloyd Welsh; grey-haired, mature. Occasional use from 1925. *Other forms*: Floyd, Loy. *Variant*: Llwyd (Welsh).

Logan Scottish Gaelic; little hollow.

Lomas, Lomax Old English; by the pool.

Lon Basque; lion.

Lorcan Irish Gaelic; fierce.

Loren A form of Laurence. (See Gender-neutral names.)

Lorin A form of Laurence.

Lou A form of Louis. *Other form*: Louie. (See Gender-neutral names.)

Louis A French form of the Old German name Ludwig, meaning famous in battle. Occasional use from 1900 rising to light use in 1990. *Other forms*: Elois, Lew, Lewie, Lewis, Lou, Louie, Lui. *Variants*: Koldo (Basque); Ludek, Ludvik (Czech); Lodewijk (Dutch);

Aloys, Clovis (French); Lodevig, Lothar, Ludwig
(German); Lui (Hawaiian); Lugaidh (Irish Gaelic);
Lodovico, Ludovico, Luigi (Italian); Lutek (Polish);
Ludis (Russian); Ludvig (Scandinavian); Ludovic
(Scottish); Luthais (Scottish Gaelic); Luis (Spanish);
Ludvik (Swedish).

Lowell Old English; beloved.

Lucas A Latin form of Luke. Occasional use from 1935.
Other form: Lukas.

Lucian Latin; from the Roman name Lucius, meaning
light.

Lucien A French form of Lucian. Occasional use 1955–75.
Variants: Lucienne (French); Luciano (Italian); Lucais
(Scottish Gaelic). (See Gender-neutral names.)

Ludovic A Scottish form of Louis. *Variant*:
Maoldomhnaich (Scottish Gaelic).

Lukas A German form of Luke.

Luke Greek; man from Lucania, a district in southern
Italy. Occasional use from 1900 falling out of use by
1925. Revived in 1960 and rose steadily into heavy use
by 1990. *Variants*: Luk (Cornish); Lukas (Czech); Lucas
(Dutch); Luc, Lucien (French); Lukas (German); Loukas
(Greek); Luc (Irish); Lucas (Irish Gaelic); Luca, Lucano
(Italian); Lukasz (Polish); Luka Lukasha (Russian);
Lucais, Lucas (Scottish Gaelic); Lucas, Lucio (Spanish);
Luc (Welsh).

Lumin Latin; light.

Lundy Scottish Gaelic; grove by the island.

Lyle French; from the island.

Lyndon Old English; hill with lime trees. Occasional use
from 1925 peaking in 1965. *Other form*: Lindon.

Lynton, Linton Old English; village near the brook.

Lynwood, Linwood Old English; wood near the brook.

Lysander Greek; liberator.

M

MacGill Scottish Gaelic; son of the stranger.

Mackenzie Scottish Gaelic; son of the wise ruler. (See Gender-neutral names.)

Macmillan Scottish Gaelic; son of the tonsured man (hermit or monk).

Macy French; hill, range of hills. (See Gender-neutral names.)

Maddison Old English; fortunate, good. (See Gender-neutral names.)

Madigan Possibly Irish Gaelic; a bear.

Madoc Welsh; fortunate, generous. *Other form*: Maddock.

Magee Irish Gaelic; son of Hugh.

Magen Hebrew; protector.

Magnus Latin; great.

Mahon Irish Gaelic; a bear.

Makani Tahitian; the wind.

Makoto Japanese; sincerity.

Malcolm Scottish Gaelic; disciple of St Columba. Light use from 1900 peaking in heavy use in 1950. *Other forms*: Calum, Mal. *Variant*: Maol-Caluim (Scottish Gaelic).

Malone Irish Gaelic; servant (follower) of St John.

Malvin Celtic; cultured ruler.

Manco Quechua; supreme leader.

Mandar Mandar; the name of a tribe in Indonesia.

Mandel Hebrew/German; man. *Other forms*: Mandy, Mendel.

Mandella Native American; ceremonial shield.

Mander Romany; from myself, hence my child.

Manfred Old German; man of peace. *Other form*: Mana. *Variants*: Manfried (German); Manfredo (Italian).

Manton Old English; hero's village.

Maona Winnebago; Creator, earth-maker.

Marar Watamare; land, earth.

Marc A French form of Mark. Light use from 1965 peaking in 1980. *Other form*: Marcel. *Variants*: Marzellus (German); Marcello (Italian).

Marco An Italian form of Mark.

Marcus The original Latin form of Mark. Occasional use from 1900 peaking in 1970.

Marin Latin; the sea. Associated with Marin county, California, an area with a free lifestyle.

Mario An Italian form of Marius.

Marius From the Roman clan name Marius, linked with Mars, the god of war. *Variants*: Mario (Italian); Marian (Polish); Mariano (Spanish).

Mark From the Roman name Marcus, linked with Mars, the god of war. Occasional use from 1900, rising into light use in 1955 and then rapidly into very heavy use in 1960. It peaked in 1965 and declined into light use by 1990. *Other forms*: Marc, Marcel, March, Marcus, Marius, Markus, Marsh, Martin. *Variants*: Margh (Cornish); Marek (Czech); Markus (Dutch, German); Marc, Marcel (French); Markos (Greek); Marcas (Irish and Scottish Gaelic); Marco (Italian); Marcos (Spanish, Portuguese); Marka, Markusha (Russian); Marko (Slovenian); Marc (Welsh).

Markus A Dutch and German form of Mark.

Marley Old English; lake in the meadow.

Marlin, Marlow, Marlo Forms of Merlin. (See Gender-neutral names.)

Marlon Probably derived from the surname Marlin, linked with Merlin. Occasional use from 1970 peaking in 1980.

Marquon, Marquell Forms of Mark.

Martin From the Roman name Martius, linked with Mars, the god of war. Occasional use from 1900, rising to heavy use in 1955, peaking in 1960 and declining into light use by 1990. *Other forms*: Mart, Marten, Martie, Martlet, Marty, Martyn, Mertin. *Variants*: Martinka, Tynek (Czech); Morten (Danish); Marten, Martijn (Dutch); Mertin (French); Martel (German); Martinos (Greek); Marton (Hungarian); Martain, Martan, Mairtin (Irish Gaelic); Marti, Martino (Italian); Martinas (Lithuanian); Martinho (Portuguese); Martyn (Russian); Martainn (Scottish Gaelic); Martinez, Marto (Spanish); Marten (Swedish); Martyn (Welsh).

Martyn A form of Martin. Occasional use from 1950 peaking in 1960.

Marvin Old English; friend of the sea. *Variants*: Morvan (Breton); Mervin (Irish).

Masamba Yao; leaves.

Mason Old French; stone-cutter.

Matai Samoan; chief.

Matalino Visayan; bright.

Mathew A form of Matthew. Occasional use from 1965 peaking in 1970.

Matthew Hebrew; gift of God. Light use from 1900, increasing from 1961 steadily towards its peak of very heavy use by 1990. *Other forms*: Mat, Mathew, Matt, Matthias, Matty, Mayo. *Variants*: Mateos (Armenian); Matai (Basque); Matei (Bulgarian); Matej, Matek (Czech); Mattaeus (Danish); Matheus (Dutch); Matthieu (French); Matthaus, Matthias (German); Matthaios (Greek); Makaio (Hawaiian); Matyas (Hungarian); Maitiu, Matha (Irish Gaelic); Matteo (Italian); Matas, Matiss (Latvian); Motiejus (Lithuanian); Matteus (Norwegian); Mateusz, Matyas (Polish); Mateus (Portuguese); Matfei, Matvey, Motya (Russian); Mata (Scottish Gaelic); Mateo, Matias (Spanish); Mathias, Matteus, Mattias (Swedish); Matviy (Ukrainian); Mathew (Welsh).

Maurice Latin; dark-skinned. Or Irish Gaelic; sea choice. Light use from 1900 peaking in 1935. *Other forms*: Maurey, Maurie, Maury, Mo, Morrie, Morris, Morry. *Variants*: Maurits (Dutch); Maur (French); Moritz (German); Mauli (Hawaiian); Muiris (Irish Gaelic); Maurizio (Italian); Mavriki (Russian); Maurits (Scandinavian); Maolmuire, Muireach (Scottish Gaelic); Mauricio (Spanish); Meurig (Welsh).

Maverick American; independent, free. Derived from the name of Samuel Maverick, a Texan who owned but did not brand cattle.

Max A form of Maximilian. Occasional use from 1935 peaking in 1990. *Other forms*: Maks, Maxy.

Maxie A form of Maximilian. (See Gender-neutral names.)

Maximilian Latin; great. Occasional use from 1965. *Other forms*: Mack, Maks, Max, Maxey, Maxie, Maxim, Maxwell, Maxy. *Variants*: Maxim (Czech); Maximilianus (Dutch); Maximilien, Maxime (French); Maximalian (German); Makszi, Miksa (Hungarian); Massimiliano, Massimo (Italian); Maksim, Sima (Russian); Maximiliano, Maximo (Spanish); Macsen (Welsh).

Maxwell Scottish Gaelic/Old English; Magnus's stream. Occasional use from 1935.

Maynard Old German; strong and powerful.

Mayo Scottish Gaelic; plain of the yew trees.

Mazin, Mazzi Arabic; proper.

Mazon Probably Illinois; nettle.

Mead, Meade Old English; meadow.

Meldon Old English; mill on the hillside.

Melvin Old English; friendly counsellor. Occasional use 1900–80. *Other forms*: Malvin, Mel, Melvyn, Vinny, Vynnie. *Variant*: Melfyn (Welsh).

Melvyn A form of Melvin. Occasional use 1935–80 peaking in 1950.

Meredith Welsh; defender of the sea. *Variant*: Mereddud (Welsh). (See Gender-neutral names.)

Merlin Welsh; sea fort. *Variant*: Marlon (French). (See Gender-neutral names.)

Merrick A Welsh form of Maurice.

Merton Old English; sea town.

Mervyn Welsh; sea fort. Occasional use 1925–60.

Meryn A Cornish name of uncertain meaning. *Other form*: Merryn.

Micah Hebrew; who is like God? *Other forms*: Mica, Micaiah, Micha, Michah. (See Gender-neutral names.)

Michael Hebrew; who is like God? Light use from 1900 rising to very heavy use at its peak in 1950. It then declined slowly but was still in heavy use in 1990. *Other forms*: Micah, Michal, Mick, Mickey, Mickie, Micky, Mikael, Mike, Mikey, Mikkel, Misha, Mitch, Mitchel, Mitchell, Mychal. *Variants*: Mikel (Basque);

Mikael (Breton); Mihail (Bulgarian); Myghal (Cornish);
Michal, Misko (Czech); Mikkel (Danish); Michiel
(Dutch); Mihkel (Estonian); Mika, Mikko (Finnish);
Michal, Michel (French); Mikhalis, Mikhos (Greek);
Mikaele (Hawaiian); Mihal, Mihaly, Miska
(Hungarian); Micheal (Irish Gaelic); Michele (Italian);
Mikelis (Latvian); Mikas, Mikelis (Lithuanian); Mikkel
(Norwegian, Danish); Michal, Michalek (Polish);
Miguel (Portuguese); Mihail, Mihas (Romanian);
Michail, Mikhail, Mischa, Misha, Mishka, (Russian);
Micheil (Scottish Gaelic); Mikal (Slavonic); Micho,
Miguel, Miki (Spanish); Mikael (Swedish); Mahailo
(Ukrainian); Meical (Welsh).

Michal A Czech form of Michael. (See Gender-neutral
names.)

Mikael A Swedish form of Michael.

Mikal A Slavonic form of Michael.

Mikasi Omaha; coyote, hence shrewd, resourceful.

Mikkel A Norwegian form of Michael.

Milan Slavonic; beloved.

Miles Possibly Old German; generous. Occasional use
from 1965. *Other forms*: Mills, Milo, Myles. *Variants*:
Milo (Irish); Maolra (Irish Gaelic); Mael-Moire (Scottish
Gaelic).

Milton Old English; village near the mill. Occasional use
1900–80. *Other forms*: Millard, Mills, Milt, Miltie, Milty.

Mingan Native American; grey wolf.

Mingo A form of Domingo, a Spanish version of
Dominic.

Misha, Mishka Russian forms of Michael.

Mitchell A form of Michael. Occasional use from 1935
peaking in 1990. *Other form*: Mitch.

Mohammed Arabic; greatly praised. Occasional use from 1945 rising to light use in 1995. *Other forms*: Mohamed, Mohammad. Muhammed. *Variant*: Mahomet (Turkish).

Mohan Sanskrit; delightful.

Montague Latin; mountain. Occasional use 1900–35. *Other forms*: Montagu, Monty. *Variant*: Montel (Spanish).

Montel A Spanish form of Montague.

Montgomery Old French; rich man's hill. *Other form*: Monty. *Variant*: Monte (Spanish).

Monty A form of Montague or Montgomery.

Morgan Celtic; sea bright. *Other forms*: Morgen, Morgun, Morrgan. (See Gender-neutral names.)

Morley Old English; meadow or clearing by the moors.

Morris A form of Maurice. Occasional use 1900–55. *Other forms*: Maurie, Morey, Morrey, Morrie, Morrison, Morry.

Morton Old English; village by the moor.

Morven Irish Gaelic; great fair one. *Other form*: Morvan.

Moses Possibly Hebrew; saviour. *Variants*: Mousa (Arabic); Mozes (Dutch); Moise (French); Maois, Maoise (Irish Gaelic); Moszek (Polish); Mosya (Russian); Moishe (Yiddish).

Moultrie Possibly Scottish Gaelic; sea warrior.

Mugamba Runyoro; great talker.

Muir Scottish Gaelic; dweller by the moor.

Mulogo Musoga; shaman, wizard.

Mungo Scottish Gaelic; amiable.

Munro, Munroe Irish Gaelic; mouth of the river. *Variant*: Mac an rothaich (Scottish Gaelic).

Murdoch Scottish Gaelic; sea warrior. *Other forms*: Murdo, Murdock. *Variant*: Murtagh (Irish Gaelic).

Murphy Irish Gaelic; sea warrior. (See Gender-neutral names.)

Murray Scottish Gaelic; seaboard settlement. Occasional use from 1935. *Other form*: Murry. *Variant*: Moirreach (Scottish Gaelic).

Musoke Rukonjo; born while a rainbow was in the sky.

Mycroft Old English; marsh homestead.

Myo Burmese; city.

N

Nain Hebrew; pleasant.

Nairn Celtic; dweller by the alder tree.

Najji Muganda; second child.

Nakos Arapaho; sage, wise.

Namid Chippewa; star dancer.

Nanda Sanskrit; joy. (See Gender-neutral names.)

Nando A German form of Ferdinand. Old German; prepared for the journey.

Nangila Abaluhya; born on a journey.

Nantan Apache; spokesman.

Naralian Australian; lover of the sea.

Nardo Old German; strong, hardy.

Narok Masai; a place-name in Kenya.

Nashashuk Fox, Sauk; loud thunder.

Nathan Hebrew; God has given. Occasional use from 1960 peaking in light use in 1990. *Other forms*: Nat, Nate. *Variant*: Natan (Spanish).

Nathaniel Hebrew; God has given. Occasional use from 1900. *Variants*: Nathanael (French); Nataniele (Italian); Natanael (Spanish).

Navin Hindi; new.

Neal A form of Neil. Occasional use from 1950.

Ned A form of Edward.

Neil Irish Gaelic; champion. Light use from 1935 peaking in heavy use in 1975. *Other forms*: Neal, Neale, Neall, Neill, Nelson, Nial, Niall, Nyles. *Variants*: Niall (Irish and Scottish Gaelic); Nilya (Russian); Niels, Nils, Njal (Scandinavian).

Nelson Son of Neil. Occasional use from 1900 peaking in 1925.

Nevil A form of Neville. Occasional use 1925–65.

Neville French; new town. Occasional use from 1925. *Other forms*: Nev, Nevil, Nevill.

Nevin Irish Gaelic; holy one. *Other forms*: Nevan, Niven.

Newton Old English; from the new village.

Niall An Irish and Scottish Gaelic form of Neil. Occasional use from 1965.

Niam Irish Gaelic; champion.

Nicholas Greek; victory people. Occasional use from 1900 peaking in heavy use in 1975. *Other forms*: Cole, Collis, Nic, Nick, Nickie, Nicky, Nicol, Nikki, Nilo. *Variants*: Nigoghos (Armenian); Mikolas (Basque); Nicca (Cornish); Niki, Nikulas (Czech); Niels (Danish); Klaas, Nicolaas (Dutch); Nikolai (Estonian); Lasse, Niilo (Finnish); Colas, Colin, Nicolas, Nicole (French); Claus, Klaus, Niklaus, Nikolas (German); Nikolos, Nikos (Greek); Nikolao (Hawaiian); Miklos (Hungarian); Nicol, Nioclas (Irish Gaelic); Cola, Nicola, Nico, Nicolo, Niccolo (Italian); Kola, Niklaus (Latvian); Nikolajus (Lithuanian); Niklas, Nils (Norwegian); Mikolaj, Milek, Milosz (Polish); Nicolao (Portuguese); Nicolae (Romanian); Kolya, Nicola, Nicolai, Nikita,

Nikolai (Russian); Nicol (Scottish); Neacal (Scottish Gaelic); Nicolao, Nicolas (Spanish); Niklas, Nils (Swedish); Mikolai, Mykola (Ukrainian).

Nicky A form of Nicholas. (See Gender-neutral names.)

Nicolas A form of Nicholas. Occasional use from 1960.

Nigel Latin; black. Occasional use from 1925. *Other forms*: Nige, Nye. *Variants*: Neils, Niels, Nils (Scandinavian).

Ninian Possibly Latin; full of life. *Variant*: Ninnidh (Irish Gaelic).

Niran Thai; eternal.

Nkunda Runyankore; loves those who hate him.

Noah Possibly Hebrew; long-lived. Occasional use 1900–70. *Variants*: Noach (Dutch); Noe (French); Noi, Noy (Russian); Noak (Scandinavian).

Noel French; Christmas. Occasional use 1900–80. *Other form*: Nowell. *Variants*: Nadelek (Cornish); Natale (Italian); Natal (Spanish). (See Gender-neutral names.)

Nolan Irish Gaelic; famous. Occasional use 1965–80.

Norman Old English; man from the north. Light use from 1900, peaking in heavy use in 1925 and then declining into occasional use. *Other forms*: Norm, Normand, Norrie, Norris, Norry. *Variants*: Normand (French); Normann (German); Normando (Spanish).

Norton Old English; northern village.

Norval A character in the play *Douglas* by John Home.

Norvin, Norvyn Old English; friend of the north.

Nui Rapanui; great.

O

Ocean Greek; sea, ocean. (See Gender-neutral names.)

Odo Old German; riches. *Variants*: Othon (French); Otto

(German); Otello (Italian); Otek, Tonek (Polish); Otilio, Tilo (Spanish).

Ogden Old English; oak tree valley.

Ogima Chippewa; chief.

Oisin French; bird, hence a free spirit.

Oko Ga; older twin.

Okon Efik; born at night.

Okuth Luo; born during a rain shower.

Olaf Old Norse; ancestor. *Variants*: Olof (Icelandic); Amhlaoibh (Irish Gaelic); Olav (Scandinavian); Aulay (Scottish); Amhlaidh (Scottish Gaelic).

Oliver Latin; olive tree. Occasional use from 1900 rising to a peak of light use in 1990. *Other forms*: Olivier, Ollie, Olly. *Variants*: Olivier (French); Oliwa (Hawaiian); Oilibhear (Irish Gaelic); Oliviero (Italian); Oliverio (Spanish).

Olivier A French form of Oliver.

Ollie A form of Oliver. (See Gender-neutral names.)

Omar Arabic; most high. *Variant*: Omari (Swahili).

O'Neil Irish Gaelic; son of Neil.

Oram Old English; riverbank enclosure.

Oran Celtic; coldwater spring.

Orban Latin; a globe, hence the world.

Orde Old English; spear.

Ordway Old English; ridgeway path.

Oren, Orin Irish Gaelic; dark-haired.

Orien Latin; east, the Orient.

Orion Greek; son of fire. A hunter who became a constellation in Greek mythology. *Variant*: Zorion

(Basque).

Orlan, Orlen Latin; golden.

Orlando An Italian form of Roland.

Orson Latin; a bear. *Variants*: Urson (French); Orsino (Italian).

Orton Old English; shore town.

Orville French; golden town.

Orvis A blend of Orville and Travis. *Other form*: Orvin.

Osaze Benin; whom God likes.

Oscar Old English; divine strength. Occasional use from 1900. *Other forms*: Oskar, Ossie, Ozzie. *Variants*: Asger (Danish); Oskari (Finnish); Oskar (German); Osgar (Scottish Gaelic).

Osmond, Osmund Old English; protected by God.

Otis Greek; keen of hearing.

Ottah Urhobo; thin at birth.

Owain A Welsh form of Eugene.

Owen A Welsh form of Eugene. Occasional use from 1900. *Variants*: Owain, Ywain (Welsh).

Owny, Owney Irish Gaelic; ancient, hence an old and wise soul.

P

Palmer Old English; one who carries a palm branch, hence a pilgrim.

Paris In Greek mythology the son of Priam who carried off Helen from Sparta to Troy. (See Gender-neutral names.)

Pat A form of Patrick. (See Gender-neutral names.)

Patrick Latin; noble person, patrician. Light use from

1900 peaking in 1965. *Other forms*: Paddie, Paddy, Pat, Patrice. *Variants*: Patrice (French); Patrizius (German); Pakelike (Hawaiian); Padraig (Irish Gaelic); Patrizio (Italian); Patek (Polish); Payton (Scottish); Padair, Padruig, Paruig (Scottish Gaelic); Patricio (Spanish); Padrig (Welsh).

Patrin Romany; trailblazer.

Patton Old English; from the warrior's estate.

Paul Greek; small. Light use from 1925, peaking in very heavy use in 1965 and then declining into light use by 1990. *Other forms*: Poul, Powle. *Variants*: Pau (Catalan); Pawly (Cornish); Pavel (Czech); Poul (Danish); Paavo, Pavo (Finnish); Paulin (German); Palika (Hungarian); Pall (Icelandic); Pol (Irish and Scottish Gaelic); Paulino, Paulo (Italian); Pawel (Polish); Pashka, Pava, Pavel, Pavlik (Russian); Pablo (Spanish); Pal (Swedish); Pawl (Welsh).

Paxton Latin; peaceful village.

Payton, Peyton Old English; from the warrior's farm.

Pedrek, Pedrick, Petroc Names linked with Petrock, a Cornish saint's name of uncertain meaning.

Pelham Old English; Peola's homestead.

Penn Old English; enclosure.

Penryn Cornish; headland.

Percival A French name meaning valley piercer invented by the historian of the Grail legends, Chretien de Troyes. Occasional use from its peak in 1900 to 1950. *Other forms*: Perceval, Percy. *Variants*: Perceval (Old French); Parzifal (German).

Percy A form of Percival. Heavy use at its peak in 1900, then declined and fell out of use by 1950. Small revival in 1990.

Peregrine Latin; wanderer. *Variants*: Peregrin (German); Pellegrino (Italian).

Perry A form of Peregrine. Occasional use from 1965. *Other forms*: Peri, Perri.

Peter Greek; a rock. Light use from 1900, rising into heavy use by 1925 and very heavy use by 1935. Peaked in 1950 and had declined into light use by 1990. *Other forms*: Per, Perkin, Pernell, Pete, Pierce, Piers. *Variants*: Boutros (Arabic); Bedros (Armenian); Pello, Peru (Basque); Piotr (Bulgarian); Pere (Catalan); Petrik; Petr (Czech); Peder, Preben (Danish); Piet, Pieter (Dutch); Pekka (Finnish); Pierre, Pierot (French); Petrus (German); Petros, Takis (Greek); Pekelo (Hawaiian); Feoras, Peadar, Piaras (Irish Gaelic); Piero, Pietro (Italian); Peteris (Latvian); Petras (Lithuanian); Peder, Peer, Per (Norwegian); Pietrek, Piotr (Polish); Petar, Petru (Romanian); Petya, Pyotr (Russian); Peadair (Scottish Gaelic); Pjotr (Slavonic); Pedro (Spanish, Portuguese); Peder, Per, Petter (Swedish); Petro (Ukrainian); Pedr (Welsh).

Philip Greek; lover of horses. Light use from 1900 peaking in heavy use in 1960. *Other forms*: Phil, Phillip, Phip, Pip. *Variants*: Filip (Czech); Philippus (Dutch); Philippe (French); Philipp (German); Phillipos (Greek); Pilipo (Hawaiian); Pilib (Irish Gaelic); Filippo (Italian); Filipek, Fil (Polish); Filya (Russian); Filip (Scandinavian); Filib (Scottish Gaelic); Felipe (Spanish); Phylip (Welsh).

Phillip A form of Philip. Occasional use from 1925 peaking in 1950.

Piers A form of Peter. Occasional use from 1950. *Other form*: Pierce. *Variants*: Per, Perig (Breton); Feoras, Ferris, Piaras (Irish Gaelic).

Pillan Araucanian; supreme essence. The name of the Araucanian god of thunder.

Powell Celtic; alert, watchful.

Precious Latin; of great price. (See Gender-neutral names.)

Presley Old English; priest's meadow.

Preston Old English; from the priest's estate.

Q

Quaid A character in the novel *Total Recall* by Piers Anthony.

Quan Comanche; fragrant.

Quentin Latin; the fifth. Occasional use 1955–65. *Other forms*: Quenton, Quint, Quintin, Quinton. *Variants*: Quintus (German); Quintilio, Quinto (Italian); Caointean (Scottish Gaelic).

Quillan Irish Gaelic; cub.

Quincy French/Latin; fifth son.

Quinn Irish Gaelic; counsel. *Other form*: Quint. (See Gender-neutral names.)

Quinton A form of Quentin.

R

Radford Old English; river crossing with reeds.

Radnor Old English; shore with reeds.

Raleigh Old English; meadow of the roe deer.

Ralph Old Norse; wolf counsel. Occasional use from 1900, peaking in 1925 and then declining and falling out of use by 1990. *Other forms*: Rafe, Ralf, Randolph, Raul. *Variants*: Raw (Cornish); Raoul (French); Rolf

(German); Radhulbh (Irish Gaelic); Raul (Italian, Spanish); Rolle (Swedish).

Ramon A Spanish form of Raymond. Occasional use 1925–55. *Other form*: Raman.

Ramsay, Ramsey Irish Gaelic; raven's island.

Randal, Randall Forms of Randolph. (See Gender-neutral names.)

Randolph Old English; wolf shield. *Other forms*: Randal, Randolf, Randy, Rannulph. *Variant*: Rannulbh (Irish Gaelic). (See Gender-neutral names.)

Randy A form of Randolph. (See Gender-neutral names.)

Ransley Old English; raven meadow.

Raphael Hebrew; God has healed. Occasional use from 1980. *Other forms*: Rafael, Rafi. *Variants*: Rafaelle (French); Raffaele, Raffaello (Italian); Rafal (Polish); Rafael (Spanish).

Raven Old Norse; raven. (See Gender-neutral names.)

Rawley Old English; deer meadow.

Ray A form of Raymond. Occasional use 1950–70.

Raymond Old German; wise protection. Light use from 1900, peaking in heavy use in 1935 and then declining steadily until it fell out of use in 1990. *Other forms*: Ray, Raymund, Reamonn. *Variants*: Rajmund (Czech); Ramone (Dutch); Aymon (French); Raimund, Reimund (German); Reamann, Lei (Hawaiian); Reamonn (Irish Gaelic); Raimondo (Italian); Raimundo (Portuguese); Reimond (Romanian); Raimundo, Raman, Ramon, Mundo (Spanish).

Reagan, Regan Irish; king. (See Gender-neutral names.)

Redford Old English; river crossing with reeds.

Reece A form of Rhys. Occasional use from 1990.

Reed Old English; red-haired. *Other form*: Reid.

Reeve Old English; magistrate.

Reginald Old Norse; strong counsel. Light use from 1900, peaking in 1925 and then declining and falling out of use in 1980. *Other forms*: Reg, Reggie, Rene, Reynold. *Variants*: Reinold (Dutch); Reginauld, Renault, Rene (French); Reinald, Reinwald (German); Raghnall (Irish Gaelic); Reginaldo, Rinaldo (Italian); Reginaldo, Reinaldo, Naldo (Spanish); Reinhold (Swedish, Danish).

Rehema Kiswahili; second-born son.

Reiss A form of Rhys. Occasional use from 1990.

Remington Old English; village near the border.

Rene A French form of Reginald. Occasional use 1900–50. *Other form*: Ren. (See Gender-neutral names.)

Reuben Hebrew; behold a son. Occasional use from its peak in 1900 but now in decline. *Other forms*: Reuven, Revie, Rube, Ruben, Rubin, Ruby, Ruvane. *Variants*: Ruupeni (Finnish); Ruben (Spanish); Rouvin (Greek); Ruvim (Russian).

Rex Latin; king. Occasional use from its peak in 1935.

Reynor Old German; brave counsel. *Other form*: Rayner. *Variants*: Rainier (French); Rainer (German); Rainerio (Italian); Ragnar (Scandinavian).

Rhesa Chaldean; prince.

Rhys Welsh; ardour. Occasional use from 1980. *Other forms*: Reece, Reese, Reiss, Rey, Rhett, Rhice.

Richard Old German; strong ruler. Light use from 1900, rising into heavy use in 1950 and peaking in very heavy use in 1965. Now slowly declining again. *Other forms*: Diccon, Dick, Dickie, Dicky, Dix, Dixy, Hickson, Hudd, Ric, Rich, Richie, Rick, Ricky, Ritchie. *Variants*:

Hicca (Cornish); Richart (Dutch); Arri, Riki (Estonian); Reichard, Richart (German); Rihardos (Greek); Likeke (Hawaiian); Rikard (Hungarian); Riocard, Risteard (Irish Gaelic); Riccardo (Italian); Rysio (Polish); Rostik, Rostya (Russian); Rikard (Scandinavian); Ruiseart (Scottish Gaelic); Ricardo, Rico, Riqui (Spanish).

Ricky A form of Richard. Occasional use from 1960 peaking in 1985 and 1990. *Other forms*: Rick, Rik.

Riley, Ryley Old English; rye meadow. (See Gender-neutral names.)

Rimmon Persian; the angel of the storm in Persian mythology.

Ringo Japanese; apple. Or a reference to a habit of wearing rings.

Rio Spanish; river. (See Gender-neutral names.)

Riordan Irish Gaelic; descendant of a royal bard.

Ripley Old English; long clearing. (See Gender-neutral names.)

River Old French; river. (See Gender-neutral names.)

Roald Scandinavian; famous power.

Robbie A form of Robert. Occasional use from 1965 peaking in 1990. (See Gender-neutral names.)

Robert Old English; bright fame. Heavy use from 1900, peaking in very heavy use in 1950 and then declining slowly into heavy use by 1990. *Other forms*: Bob, Bobby, Dob, Hob, Hodge, Rab, Rob, Robbie, Roberts, Robin, Robson, Rory, Nobby. *Variants*: Bobek (Czech); Robard, Robers, Robin (French); Robrecht, Rupert, Ruprecht (German); Lopaka (Hawaiian); Robi (Hungarian); Riobard, Roibeard (Irish Gaelic); Roberto, Ruperto (Italian); Rosertas (Lithuanian); Railbeart, Roban (Scottish Gaelic); Roberto (Spanish); Rhobet, Robet, Robyn (Welsh).

Rock Latin; a stone. *Other forms*: Rocklin, Rocklyn. *Variants*: Roch (French); Rochus (German, Dutch); Rocco (Italian).

Rockford Old English; rocky river crossing.

Rockley Old English; rocky field.

Rockwell Old English; rocky spring.

Roderick Old German; famous ruler. Occasional use from 1925, peaking in 1955 and falling out of use in 1975. There was a small revival in 1990. *Other forms*: Rod, Roddy. *Variants*: Roderique (French); Roderich (German); Ruaidhri (Irish Gaelic); Rodrigo (Italian); Rurich, Rurik (Russian); Ruairidh (Scottish Gaelic); Rodrigo, Ruy (Spanish).

Rodney Old English; cleared land near water. Occasional use 1925–80. *Other forms*: Rod, Rodders, Roddy.

Rogan Scottish Gaelic; red-haired.

Roger Old English; famous warrior. Occasional use from 1900 peaking in light use in 1950. *Other forms*: Rodge, Rodger, Roj. *Variants*: Rutger (Dutch); Rudiger, Rudi (German); Rogerios (Hungarian); Ruggiero (Italian); Gerek (Polish); Rogerio (Spanish).

Rohan Sanskrit; ascending, healing. Also associated with *The Lord of the Rings* by Tolkien. (See Gender-neutral names.)

Rohin Hindi; the upward path.

Roland Old German; famous land. Occasional use from 1900 peaking in 1925. *Other forms*: Orlando, Rolland, Rollo, Rowland. *Variants*: Roeland (Dutch); Orlando, Ruland (German); Lorand, Lorant (Hungarian); Rodhlann, Rodhulbh, Rolann (Irish Gaelic); Orlando, Rolando (Italian); Rolek (Polish); Lando, Orlo, Rolando, Roldan (Spanish); Rolant (Welsh).

Romney Old English; broad river.

Ronald Old Norse; strong counsel. Occasional use from 1900 peaking in very heavy use in 1935. *Other forms*: Ron, Ronnie, Ronny. *Variants*: Raghnall (Irish Gaelic); Ronaldo (Italian); Ranald (Scottish); Raghnall (Scottish Gaelic); Renaldo (Spanish).

Ronan Irish Gaelic; little seal.

Ronnie A form of Ronald. Occasional use 1925–85.

Ronson Scottish; son of Ronald.

Rory Scottish Gaelic; red-haired. Occasional use from 1965 peaking in 1990. *Other forms*: Rorey, Rorie. *Variants*: Ruaidhri (Irish Gaelic); Ruairidh, Ruaridh (Scottish Gaelic); Rurik (Slavonic).

Roscoe Scandinavian; deer forest.

Ross Scottish Gaelic; cape. Occasional use from 1950 peaking in 1990. *Variants*: Ros, Rosach (Scottish Gaelic).

Rowan Scottish Gaelic; red-haired. (See Gender-neutral names.)

Rowland A form of Roland. Occasional use 1900–80.

Roy Scottish Gaelic; red-haired. Occasional use from 1900 peaking in heavy use in 1935. *Other forms*: Royle, Royston. *Variants*: Loe (Hawaiian); Ruffino (Italian); Rory (Scottish); Rey (Spanish).

Royce Probably Old German; kind fame.

Roydon Old English; hill where rye grows.

Royston German/Old French; Rohesia's cross. Occasional use 1925–85. *Other form*: Roystan.

Rudolf Old German; famous wolf. *Other forms*: Dolf, Rudi, Rudy. *Variants*: Rudek (Czech); Rodolphe (French); Rudi (German); Rezso (Hungarian); Rudolfo, Rudolpho (Italian); Rodolfo (Spanish).

Rudyard Old English; red enclosure.

Rufus Latin; red-haired.

Ruhakana Rukiga; fond of debate, argumentative.

Rupert A German form of Robert. Occasional use form 1925.

Ruskin Old German; red-haired child.

Russell French; red-haired. Occasional use from 1900 peaking in light use in 1960. *Other forms*: Russ, Russel, Rusty. *Variants*: Lukela (Hawaiian); Rosario (Italian).

Ryan Scottish Gaelic; little king. Occasional use from 1970 peaking in heavy use in 1990. *Other forms*: Rian, Ry, Rye, Ryen.

Ryder Old English; knight, rider.

Rydon Old English; Rye valley.

Ryker Scottish Gaelic; one who reaches or strives.

Rylan Old English; place where rye grows.

Ryman Old English; rye seller.

S

Sasha A Russian form of Alexander. (See Gender-neutral names.)

Sage From the name of the herb. (See Gender-neutral names.)

Salim Arabic; flawless, whole. *Variant*: Salman (Czech).

Sam A form of Samuel. Occasional use from 1925 peaking in light use in 1990. (See Gender-neutral names.)

Samar Hebrew; guarded by God.

Sammy A form of Samuel. Occasional use from 1980.

Sampson Possibly Hebrew; child of Shamash the sun god. *Variants*: Sansone (Italian); Sanson (Spanish).

Samuel Hebrew; heard by God. Light use from its peak in 1900, declining into occasional use by 1950 but then reviving again into heavy use in 1990. *Other forms*: Sam, Sami, Sammie, Sammy. *Variants*: Samko, Samo (Czech); Zamiel (German); Samouel (Greek); Shem (Hebrew); Kamuela (Hawaiian); Samu (Hungarian); Somhairle (Irish Gaelic); Salvatore, Samuele (Italian); Samaru (Japanese); Simao (Portuguese); Samvel (Russian); Somhairle (Scottish Gaelic); Sawyl (Welsh).

Sandon Old English; dweller on the sandy down.

Sandusky Wyandot; the name of a river in Ohio.

Sandy A form of Alexander. Occasional use from 1965. *Variant*: Sandaidh (Scottish Gaelic). (See Gender-neutral names.)

Sanford Old English; sandy river crossing.

Sanjay Sanskrit; triumphant.

Saxon Old English; people of the swords.

Schuyler Dutch; shelter, or wise man.

Scott Old English; from Scotland. Occasional use from 1950 peaking in light use in 1990. *Other forms*: Scot, Scottie, Scotty.

Seamus An Irish Gaelic form of James. *Other forms*: Seamas, Shamus. *Variant*: Seumas (Scottish Gaelic).

Sean An Irish Gaelic form of John. Occasional use from 1950 peaking in light use in 1965. *Other forms*: Shane, Shaughn, Shaun, Shawn. *Variants*: Sezni (Breton); Zenan (Cornish).

Seaton Old English; place by the sea. *Other form*: Seton.

Sebastian Greek; venerable. Occasional use from 1970. *Other forms*: Bastian, Seb, Sebby. *Variants*: Sebastien (French); Sebastianus (German); Sebatiano (Italian); Sevastian (Russian).

Sefton Old Norse; village where rushes grew.

Selby Old German; manor farmhouse.

Selwyn Old English; holy friend. Occasional use 1900–35.

Seraiah Hebrew; warrior of God. (See Gender-neutral names.)

Seth Hebrew; to set.

Seton Old English; dweller by cultivated land.

Seymour Old English; moor by the sea.

Shaka Zulu; first, founder.

Shane An Anglicized form of Sean. Occasional use from 1955 peaking in 1990. *Other form*: Shayne.

Shanto Bengali; quiet one.

Sharad Gujarati; autumn.

Shaun A phonetic form of Sean. Occasional use from 1955 peaking in light use in 1965. *Other form*: Shawn.

Shaw Old English; dweller by the wood.

Shawn A form of Shaun. Occasional use 1965–85.

Shay Irish Gaelic; courteous. *Other form*: Shael.

Shayne A form of Shane. Occasional use 1980–5.

Sheldon Old English; sheltered hill.

Shenton Old English; bright village.

Sheridan Irish Gaelic; eternal treasure.

Sherman Old English; shearman (cutter of nap from woollen cloth).

Shiloh Possibly Hebrew; tranquillity. In the Bible, a place near Jerusalem. *Other form*: Shilo. (See Gender-neutral names.)

Sholto Old French; sultan.

Shosan Hebrew; praise, affection.

Sidney Norman French; from the French place-name
Saint-Denis. Heavy use at its peak in 1900 then steadily
declining until it fell out of use in 1985. *Other forms*:
Sid, Syd, Sydney. *Variants*: Sidonio (Spanish). (See
Gender-neutral names.)

Siegfried Old German; victorious peace. *Other forms*:
Seifert, Sig, Sigfrid, Siggy, Ziggy. *Variants*: Sigfroi
(French); Szygfrid (Hungarian); Sigefriedo (Italian);
Sigvard (Norwegian); Zygi (Polish); Siguefredo
(Portuguese); Zigfrid (Russian); Sigfredo (Spanish).

Sigmund Old German; shield of victory. *Other forms*: Sig,
Siggy, Sigmond. *Variants*: Sigismundus (Dutch);
Sigismond (French); Zsigmond (Hungarian);
Sigismondo (Italian); Zygmunt (Polish); Sigismundo
(Spanish).

Silas Latin; from Silvanus, the Roman god of woodland.
Variants: Silvain (French); Silvanus (German); Silvano
(Italian); Silvio (Spanish).

Silvester Latin; woody, rural. *Other form*: Sly. *Variants*:
Sylvestre (French); Silvestro (Italian).

Simba Kiswahili; lion, strong person.

Simcha Hebrew; joy.

Simeon Hebrew; listen attentively. Occasional use
1965–85.

Simon A form of Simeon. Occasional use from 1900,
peaking in heavy use in 1970 and then declining into
light use by 1985. *Other forms*: Cimon, Cy, Si, Sim, Simi,
Simm, Simpson, Sy. *Variants*: Samein (Arabic); Simeon
(French); Simeon, Sim (German); Semon (Greek);
Shimon (Hebrew); Siomon (Irish Gaelic); Simone
(Italian); Simao (Portuguese); Simion (Romanian);

Semjon (Russian); Sim, Simidh (Scottish Gaelic); Ximenes (Spanish); Seimon (Welsh).

Sinclair From the French place-name St Clair.

Skeeter Old English; swift.

Skelly Scottish Gaelic; storyteller.

Sky Old English; vault of heaven, sky, hence high aspirations. (See Gender-neutral names.)

Skyler Dutch; scholar. (See Gender-neutral names.)

Sloan Scottish Gaelic; warrior. (See Gender-neutral names.)

Solomon Hebrew; peace. Occasional use 1900–85. *Other forms*: Salomon, Salo, Saloman, Sol, Sollie, Solly, Zalman, Zelmo, Zollie, Zolly. *Variants*: Sulaiman (Arabic); Selevan (Cornish); Salamun (Czech); Salomo (Dutch, German); Salomon (French, Spanish); Shlomo (Hebrew); Salamon (Hungarian); Solamh (Irish Gaelic); Salomone (Italian); Salamen (Polish); Salomon, Salomo (Scandinavian).

Somerset Old English; place of the summer settlers.

Songan Native American; strong.

Sonny A form of Orson, Grayson, etc. (See Gender-neutral names.)

Sorrell, Sorrel Scandinavian; Viking. Or French; chestnut-coloured. *Variant*: Soren (Swedish).

Spencer Old English; dispenser of provisions. Occasional use from 1960 peaking in 1975. *Other forms*: Spence, Spenser.

Spike Old English; ear of grain. *Other form*: Spyke.

Spokane Siwash; sun.

Stafford Old English; riverbank landing place.

Stanford Old English; rocky river crossing.

Stanley Old English; stony meadow. Light use from 1900, peaking in heavy use in 1925 and then declining and falling out of use by 1990. *Other forms*: Stan, Stanleigh, Stanly, Stanton.

Stanton Old English; village near the stony field.

Star, Starr Old English; star.

Stedman Old English; owner of a farm.

Stefan A German and Russian form of Stephen. Occasional use from 1955 peaking in 1985.

Stephen Greek; crown. Light use from 1900, peaking in very heavy use in 1955 and then declining into light use again by 1990. *Other forms*: Stefan, Stephan, Stevan, Steve, Steven, Stevie, Stevy. *Variants*: Esteve (Catalan); Stepka (Czech); Tapani, Teppo (Finnish); Etienne, Stephane (French); Stefan, Stephan, Steffen (German); Stavros, Stefanos, Stephanos (Greek); Kiwini (Hawaiian); Estevan, Istvan, Stephan (Hungarian); Stiana, Stiofan (Irish Gaelic); Stefano (Italian); Steffen (Norwegian); Szczepan (Polish); Estevao (Portuguese); Stefan, Stenya, Stepan (Russian); Steaphan (Scottish Gaelic); Esteban, Teb (Spanish); Stefan, Staffan (Swedish); Steffan, Ystffan (Welsh).

Steven A form of Stephen. Light use from 1950 peaking in heavy use in 1975. *Other forms*: Steve, Stevie.

Stewart A form of Stuart. Occasional use from 1900 peaking in 1960. *Other forms*: Steward, Stewie.

Stirling, Sterling Old English; without blemish.

Storr Old Norse; big.

Strachan Irish Gaelic; minstrel.

Strephon Greek; to turn. Invented by W. S. Gilbert for the operetta *Iolanthe*.

Struan Scottish Gaelic; stream.

Stuart Old English; chief of the royal household. Occasional use from 1900 peaking in heavy use in 1975. *Other forms*: Stewart, Stu, Stuie. *Variant*: Stiubhart (Scottish Gaelic).

Suamico Menominee; sandbar.

Sullivan Irish Gaelic; keen-eyed.

Susco Patwin; a Native American village name.

Swango Algonquian; eagle.

Sydney A form of Sidney. Light use from its peak in 1900, steadily declining until it fell out of use in 1960. There was a small revival in 1990. *Other form*: Syd. (See Gender-neutral names.)

T

Taamiti Lunyole; brave.

Tabor Persian; drummer.

Taggart Irish Gaelic; son of the priest.

Tai Chinese; peace.

Taj Urdu; crown.

Takoda Sioux; friend to all.

Talan Cornish/Breton; forehead, hence intelligence.

Taliesin Welsh; radiant brow. The name of a legendary Welsh poet. *Other form*: Talieson.

Taliki Hausa; man.

Talli Lenape; legendary hero.

Tally Aramaic; young lamb. (See Gender-neutral names.)

Tambaran Papuan; men's clubhouse or meeting place.

Tanek Greek; immortal. *Variants*: Atek (Polish); Tanas (Russian).

Tangye Possibly Breton; fire dog. A useful name for a

child born under this sign in Chinese astrology. (See Gender-neutral names.)

Tao Chinese; life-force or essence.

Tareth An anagram of T(he) earth.

Tarik Arabic; conqueror. *Other forms*: Tarek, Tari, Tariq.

Tarn Old Norse; lake in the mountains.

Taro Japanese; first son, big boy.

Tarok Tarok; the name of a tribe in Nigeria.

Taron A blend of Tad and Ronald.

Tarquin An Etruscan name of uncertain meaning. Tarquinius was the name of two of the early kings of Rome.

Tarwyn, Tarwin Welsh/Old English; white rock.

Tas Romany; bird's nest.

Tate Old English; cheerful. Or Native American; great talker. *Other form*: Tait.

Tau Tswana; lion.

Tavi, Tavey Aramaic; good.

Tavis Celtic; son of David.

Tay From the Scottish river name.

Taylor Old English; worker with cloth. (See Gender-neutral names.)

Taz Arabic; shallow cup.

Teague Celtic; poet.

Tembo Swahili; elephant.

Terence Latin; from the Roman clan name meaning gracious. *Other forms*: Tel, Telly, Terrance, Terrell, Terrence, Terry, Torn, Torrance, Torrey. *Variants*: Toirdealbhach (Irish Gaelic); Terenziano (Italian); Terencio (Spanish).

Terran Latin; dweller on planet Earth.

Terrence A form of Terence. Occasional use 1935–85.

Terry A form of Terence. Occasional use from 1925 peaking in 1965. (See Gender-neutral names.)

Tevin A blend of Terence and Kevin.

Thaddeus Greek; courageous. *Other forms*: Tad, Thad, Thadeus. *Variants*: Thadee (French); Thaddaus (German); Tadeo, Thaddeo (Italian); Tadek (Polish); Tadeo (Spanish); Fadey (Ukrainian).

Thane Scottish; warrior lord.

Theo A form of Theodore. Occasional use from 1990.

Theodore Greek; gift of God. *Variants*: Todor (Basque); Teodus (Czech); Theodorus (Dutch); Theodor (German); Teodoro (Italian, Spanish); Tedorik, Tolek (Polish); Fedor, Fedya, Fyodor (Russian); Feodor (Slavonic); Tewdr, Tudor (Welsh).

Theon Greek; godly.

Theron Greek; hunter.

Thomas Aramaic; twin. Very heavy use from its peak in 1900 then declining into occasional use by 1960. Started to revive almost at once and climbed back to very heavy use again by 1990. *Other forms*: Tam, Thom, Thompson, Tom, Tomas, Tommie, Tommy. *Variants*: Toomas (Estonian); Tuomo (Finnish); Thumas (French); Thoma (German); Tamas, Tomi (Hungarian); Tomas (Irish Gaelic); Tomaso, Masaccio (Italian); Tomelis (Lithuanian); Tomek (Polish); Toma (Romanian); Foma (Russian); Tam, Tavish, Tevis (Scottish); Tomas (Scottish Gaelic); Tomos (Slavonic); Chumo, Tomas (Spanish); Tomas (Swedish); Tomos, Twm (Welsh).

Thorin Old Norse. Thor was the Scandinavian god of thunder. *Other forms*: Thor, Thorkel.

Thornton Old English; village surrounded by thorns.

Thurstan, Thurston Old English; Thor's stone.

Tierney Irish Gaelic; lord.

Tiger Greek; tiger. *Variants*: Tigre (French); Tora (Japanese).

Timothy Greek; honouring God. Occasional use from 1900 peaking in light use in 1965. *Other forms*: Tim, Timmie, Timmy, Tymon. *Variants*: Timotei (Bulgarian); Timo (Finnish); Timothee (French); Timotheus (German); Timotheos (Greek); Kimokeo (Hawaiian); Timot (Hungarian); Tadhg, Tiomoid (Irish Gaelic); Timoteo (Italian); Timoteus (Norwegian, Swedish); Tymek, Tymon (Polish); Timoteo (Portuguese, Spanish); Timka, Timofey, Timok (Russian); Timotheus (Welsh).

Tobbar Romany; life's open road.

Tobias Hebrew; God is good. Occasional use 1980–5. *Other forms*: Tobin, Toby, Tobyn. *Variants*: Tobie (French); Tobias (German); Tiobi, Tioboid (Irish Gaelic); Tobia (Italian); Tobias (Spanish).

Toby A form of Tobias. Occasional use from 1965 peaking in 1985. *Other forms*: Tobe, Tobey, Tobie, Tobye.

Todd Old English; fox hunter. Occasional use from 1965 peaking in 1990. *Other forms*: Tad, Tod, Toddie, Toddy.

Tohon Native American; cougar.

Tolman Old English; collector of tolls.

Tom A form of Thomas. Occasional use from 1900, falling out of use in 1955 but reviving into occasional use again in 1975. *Other forms*: Tommie, Tommy. *Variant*: Teo (Vietnamese).

Tombe Kakwa; northerner.

Tommy A form of Thomas. Occasional use from 1980.

Tony A form of Anthony. Light use from 1935 peaking in

1965. *Variants*: Tonda (Czech); Tonjes (German); Tonio (Italian, Portuguese); Tonek (Polish).

Topaz Greek; yellow gemstone. (See Gender-neutral names.)

Topock Mohave; bridge.

Tor Tiv; king.

Torin, Torunn Irish Gaelic; thunder chief.

Tork, Torc Celtic; gold neckring (a symbol of wealth and power amongst the Celtic peoples).

Torquil Old Norse; Thor's cauldron.

Torr Old English; from the tower.

Torrence Irish Gaelic; tall tower. (See Gender-neutral names.)

Torsten Old German; rock of Thor. The name of the rock upon which Thor hammered out his magical swords.

Torvald Old Norse; ruler by Thor's grace.

Tory A form of Torr. (See Gender-neutral names.)

Trahern Welsh; strong as iron.

Travis, Travers Old English; tollbridge keeper.

Tremaine, Tremayne Scottish Gaelic; house of stone.

Trenton, Trent Latin; torrent.

Trevor Welsh; great (or sea) homestead. Occasional use from 1900 peaking in light use in 1955. *Variants*: Trebor, Trefor (Welsh).

Trey Middle English; third-born.

Trini Spanish; trinity.

Tristan Probably Celtic; noise, din. Occasional use from 1970 peaking in 1980. *Other forms*: Treston, Tris, Tristen, Tristin, Trystan. *Variants*: Tristram (Cornish); Tristano (Italian); Trystan (Welsh). (See Gender-neutral names.)

Troy Irish Gaelic; foot soldier. Occasional use from 1965 peaking in 1970. *Variant*: Koi (Hawaiian).

Truman Old English; faithful, honest man.

Tuan Vietnamese; goes smoothly.

Tuari Laguna; young eagle.

Tucker Old English; a fuller of cloth.

Tyler Middle English; roof-builder. Occasional use from 1975.

Tymon A form of Timon, a character in Shakespeare's play *Timon of Athens*.

Tynan Celtic; dark.

Tyree Scottish Gaelic; island dweller.

Tyrone From the name of the Irish county. *Other form*: Tyron. Occasional use from 1960.

Tyson Son of Ty. Occasional use from 1990.

U

Uffa A form of Ulrich. Old German; powerful fortune.

Ultan Irish Gaelic; Ulsterman.

Ulysses Possibly Etruscan; wanderer. This is the Latin form of Odysseus, the name of the Greek hero of Homer's epic poem *The Odyssey*. *Variants*: Ullioc (Irish Gaelic); Ulisse (Italian); Ulises (Spanish).

Umar Arabic; flourishing.

Umi Yao; life.

Urban Latin; city dweller. *Variants*: Urbaine (French); Urbain (German); Orban (Hungarian); Urbano (Italian); Urvan, Urvon (Russian).

V

Vadin Hindi; talker.

Valentine Latin; healthy, vigorous. Occasional use 1900–70. *Other forms*: Val, Valentin. *Variants*: Valentijn (Dutch); Valentin (French, German); Balint (Hungarian); Bhailintin (Irish Gaelic); Valentino (Italian); Walenty (Polish); Uailean (Scottish Gaelic); Valencio (Spanish); Folant (Welsh).

Van Dutch; from, implying noble descent.

Vance Old English; dweller near a marsh.

Vardon Old English; green hill.

Vartan Armenian; rose grower.

Vaughan Welsh; little. Occasional use 1950–85. *Other form*: Vaughn.

Venn Celtic; fair.

Vere Latin/French; true.

Vernon Old French; alder tree. Occasional use from its peak in 1925 falling out of use in 1975. *Other forms*: Varney, Vern.

Victor Latin; victory. Light use from 1900, peaking in 1925 and declining into occasional use by 1970. *Other forms*: Vic, Vito. *Variants*: Victoir (French); Viktor (German); Wikoli (Hawaiian); Buadhach (Irish Gaelic); Vittorio (Italian); Wiktor (Polish); Vitor (Portuguese); Vitenka, Vitya (Russian); Victorio, Vito, Vitorio (Spanish).

Vincent Latin; to conquer. Occasional use from 1900 peaking in 1925. *Other forms*: Vin, Vince, Vinnie, Vinny, Vinson. *Variants*: Vicenc (Catalan); Cenek, Vinca, Vincenek (Czech); Vincentius (Dutch); Vincente (French); Vincenz (German); Binkentios (Greek); Vince,

Vinci (Hungarian); Uinseann, Uinsionn (Irish Gaelic);
Enzo, Vincente, Vincenzo (Italian); Wincenty (Polish);
Kesha, Vikenti, Vikesha (Russian); Chenche, Vicente
(Spanish).

Vyvyan Latin; alive, lively. *Variant*: Vivien (French).
(See Gender-neutral names.)

W

Wade Old English; river crossing. Occasional use
1955–65.

Wainwright, Wain Old English; wagon maker.

Walden Old French; woods.

Waldo Old English; ruler. *Other form*: Waldron.

Wallace, Wallis Old French; stranger. *Other forms*: Wallas,
Walsh. *Variant*: Wallach (German).

Walter Old German; ruling people. Heavy use at its peak
in 1900, then declining into occasional use and falling
out of use by 1985. *Other forms*: Waldo, Wallie, Wally,
Walt, Wat, Wilt. *Variants*: Vladko (Czech); Gautier
(French); Walther (German); Uaitar, Ualtar (Irish
Gaelic); Gualtiero (Italian, Spanish); Waldemar
(Lithuanian); Ladislaus (Polish); Vladimir, Volya
(Russian); Bhatar, Bhaltair (Scottish Gaelic); Gualberto
(Spanish); Valter (Swedish); Gwalter (Welsh).

Walton Old English; walled village.

Ward Old English; to guard, hence guardian, protector.

Warner Possibly Old German; protecting warrior.
Variant: Werner (German).

Warren Middle English; to preserve. Occasional use
from 1935 peaking in the 1970s. *Other forms*: Varner,
Waring.

Waylon, Wayland Old English; land near the highway.

Wayne Welsh; meadow. Occasional use from 1950 peaking in light use in 1965. *Other forms*: Dwaine, Dwayne, Wene. *Variant*: Wene (Hawaiian).

Weldon Old English; willow trees on the hill.

Wendel, Wendell Old German; wanderer.

Wescott Old English; western cottage.

Wesley Old English; west meadow. Occasional use from 1900 peaking in the 1980s. *Other forms*: Wes, Westleigh. *Variant*: Wexel (Czech).

Westby Old English; western farmstead.

Westin Old English; western stream.

Westley A form of Wesley. Occasional use 1975–80.

Weston Old English; western village.

Weylin Celtic; son of the wolf.

Wilber, Wilbur Old English; willow town.

Wilfred Old English; hope for peace. Light use from 1900, peaking in 1925 and falling out of use by 1970. *Other forms*: Wilfrid, Wilfryd. *Variants*: Wilfried (German); Wilfredo (Spanish); Vilfred (Scandinavian).

Willard Old German; strong-willed, resolute.

William Old German; resolute protector. Very heavy use from its peak in 1900, declining into light use by 1970 but then steadily increasing again towards heavy use by 1990. *Other forms*: Bill, Billie, Billy, Gwylim, Wil, Will, Willie, Willis, Willy, Wilmer, Wilson. *Variants*: Wella (Cornish); Vilek, Viliam (Czech); Willem, Wim (Dutch); Guillaume (French); Wilhem, Willi (German); Vasilios, Vassos (Greek); Wiliama (Hawaiian); Vili (Hungarian); Liam, Uilliam (Irish Gaelic); Guglielmo (Italian); Wilek (Polish); Vasily, Vasya (Russian); Uilleam (Scottish Gaelic); Blaz (Serbo-Croatian);

Guillermo (Spanish); Vilhelm (Swedish); Gwilym (Welsh).

Willie A form of William. Occasional use 1900–65. *Other form*: Willy.

Wilson Son of William. Occasional use 1935–55.

Windsor Old English; river bank with a winch.

Wingate, Wyngate Old English; victory gate.

Winmer Old English; famous friend.

Winnie A form of Winston. (See Gender-neutral names.)

Winston Old English; Wine's farm. Occasional use 1900–70. *Other forms*: Winnie, Winny.

Wolf A form of Wolfgang. Old German; wolf path or way.

Woodrow Old English; row of cottages in a wood.

Wyman Old English; warrior.

Wymer Old English; famous in battle.

Wynford Welsh; white torrent.

Wynton, Winton Welsh/Old English; white farm.

Wystan Old English; battle stone.

X

Xandi A Galician form of Sandy.

Xavier Spanish; new house. *Other forms*: Xavian, Xavon, Zavier. *Variants*: Javier (Basque); Xaver (German); Xavon (Hungarian); Zaverio (Italian); Xever (Spanish).

Xenos Greek; stranger.

Xingu Arawakan; the name of a river in southern Brazil.

Xylon Greek; forest.

Y

Yale Scottish; vigorous.

Yancy, Yancey Forms of Jansen. Dutch; son of John. (See Gender-neutral names.)

Yanto A Welsh form of John.

Yesten, Yestin Cornish forms of Justin.

Yolo Native American; place where rushes grow.

Yonah Cherokee; a bear.

Yovan A form of Jovan.

Yul Mongolian; beyond the horizon.

Yutan Otoe; chiefs.

Yves A French form of Ivor. *Variants*: Ivo (German); Iwo (Polish).

Z

Zachary A form of Zachariah. Hebrew; Jehovah has remembered. Occasional use from 1980. *Other forms*: Zach, Zack, Zak, Zeke. *Variants*: Sakeri (Danish); Sakari (Finnish); Zacharie (French); Zacharias (German); Zako (Hungarian); Zaccaria (Italian); Zacarias (Portuguese, Spanish); Sachar, Zakhar, Zasho (Russian); Zakarias, Zakris (Scandinavian); Zakarij (Slavonic).

Zade Yiddish; grandfather.

Zadok Hebrew; righteous.

Zak A form of Zachary. Occasional use from 1965. *Other form*: Zack.

Zakari Hebrew; bright, clear.

Zaki Arabic; bright.

Zale Greek; sea-strength.

Zander A Greek form of Alexander.

Zane Italian; clown.

Zareb Sudanese; protector against enemies.

Zarek Polish; may God protect the king.

Zaskar Kashmiri; the name of a mountain range in Kashmir.

Zebedee Hebrew; gift of God.

Zed A form of Zedekiah. Hebrew; God's justice.

Zefram, Zephram Hebrew; fruitful.

Zeke Arabic; intelligent. Or a form of Ezekiel. Hebrew; may God strengthen.

Zelick Yiddish; happy, fortunate. *Other forms*: Selig, Zelig.

Zemar Dari; lion.

Zen Japanese; meditation.

Zenda A Czech form of Eugene. (See Gender-neutral names.)

Zendik Persian; sacred.

Zennor From the Cornish saint's name of uncertain meaning.

Zenon Greek; hospitality.

Zephan A form of the Hebrew name Zephaniah; the meaning is uncertain. *Other form*: Zevan.

Zeroun Armenian; wise and respected.

Zetan Hebrew; the olive tree.

Zimra Hebrew; song of praise.

Zio Hebrew; excellent.

Ziven Slavonic; vigorous.

Zohar Hebrew; radiant light.

Zoltan Arabic; ruler.

Zorba Greek; live each day.

Further reading

This is a list of key books consulted during the preparation of this dictionary. More extensive bibliographies can be found in the works by Dunkling and Gosling, and Hanks and Hodges. The date given is the date of the first edition unless otherwise specified.

Bice, Christopher. *Names for the Cornish*, Dyllansow Truran, Truro, Cornwall, 1984

Browder, Sue. *The New Age Baby Name Book*, Workman Publishing, New York, 1987

Brown, Michele. *The New Book of First Names*, Corgi Books, London, 1985, republished by Greenwich Editions as *The Baby Name Book*.

Cresswell, Julia. *Irish First Names*, HarperCollins, London, 1996

Crystal, David. *The Cambridge Encyclopedia of Language*, Cambridge University Press, Cambridge, 1987

Dunkling, Leslie. *Scottish Christian Names*, Johnston and Bacon, Edinburgh, 1978

Dunkling, Leslie. *The Guinness Book of Names*, 7th edn, Guinness Publishing, London, 1995

Dunkling, Leslie, and Gosling, William. *Everyman's Dictionary of First Names*, Dent, London, 1983

Ekwall, Eilert. *The Concise Oxford Dictionary of English Place-names*, 4th edn, Oxford University Press, Oxford, 1960

Ellefson, Connie Lockhart. *The Melting Pot Book of Baby Names*, 3rd edn, Betterway Books, Cincinnati, OH, 1995

Gruffudd, Heini. *Welsh Names for Children*, Y Lolfa, Talybont, Ceredigion, 1980

Hanks, Patrick, and Hodges, Flavia. *A Dictionary of Surnames*, Oxford University Press, Oxford, 1988

Hanks, Patrick, and Hodges, Flavia. *A Dictionary of First Names*, Oxford University Press, Oxford, 1990

Lansky, Bruce. *The Very Best Baby Name Book in the Whole Wide World*, Meadowbrook Press, Deephaven, MN, 1979

Lansky, Bruce, *35,000+ Baby Names*, Meadowbrook Press, Deephaven, MN, 1995

Merry, Emma. *First Names*, HMSO, London, 1995

Nicholson, Louise. *The Best Baby Name Book*, Thorsons, London, 1985

Paix, Yvonne de La. *Just the Perfect Name*, Avery Publishing, New York, 1997

Peterson, Sarah. *The Book of Names*, Tyndale House, Wheaton, IL, 1997

Reaney, P. H. *A Dictionary of British Surnames*, Routledge & Kegan Paul, London, 1961

Revard, Carter. 'Traditional Osage Naming Ceremonies: Entering the Circle of Being', in *Recovering the Word: Essays on Native American Literature*, Brian Swann and Arnold Krupat (eds.), University of California Press, Berkeley, CA, 1987

Rule, Lareina. *Name Your Baby*, Bantam Books, New York, 1963

Spence, Hilary. *The Complete Book of Baby Names*, Foulsham, Slough, Berkshire, 1993

Spence, Jane. *The Virgin Book of Baby Names*, Virgin Books, London, 1993

Stewart, George. *A Concise Dictionary of American Place-Names*, Oxford University Press, Oxford, 1985

Todd, Loreto. *Celtic Names for Children*, O'Brien Press, Dublin, 1998

Wilson, Stuart. *The Pan Guide to Babies' Names*, Pan, London, 1994

Withycombe, E. G. *The Oxford Dictionary of English Christian Names*, Oxford University Press, Oxford, 1945.

Acknowledgements

My thanks to the following individuals who supplied names or access to name lists: Martin Holyoak, Matthew Selley and Rowan Duxbury, Durga Das and Hari Sudha, Tatanya McClurg, Barbara White and Stephanie Ewings. And a special thank you to Joanna Prentis, my friend and colleague in our past-life group; without your help, Jo, I would never have encountered the concept of the Angel of the Name.

No one writes a name book in a vacuum. All writers in this field build upon the work of the other name book authors, and I am indebted to the many published sources listed in 'Further Reading' on page 363. I am particularly indebted to Leslie Dunkling and Emma Merry, and to Sue Browder whose *New Age Baby Name Book* inspired me to present foreign language variants alphabetically by source. My profound thanks to all these authors; this book could never have been written without you.

However, the central core of new names found in this book came from my own research. During this research I wrote to 139 Steiner/Waldorf Schools throughout the English-speaking world. I am most grateful to the many schools who responded, and I acknowledge their help by listing these schools here.

United States of America

Live Oak Waldorf School, Applegate, California.
Mountain Meadow Waldorf School, Calpella, California.
The Waldorf School of Mendocino County, Calpella,
    California.
Mariposa Waldorf School, Cedar Ridge, California.
East Bay Waldorf School, Emeryville, California.
Chicago Waldorf School, Chicago, Illinois.
The Merriconeag School, Freeport, Maine.
Cape Ann School, Gloucester, Massachusetts.
The Waldorf School, Lexington, Massachusetts.
Minnesota Waldorf School, Roseville, Minnesota.
The Waldorf School of Princeton, Princeton, New Jersey.
The Waldorf School of Garden City, Garden City,
    New York.
Mountain Laurel School, New Paltz, New York.
Eugene Waldorf School, Eugene, Oregon.
Light Valley Waldorf School, Jacksonville, Oregon.
Portland Waldorf School, Portland, Oregon.
Kimberton Waldorf School, Kimberton, Pennsylvania.
Austin Waldorf School, Austin, Texas.

United Kingdom

Dartington Steiner School, Dartington, Devon.
Plymouth Rudolf Steiner School, Plymouth, Devon.
The Holywood Rudolf Steiner School, Holywood, County
    Down.
Nant-Y-Cwm Rudolf Steiner School, Clunderwen, Dyfed.
Folly Farm School, Ringwood, Hampshire.
Rudolf Steiner School, Kings Langley, Hertfordshire.
North London Rudolf Steiner School, London.
Michael Hall, Forest Row, Sussex.

ACKNOWLEDGEMENTS

Sheffield Steiner School, Sheffield, Yorkshire.
York Steiner School, York, Yorkshire.

Australia

Eukarima School, Bowral, New South Wales.
Melbourne Rudolf Steiner School, Warranwood, Victoria.
Perth Waldorf School, Hamilton Hill, Western Australia.

Canada

Nelson Waldorf School, Nelson, British Columbia.
The Vancouver Waldorf School, North Vancouver, British
  Columbia.
London Waldorf School, London, Ontario.

South Africa

The Roseway Waldorf School, Hillcrest, Natal.

www.panmacmillan.com

.

www.ingramcontent.com/pod-product-compliance
Ingram Content Group UK Ltd.
Pitfield, Milton Keynes, MK11 3LW, UK
UKHW040641280225
455688UK00002B/50